The Digital Musician

The aim of *The Digital Musician* is to explore what it means to be a musician in the digital age. It examines musical skills, cultural awareness and artistic identity, through the prism of recent technological innovations. New technologies, and especially the new digital technologies, mean that anyone can produce music without musical training. *The Digital Musician* asks *why* make music? *what* music to make? and *how do we know what is good?* The answers involve developing a personal aesthetic, an awareness of the context for one's work, and certain musical and technical abilities.

Unlike many other books on music technology *The Digital Musician* considers the musician, rather than the technology. It is a synthesis of ideas that are influential in music and relevant to the digital age. These are integrated with a discussion of the technology and its implications for the musician. Technical issues are outlined and bibliographic references supplied for further study; however, this book does not provide a 'how-to-make-computer-music' reference manual. Instead, it concentrates on musical creativity with new technologies.

Designed to function as a complete and stand-alone text, it includes the enhancement of using a MOO (Multi-user domain, Object-Orientated), which is a virtual world capable of supporting multimedia.

Andrew Hugill is a composer, writer and Director of the Institute of Creative Technologies (IOCT) at De Montfort University, Leicester, UK, where he also founded the Music Technology programme.

The Digital Musician

Andrew Hugill

Routledge
Taylor & Francis Group

NEW YORK AND LONDON

First published 2008
by Routledge
270 Madison Ave, New York, NY 10016

Simultaneously published in the UK
by Routledge
2 Park Square, Milton Park, Abingdon, Oxon OX14 4RN

Routledge is an imprint of the Taylor & Francis Group, an informa business

© 2008 Taylor & Francis

Typeset in Goudy and Gill Sans by The Running Head Limited, Cambridge, UK.
Printed and bound in the United States of America on acid-free paper by
Edwards Brothers, Inc., Ann Arbor, MI.

Library of Congress Cataloging in Publication Data
A catalog record has been requested for this book

ISBN 10: 0–415–96215–3 (hbk)
ISBN 10: 0–415–96216–1 (pbk)
ISBN 10: 0–203–93565–9 (ebk)

ISBN 13: 978–0–415–96215–5 (hbk)
ISBN 13: 978–0–415–96216–2 (pbk)
ISBN 13: 978–0–203–93565–1 (ebk)

Cover image: Paul Gauguin, French, 1848–1903, *Where Do We Come From? What Are We?
Where Are We Going?*, 1897–98, oil on canvas, 139.1 x 374.6 cm (54¾ x 147½ in.), Museum
of Fine Arts, Boston, Tomkins Collection/Arthur Gordon Tompkins Fund, 36.270

Contents

Figures and tables

Figures

Tables

Preface

In *The Digital Musician*, the word 'musician' is extended to cover all those working creatively with sound. Resistance to this extension is fairly strong from both the traditional musicians (who play 'notes' on 'instruments') and from the sonic artists (who want to lose the connotations of 'music'). However, I take the view that music is the name given to the organisation of sound (and silence) and that both groups have a great deal in common, whether they accept it or not. I therefore do not shrink from applying some useful 'musical' ideas to the field of music technology, nor from cheerfully ignoring those aspects of music which are irrelevant or useless when working with the new technologies.

The aim of this book is to describe a new kind of 'digital' musician. To this end, I examine issues of cultural awareness, artistic identity and musical skills, through the prism of recent technological innovations. The book has come about because of a seismic shift in 'music' and particularly music education over the past ten or fifteen years. Many universities now offer programmes in 'music technology', a subject which was once the exclusive domain of engineers, organologists and acousticians. What has greatly accelerated the change is, of course, the advent of the personal computer and, hence, the ready availability of sophisticated audio manipulation and music production tools. The phrase 'music technology', then, is code for creative music production, often using digital technologies.

Most of the existing books on music technology (and there are many) concentrate on the *technology*. There are good reasons for this: it can be complicated and difficult; most students want to know *how* to do things; aesthetic issues are hard to discuss; the world is changing fast; and so on. A smaller number of books focus on the musical or artistic aspects of sonic manipulation, exploring this or that approach to electronic, electro-acoustic or computer music, sonic art, sound-art and sound design.

The Digital Musician, on the other hand, is about the musician. It is the result of more than ten years of research and is a synthesis of ideas that are influential in music and relevant to the digital age. These ideas are integrated with a discussion of the technology and its implications for the musician. Technical issues are outlined where appropriate and bibliographic references supplied for further study: however, this book does not provide a 'how-to-make-computer-music' reference manual, of which there are many good examples already in existence. Instead, it concentrates on questions raised for the individual musician by all this potential to make music: What music? What is there to 'say'? Why create music? What about existing music – how to approach that? Which music to approach? How do we know what is good?

The answers to these questions involve developing a personal aesthetic, an awareness of the context for the work, specific musical and technical abilities and an individual identity. Digital musicians must find a distinctive musical 'voice'. They may build on what has gone before, or they may sidestep existing work. Either way, they become a new kind of musician: one who originates *and* performs, who creates *and* produces, and who harnesses the potential of technology in new and exciting ways.

This human focus created two problems in writing the book. The first was how much technical information to include? Given that it is well explained elsewhere, an initial decision might have been: none at all. However, to omit technical discussion entirely would have led to a lack of clarity about the precise nature of the subject. I therefore set out to provide a map of the territory the digital musician inhabits. The scale of the map may be large, but the landscape must be clearly indicated. The overlapping fields of science, technology, music and ideas are significant features on the map. They are consequently described in sufficient detail to be recognisable as such.

This led on to a second problem: to what level of detail? More or less all the chapter headings, and sub-headings, could become a book in their own right. In fact, books do exist on most of the topics, as the recommended reading lists will show. The digital musician is expected to cover an enormous range and diversity of knowledge and plainly cannot become an expert in *all* these areas. *The Digital Musician* therefore covers only *one* subject in sufficient detail: the digital musician. All the chapters and sub-chapters are doorways into areas for further activity, research or study. Throughout the book there are symbols to indicate these, as follows:

- ● refers to one of the **creative projects** in Chapter 10
- ■ recommends **further reading** around a topic
- ▲ indicates a **listening list.**

It is probable that the readers will eventually want to specialise in one or more of the larger areas, and the given projects and recommended reading and listening lists should support that.

Although the book is timely, it is also important that it is sustainable, that it remains relevant in the future. Technology changes so rapidly that there is a danger of instant obsolescence. To that end, I avoid discussion of the particulars of current software or equipment but focus instead on generic tools and ideas. So, the properties of sound, microphones, loudspeakers, computer processes will all be part of the musician's environment for the foreseeable future.

A particular piece of software, or electronic widget, or amazing gadget, may not be so important in a few years' time. Music itself constantly goes through many changes in fashion and taste. *The Digital Musician* concerns itself with ideas that should be relevant in *any* musical situation and for many years to come.

It will be noticed that the 'new technologies' described in the book are predominantly digital but not exclusively so. Neither analogue electronic technologies nor, indeed, mechanical technologies, are necessarily excluded from the picture that emerges. Musicians will always use whatever technology seems appropriate for the given purpose. What has changed is the arrival of these digital technologies, which have shifted our understanding of all other technologies, so much so that music today is assimilated through an inherently digitised culture and mindset. The 'digital musician', therefore, is not one who uses *only* those technologies but is rather a product of the digital culture. This idea will be developed through the book.

Another, literal, interpretation of the phrase 'digital musician', might lead to the assumption that the subject here is machine musicianship, or the computer itself as musician. This possibility is also not excluded: artificial intelligence, algorithmic composition and various forms of automation and networked interactivity are all discussed. However, these are always presented in the context of a human exchange. Once again, the interest lies in the people rather than the equipment. The ambiguity of 'digital musician' is embraced as a positive reflection of the state of these new kinds of musicians.

To the educators

The Digital Musician is intended first for university and college students who are beginning to come to terms with fairly advanced use of technology. Such students have a natural tendency to become obsessed with what their equipment does and how they can best implement the known techniques. By stressing the discovery of an individual voice, I try to open their minds to possibilities that they had not previously considered. In my experience, students will often postpone the creation of interesting work until they own this piece of kit, or that piece of software, or until they have mastered this or that *really cool* technique. It is a premise of *The Digital Musician* that good music can be made at any stage, with any equipment and using any technique.

The book is constructed in such a way as to allow sessions, or series of sessions, to be developed around a particular topic or theme. It will be observed that almost every sub-heading comes with an associated project and some recommended further reading. One way of using the book, therefore, is to start with a creative or listening project and use this as a stimulus for discussion of the more theoretical aspects raised in the earlier chapters.

The creative projects attempt to apply the key concepts and ideas to a range of practical scenarios with the aim of improving the individual's ability to interact with their own work and with the work of other people. The projects may be assigned individually or to groups and will also provide good classroom material. They are all capable of repetition, fairly open-ended and should always produce interesting and varied results. The listening projects are designed to widen musical experience and knowledge as well as to illustrate some key historical and contemporary themes and trends.

All the projects are quite diverse: some could potentially take several weeks to complete, whereas others are simpler exercises. Some require a lot of preparation and technical equipment; others are almost 'lifestyle' undertakings that require nothing more than a little forethought. Clearly the educator needs to exercise judgement in deciding which projects to undertake.

In addition, there are several 'case studies' of musicians working in various ways. These take the form of interviews which ask questions drawn from the main themes of the book. It is interesting to compare the various responses and identify common threads. It is also hoped that such 'real world' stories will prove inspirational for aspiring musicians.

To summarise, therefore, this book could be used in the following ways, by:

- reading as a stimulus to creative and critical thought and enquiry
- undertaking specific projects and building a session or part of a programme around them
- basing sessions on sections of the book, supplemented by selected projects as supporting activities or assessable components.

To the students

If there is one thing that should emerge from these pages, it is the benefit of collaboration and cooperation, of social exchange, in music. The music-technology workstation, whether fixed or portable, and the general culture of individualism around today, tends to reinforce a natural interest in your own progress, your own marks. This is perfectly understandable but can also be a problem in musical development. It is my stated aim that you should develop your own musical 'voice' which is distinctive and individual. Paradoxically, the best way to achieve that is to become aware of what others are doing and to work with them. This will have the beneficial effect of helping to shape and define your individual identity. Just as no sound exists in a vacuum, so no musician can grow in isolation.

Another important thing is to develop your ability to discriminate. This applies at the level of sound and music but also at the level of ideas and knowledge. The vast amount of unfiltered, indiscriminate, information available today, particularly through the Internet, should be treated with caution. It *is* wonderful to be able to access instantaneously an answer to some of the most awkward or obscure questions. However, that answer does not necessarily always come from an authoritative source. Academic books such as this one have been through a fairly stringent 'peer-review' process by experts in the field. This does not, of course, guarantee that they are absolutely right about everything, but it does shorten the odds.

My main hope is that this book will stimulate, inform and inspire you in roughly equal measure. There is a great deal of both theoretical and practical material in its pages, but in Chapter 9 there is a summary of 'real world' advice and interviews with a number of people who are actually making a living as digital musicians. Most students, quite rightly, want to know where their chosen study will lead in terms of career or life path. The days of a single job for life have largely gone, and the digital world is both fluid and diverse. *The Digital Musician* reflects upon that and offers some pointers that will be useful in any situation. But mostly it focuses upon the wonderfully rich, exciting and beneficial ways in which music can be made today.

To summarise, you could use this book in the following ways, by:

- reading through to build up a general picture of the scope of the territory
- undertaking specific projects and creating new music and ideas from them
- exploring further beyond the sections of the book that seem particularly interesting or relevant, using the recommended reading and listening lists as a guide.

Web resources

The Digital Musician website is located at www.digitalmusician.org and contains all sorts of additional materials, including: a complete bibliography, further support for the projects, suggested assessment strategies, colour illustrations and movies, sound clips and examples referenced in the text and many other resources. It also includes a link to a unique online educational environment called 'MusiMoo', which is a virtual world for digital music that I have developed and offer to readers as an 'optional extra' to be used as you wish. In the event that the website is password protected, the guest username will be 'digital' and the password 'musician'. Login details for MusiMoo will be given separately on the website.

The Digital Musician can also be found at
www.routledge.com/textbooks/9780415962162/.

Acknowledgements

Many thanks are due to the following colleagues, for giving generously of their time, being interviewed for this book, or offering critical feedback and advice: Newton Armstrong, Simon Atkinson, Peter Batchelor, Bret Battey, Howard Burrell, Evan Chambers, Todd Coleman, Peter Elsea, Rebekah Harriman, Ronald Herrema, Elizabeth Hinkle-Turner, David Houghton, Andy Hunt, Leigh Landy, Philip Martin, Dimitris Moraitis, Gary Lee Nelson, John Richards, Julian Rohrhuber, Geoff Smith, Tim O'Sullivan, Sue Thomas, Barry Truax and Ge Wang.

I would also like to thank the following for making materials available to me or poviding illustrations: Matthew Adkins, Peter Batchelor, Annie Cattrell, Eric Charry, John Dack, Sidney Fels, Ambrose Field, Rob Godman, Morten Kringelbach, James Mooney, Tony Myatt, Christine North, Garth Paine, Claude Schryer, Nina Sellars, Philip Tagg and Scott A. Wyatt.

Many thanks too to the 'case studies': Oswald Berthold, Nick Collins, Julio d'Escriván, Chris Joseph, Thor Magnusson, Kaffe Matthews, Randall Packer, Quantazelle, John Richards, Sophy Smith, Atau Tanaka, Martyn Ware.

Extra special thanks go to: Simon Emmerson, who gave selflessly of his time and vast expertise throughout the process of writing, and whose parallel blog kept me going; Constance Ditzel, my editor; Denny Tek at Routledge; Carole Drummond at The Running Head; Liz O'Donnell for her copy-editing; and my wife, Louise, without whom . . .

This book is dedicated to my students, past, present and future, with grateful thanks for all they have taught me.

Illustrations

All copyrighted illustrations are used with permission. The author gratefully acknowledges the help of the copyright holders. The unacknowledged illustrations below are by the author. The illustrations by Nina Sellars and Peter Batchelor were created especially for this book.

Figure 1.1 © NASA
Figure 2.1 © Nina Sellars

Figure 2.2 © Dr Spiro Comis/Wellcome Trust Medical Picture Library
Figure 2.3 © Dr David Furness/ Wellcome Trust Medical Picture Library
Figure 2.4 © C. R. Nave, Georgia State University
Figures 2.5, 3.4 Wellcome Trust Medical Picture Library
Figures 2.6–2.10 © Dr Morten Kringelbach
Figure 2.11 © Tony Myatt and Peter Fluck
Figures 3.1, 3.6–3.15, 3.17, 3.19, 4.1–4.4, 4.6–4.8, 4.10–4.12 © Peter Batchelor
Figures 3.2, 4.13 © Barry Truax
Figure 3.16 © Raimund Specht, Avisoft Bioacoustics www.avisoft.com
Figure 3.20 © Schotts Ltd
Figure 4.5 © Atau Tanaka
Figure 4.9 © Peter Batchelor and Jonty Harrison
Figure 4.14 © Iannis Xenakis
Figure 6.1 © Scott A. Wyatt
Figure 6.2 © Claude Schryer
Figure 6.3 © Garth Paine
Figure 6.4 © MIT Media Lab
Figure 6.5 © Kaffe Matthews
Figure 6.6 © Sidney Fels
Figure 6.7 © Quantazelle
Figure 6.8 © Ge Wang

Chapter 1

New technologies, new musicians

The picture on the cover of this book – *Where Do We Come From? What Are We? Where Are We Going?* – was painted in 1897 by Paul Gauguin towards the end of his life, during his extended stay in Tahiti. It is a very large canvas – 1.39 × 3.74 metres (4' 6" × 12' 4") – and is generally considered his greatest work. Gauguin indicated that the painting should be 'read' from right to left, with the three main groups of figures illustrating the questions posed in the title. The three women with a child represent the beginning of life; the central group symbolises the daily existence of young adulthood; and in the final group, according to the artist, 'an old woman approaching death appears reconciled and resigned to her thoughts'; while at her feet 'a strange white bird . . . represents the futility of words'. Beyond this, Gauguin wanted the picture to remain a mystery. 'Explanations and obvious symbols would give the canvas a sad reality', he wrote, 'and the questions asked [by the title] would no longer be a poem.'

These are profound philosophical questions about life in general and, for Gauguin, the lack of an answer led to a failed suicide attempt soon after the picture was painted. But the way they are addressed in the painting is also an expression of a complex cultural mix. The painting is executed in the Symbolist style, and yet it shows a fascination with the folk art of Tahiti; it is the work of a French artist whose sense of cultural identity has been challenged and extended by his chosen immersion in a foreign culture.

Gauguin's questions are very relevant to today's musicians. The new technologies have transformed the way music is created and heard, composed and performed, produced and distributed. The world that surrounds the musician, the cultural context, has changed in many ways. These changes have created a new musician, who may come from a variety of backgrounds, possess all sorts of musical training and technical skills, have many different kinds of knowledge and opinions, but feels empowered by the new technologies and drawn to making music. This chapter asks Gauguin's questions (in a different order) and considers what it means to be a musician in the digital age.

What are digital musicians?

There are, of course, many different musical traditions and many different ways of classifying musicians according to their background. Some classifications are made by musicians themselves, others are made by writers, critics or academics. No single way is really satisfactory, because music tends to seep through its own porous boundaries. It is highly likely that a musician will show characteristics of more than one type.

Many musicians who knowingly work within highly established traditions, such as 'classical' music and certain forms of 'folk' music, take *pitch* as a starting point for their musical training. These musicians generally play an acoustic instrument as their main practice, and they travel a prescribed career path that involves the gradual evolution of technique and musicianship. The criteria for recognising virtuosity are clearly established, and there is broad agreement among listeners about the level that an individual musician has attained.

Indian *raga*, Javanese *gamelan*, Chinese folk music, Western classical music and some forms of jazz, are all examples of such established traditions. What these systems have in common is an established set of skills and a standard practice. The relationship with pitch is a constant, whether it is the microtonal *sruti* of the *raga*, the harmonious relationship between the instruments of the *gamelan* orchestra, the modal inflections of Chinese folk music or the twelve notes to an octave of Western music. The first piano lesson generally begins with the note 'middle C', just above the keyhole in the piano frame, the middle of the keyboard. From this fundamental understanding, a pianist's training can begin. The student follows a path prescribed by experts, usually supervised by a teacher who gives 'one-to-one' guidance through the various levels of technical mastery to the full realisation of musical potential. So 'technique' is acquired.

Another type of musician may begin with *rhythm*, or at least *beat*. This includes rock and most forms of popular music. Musicians working within this tradition tend to show a relative lack of interest in pitch when compared to the first type (although they do not ignore it completely). Bands without some sort of percussion section are rare, and, when they do appear, the instruments often emphasise rhythmic content in order to compensate. There is also general agreement about what constitutes a good musician in this field, although it is sometimes bound up with extra-musical questions such as lifestyle, image and so on. The path to success is just as difficult as that for the traditional musician and is also mapped out by convention and experts.

As you look around the world today, it is clear that this kind of musician is the most prevalent. On the island of Zanzibar, most musicians are drawn to rap, rather than the traditional *Taarab*; in Bali, the young people perform punk rock in shopping malls, in preference to *gamelan* under pagodas; in Iran, the underground-rave and heavy-metal scenes flourish in spite of attempts by the regime to limit expression to traditional Iranian forms such as the *Radif*. But in many of these cases, the musicians are concerned to introduce traditional instruments and sounds into the more Western forms. Globalisation is complex, and there is more going on here than just a Westernisation of world culture. A musical commitment to traditional music does not necessarily prevent an involvement in bands, or vice versa. Recent musical history is peppered with examples of 'classically trained' popular musicians or popular musicians who have found a voice in classical forms. Jazz seems to sit somewhere between the two. These categories are not rigid.

A third tradition starts from *timbre*. This type of musician is harder to pin down, for the simple reason that many timbre-focused artists do not consider themselves to be musicians at all, or do not use the word 'music' to describe what they produce. Into this category can be placed the majority of those working in electronic and electro-acoustic[1] music, but also sonic art, sound-art, sound design and various forms of radiophonic[2] and speech-based work. By dealing with *sounds* rather than *notes*, these musicians have changed the nature of music itself, raising questions about what is 'musical'. The conventions of music seem inadequate to describe their activities. These musicians may even begin to challenge music's very existence, since so much of their prime material is *audio* and lacks the expressive intention and cultural baggage of 'music'.

This third type of 'musician' generates and manipulates sound using electronic means. For the majority of the relatively short history of this kind of music, they have done so using non-digital technologies. The fixed elements of the music – the microphone and the loudspeaker – remain (and presumably always will remain) *analogue*, that is to say: transducers that convert sound waves into an electrical signal (in the case of the microphone) or an electrical signal into sound waves (in the case of loudspeakers). The arrival of digital technologies has effected a rapid change in, and expansion of, the techniques available to this musician.

It might be assumed that these 'technological' musicians most naturally fit into the class of 'digital musicians', but in fact this is not necessarily the case. All types of musicians have always worked with technology, and all musical instruments are an example of technological innovation and development. Even the human voice may be thought of as a technology by the singer. For each of the three types of musician described above, a new situation exists, because so many people are now faced with digital technology at some stage in their working lives. The challenge is how, and to what extent, to engage with these technologies.

'Digital musicians' are, therefore, not defined by their use of technology alone. A classical pianist giving a recital on a digital piano is not really a digital musician, nor is a composer using a notation software package to write a string quartet. These are musicians using digital tools to facilitate an outcome that is not conceived in digital terms. However, if that pianist or composer were to become intrigued by some possibility made available by the technology they are using, so much so that it starts to change the way they think about what they are doing, at that point they might start to move towards becoming a digital musician.[3]

The phrase 'digital musician' itself is only descriptive. It is the intention of this book to identify a new class of musicians, but not necessarily to rename them. 'Computer musician', 'sound artist', 'sonic artist', 'sound designer', or even just a qualified 'musician' are among the possible names for people from this group. A digital musician is one who has embraced the possibilities opened up by new technologies, in particular the potential of the computer for exploring, storing, manipulating and processing sound, and the development of numerous other digital tools and devices which enable musical invention and discovery. This is a starting point for creativity of a kind that is unlike previously established musical practice in certain respects. It also requires a different attitude of mind. These musicians will be concerned not only with *how* to do what they do, nor *what* to do, but also with *why* to make music. A digital musician, therefore, has a certain curiosity, a questioning and critical engagement that goes with the territory.

Although the digital musician could not have existed without the new technologies, that does not mean that he or she uses them exclusively. A digital musician might play an acoustic instrument, or use a non-digital electronic device, as part of their activities. In fact, this will almost certainly happen and be advantageous when it does. The difference is that those technologies will be used in conjunction with or *informed by* the digital. This 'informing' is a consequence of the changes in the state of the mind of the musician outlined above.

So what specifically distinguishes 'digital musicians' from other musicians? What skills do they possess? To be a digital musician requires:

- *aural awareness* (an ability to hear and listen both widely and accurately, linked to an understanding of how sound behaves in space and time)
- *cultural knowledge* (an understanding of one's place within a local and global culture coupled with an ability to make critical judgements and a knowledge of recent cultural developments)
- *musical abilities* (the ability to make music in various ways – performance, improvisation, composition, etc. – using the new technologies)
- *technical skills* (skill in recording, producing, processing, manipulating and disseminating music and sound using digital technologies).

These are not absolute categories: 'aural awareness' may be considered 'musical', acquiring 'cultural knowledge' will require some 'technical skills' and so on. Their interdependency is crucial, and the digital musician will not neglect any one of them. In all respects, the digital musician will be distinguished by *creativity*.

This creativity seems closest to sculpture, as the musician finds and shapes, manipulates and processes, sonic materials. To borrow the title of a book by the great Russian film-maker, Andrei Tarkovsky, it might be called *sculpting in time*. Tarkovsky himself remarked about music: 'I feel that the sounds of this world are so beautiful in themselves that if only we could learn to listen to them properly, cinema would have no need of music at all'.[4] The creative process perhaps also resembles alchemy: combining and recombining sounds, transforming them all the while, seeking the right mixture, the ideal combination.

These are musicians in a digital world and a digital culture in which sound has joined image and text as information or data, capable of endless mutation and transformation. They are musicians brought together by shared interests in a particular musical idea or form, often regardless of national boundaries or cultural heritage. The main medium is digital technology: the personal computer in all its many manifestations, from the desktop machine to the mobile phone; the network, from local area networks to the Internet; virtual worlds and artificial intelligence; multimedia and new media; software instruments and modified hardware.

Today's digital sound recording and its associated distribution and dissemination media has made all sorts of music readily available. This is far more than just a curious by-product of the development of digital media. It has fundamentally changed the cultural landscape. It affects all types of musician, but the digital musician will be the first to take this for granted, the first for whom the digital world is as 'given' as the physical world around them. For the digital musician, it is not just the technologies that are defining: it is the way they are used.

The world the digital musicians inhabit is both a perpetual horizon and a labyrinth of connections or links to the next meaningful encounter. The great challenge is to have *integrity*, to know who they are, where they are, what they are. They are on a journey without a clear destination. Perhaps they will come to a stop one day, but probably not today. The next encounter looks too intriguing, too exciting, to stop now, to stop here. Driven on by a relentless curiosity, the snail trail of their progress maps their identity as they accumulate ideas, information, stimulations and music. They move perpetually from the known to the unknown. This is what digital musicians are.

Where do they come from?

The intriguing answer to Gauguin's question is: *it does not matter where they come from*. This is the most significant change produced by the new technologies: they are pervasive. They cut across national, cultural and musical boundaries, and background is largely irrelevant. If the classical musician may be seen as 'highbrow' and the band musician as 'lowbrow', then right now a 'middlebrow' or 'nobrow' musician is emerging.[5] No form of musical knowledge, understanding or ability will be a handicap to these musicians, provided they are willing to embrace the possibilities offered by new technologies.

This applies equally well to the 'technological' musicians, for whom the process of accepting new technologies is a natural evolutionary step. Here, the challenge is to develop the *musicality* of what they do. While it is true that technology has enabled the creation of many new forms of music, this does not mean that the knowledge and understanding accumulated by the other established forms of music is now obsolete.

None of this would be possible without the ready availability of recorded sound. In his classic essay 'The Work of Art in the Age of Mechanical Reproduction'

most emotive power in the acoustic enjoyment, in its own right, that the artist's inspiration will extract from combined noises.

Here are the six families of noises of the futurist orchestra which we will soon set in motion mechanically:

1   *rumbles:* roars, explosions, crashes, splashes, booms
2   *whistles:* hisses, snorts
3   *whispers:* murmurs, mumbles, grumbles, gurgles
4   *screeches:* creaks, rustles, buzzes, crackles, scrapes
5   *noises* obtained by percussion on metal, wood, skin, stone, terracotta, etc.
6   *voices of animals and men:* shouts, screams, groans, shrieks, howls, laughs, wheezes, sobs.

In this inventory we have encapsulated the most characteristic of the fundamental noises; the others are merely the associations and combinations of these. The rhythmic movements of a noise are infinite: just as with tone there is always a predominant rhythm, but around this numerous other secondary rhythms can be felt.[9]

He duly built a Futurist orchestra consisting of *intonarumori* ('intoners' or 'noise machines') and gave several performances during 1914 in Milan and London.

Influenced by his teacher Busoni, the composer Edgard Varèse (1883–1965) complained bitterly: 'in music we composers are forced to use instruments that have not changed for two centuries'. Varèse spent the majority of his life dreaming of a day when the technologies available to him would be capable of realising his musical ideas. In his manifesto 'The Liberation of Sound', published in 1936, he wrote:

The raw material of music is sound. That is what the 'reverent approach' has made people forget – even composers. Today when science is equipped to help the composer realize what was never before possible [. . .] the composer continues to be obsessed by traditions which are nothing but the limitations of his predecessors.

[. . .] As far back as the twenties, I decided to call my music 'organized sound' and myself, not a musician, but 'a worker in rhythms, frequencies, and intensities'. Indeed, to stubbornly conditioned ears, anything new in music has always been called noise. But after all what is music but organized noises? And a composer, like all artists, is an organizer of disparate elements.

[. . .] The electronic medium is adding an unbelievable variety of new timbres to our musical store, but most important of all, it has freed music from the tempered system, which has prevented music from keeping pace with the other arts and with science. Composers are now able, as never before, to satisfy the dictates of that inner ear of the imagination. They are also lucky so far in not being hampered by aesthetic codification – at least not yet! But

I am afraid it will not be long before some musical mortician begins embalming electronic music in rules.[10]

With such passionate, even Romantic, views, it is no surprise that Varèse encountered constant obstacles to his musical expression. He composed only a handful of works, and he experienced rejection both by the general public and his professional colleagues (including Schoenberg). His attempts to convince Bell Laboratories to allow him to research electronic music during the 1920s and 1930s failed. It was only when in his seventies that the musical world and the technological world caught up with Varèse. He composed *Déserts* for orchestra and tape in 1950–1954, supported by Pierre Schaeffer who provided facilities at the Radio-diffusion-Television Francaises (RTF) studios, where he was working on *musique concrète*.[11] Finally, in 1958, Varèse was invited by the architect Le Corbusier to create *Poème Electronique* for the Philips Pavilion at the 1958 World's Fair. This was essentially a sound installation, which used 400 loudspeakers to create a walk-through sonic experience that combined synthesised and recorded and processed sounds.

In 1937, the composer John Cage (1912–1992) delivered a highly prophetic lecture in Seattle, entitled 'The Future of Music – Credo', which included the following passage:

I BELIEVE THAT THE USE OF NOISE
Wherever we are, what we hear is mostly noise. When we ignore it, it disturbs us. When we listen to it, we find it fascinating. The sound of a truck at 50 m.p.h. Static between the stations. Rain. We want to capture and control these sounds, to use them, not as sound effects, but as musical instruments. Every film studio has a library of 'sound effects' recorded on film. With a film phonograph it is now possible to control the amplitude and frequency of any one of these sounds and to give to it rhythms within or beyond the reach of anyone's imagination. Given four film phonographs, we can compose and perform a quartet for explosive motor, wind, heartbeat, and landslide.

TO MAKE MUSIC
If this word, music, is sacred and reserved for eighteenth- and nineteenth-century instruments, we can substitute a more meaningful term: organisation of sound.

WILL CONTINUE AND INCREASE UNTIL WE REACH A MUSIC PRODUCED THROUGH THE AID OF ELECTRICAL INSTRUMENTS
[. . .] The special property of electrical instruments will be to provide complete control of the overtone structure of tones (as opposed to noises) and to make these tones available in any frequency, amplitude, and duration.[12]

Cage was one of a number of experimental composers who also used computers in his composition, most notably in the work *HPSCHD* (1969), created in collaboration with Lejaren Hiller,[13] but also throughout his career as a means of generating random numbers based on the Chinese 'Book of Changes' or I Ching, and texts such as 'mesostics' in which a vertical phrase intersects horizontal lines of writing.[14]

It is beyond the scope of this book to give a complete history of the use of computers to make music. Authoritative accounts may be found in the following books:

- Chadabe, J. (1997) *Electric Sound: The Past and Present of Electronic Music.* Upper Saddle River, NJ: Prentice Hall.
- Holmes, T. (2006) *The Routledge Guide to Music Technology.* New York: Routledge.
- Manning, P. (1994, rev. 2004) *Electronic and Computer Music.* Oxford: Oxford University Press.

The first significant use of computers for music seems to have taken place in 1957 at the Bell Telephone Laboratories in New Jersey, where Max Mathews created a program called MUSIC4 to manipulate and process sound. In the same year, the first computer-generated compositions appeared, including the *Illiac Suite*, created at the University of Illinois by Lejaren Hiller and Leonard Isaacson. Europe was relatively slow to seize upon the potential of computers for music, but the establishment of the Institut de Recherche et de Coordination Acoustique/ Musique (IRCAM) in Paris, France, in 1976 seems to represent a turning point in these developments.

Of even more importance to digital musicians were: the release in 1977 of the Apple II, the Commodore PET, and the Tandy TRS-80 computers, all forerunners of today's desktop machines; the creation of the first computer network by the Advanced Research Projects Agency (ARPA, later known as the Defense Advanced Research Projects Agency, or DARPA) in February 1958, leading to the first wide area network, which was operational by 1983; the development of Digital Signal Processing (DSP) techniques for audio in the 1960s; the general adoption of the MIDI (Musical Instrument Digital Interface) specification in the early 1980s; and the creation of the World Wide Web in 1991 at the Swiss/ French particle physics laboratory Organisation européenne pour la recherche nucléaire, commonly known as CERN.

It is interesting to note that, even at the very origins of computer science, the musical possibilities offered by number-crunching machines were realised. In 1843, Lady Lovelace (Ada Byron) (1815–1852) wrote 'The Sketch of the Analytical Engine' about a calculating machine conceived by Charles Babbage at Cambridge. Babbage had already partially built a 'Difference Engine', and was planning the more sophisticated 'Analytical Engine'. This was an early model of a programmable computer, and Ada Byron immediately recognised the potential for 'universality' of the device. In the essay, she describes all aspects of Babbage's machine, including this passage about its musical application:

Again, it might act upon other things besides number, were objects found whose mutual fundamental relations could be expressed by those of the abstract science of operations, and which should be also susceptible of adaptations to the action of the operating notation and mechanism of the engine . . . Supposing for instance, that the fundamental relations of pitched sounds in the science of harmony and of musical composition were susceptible of such expression and adaptations, the engine might compose elaborate and scientific pieces of music of any degree of complexity or extent.[15]

Where are they going?

There is a danger, when contemplating the evolution of digital technology, of sounding, or even of actually becoming, *utopian*. It should be stated that these new 'digital' musicians are not inherently superior to the old musicians, and we are not heading for utopia. The phrase 'the digital world', with its global implications, seems to imply a state of affairs that holds good for everybody everywhere. This is not the case, as contemplation of a few statistics will quickly reveal.

About 2 billion people worldwide do not have any access to electricity.[16] Figure 1.1 shows a picture of the Earth at night,[17] seen from space, illustrates the distribution of electrical light.

The number of computer users is, therefore, a subset of that, and the number of computers connected to the Internet even smaller. The number of broadband users in the world in 2005 stood at 158 million,[18] compared to a world population of more than 6 billion.[19] These statistics and images give only a loose impression of the overall picture and, of course, are subject to daily fluctuation, but the main point remains: the digital 'world' is accessible only to relatively few people. In the early days of the Internet, these people were sometimes called the

Figure 1.1 Night on Earth.

'digerati'. *The Edge* gives the following definition: 'Who are the "digerati" and why are they "the cyber elite"? They are the doers, thinkers, and writers who have tremendous influence on the emerging communication revolution. They are not on the frontier, they *are* the frontier'.[20]

The numbers of the so-called digerati have now swelled considerably to include many people in the digital world, but these are still a technologically literate elite in comparison with the world's population taken as a whole. What makes the digital world so extraordinary is the way it defies geographical and national boundaries and can compress or expand time and space. The technology of the Japanese digital musician is mostly indistinguishable from his or her European counterpart, and they can and do share files across the Internet without noticeable difficulty.

It seems fairly clear that there will be a greater expansion and proliferation of digital technologies; although this will not necessarily make a better world, it does seem more or less inevitable. It also seems clear that it will rapidly become irrelevant that these are *digital* technologies, in other words that the novelty of digitisation will be replaced by a set of assumptions about their capabilities. This is in fact already happening, and many domestic appliances use computer technology for their operation without this being apparent to the consumer.

The digital music culture is increasingly an *aural* culture. Notation has a place within this culture, but the primary musical exchange is based on sounds. Since these sounds are held in digital form on digital media, their existence is abstracted even to the point of leaving no trace. The contents of a computer hard drive may be erased with ease, without destroying the drive itself. They may also be transformed into some other kind of data, modified so that their nature as sounds is changed. So the culture is based on what is heard, rather than on the written artefact. Performers devise music in real time, or over networks. Composers create music from sound recordings to be played back through loudspeaker systems. None of this is written down on paper.

One consequence is that the tendency to make a grand narrative out of the evolution of music itself will have to cease. The drawing of a single evolutionary line through classical music (Bach, Beethoven, Wagner, and so on through the breakdown of tonality); or popular music (where the blues leads to rock, where The Beatles develop beyond Gerry and the Pacemakers, where trance evolves from techno); will become a less viable method. In a world where all these musics are as accessible and available as any other, where the most 'extreme' music is equivalent to the most 'conventional' as pure digital information, evolutionary lines must be drawn in many different directions at once.

Today's musician is faced with a bewildering and exciting diversity. The full range of sound, from pure noise to a single pitch is available, as is the full range of human music. Every kind of means to manipulate these sounds is at the fingertips and often for relatively little cost. The channels of dissemination are open, and an individual working in isolation anywhere may reach a global audience.

This all means that the musician needs to develop *sensitivity*, *integrity* and *aware-*

ness. These are expressed not just in words, but in the sound itself and through the music. This requires intelligence; it requires critical reflection; it requires knowledge and understanding. The study and analysis of music is becoming increasingly relevant to the actual practice of making music.

The music to be made may 'sound like' anything at all, but the sound must be *distinct*. It is not enough merely to reproduce what has already been done. The music is a voice, a way of articulating in sound. The diversity of digital culture throws into relief the individual identity of the voice that wants to be heard. The technology of endless reproduction emphasises the need for consistent originality.

Given the breadth of these statements, the diversity of the culture, the problem of the lack of linear progression, the absence of 'tram-lines' down which to travel, the unfamiliarity of much of the terrain, and the apparent disintegration of known musical values, it might be concluded that the digital musician faces an impossible and unrewarding task. It is certainly difficult: far more is expected of these musicians than of their more narrowly focused predecessors. The compulsion to make something musical that 'speaks', that shows itself to be relevant to human existence, remains. But the means and the language with which to do this has vastly expanded.

The skills that the digital musician should possess are many and varied. These skills are currently being taught largely through 'music technology' programmes, although often with other subjects or in an interdisciplinary way. The breadth of skills required means that at some point the digital musician must make choices about which to pursue further if real depth is to be achieved. Part of the basic skill set, therefore, is the acquisition of sufficient musical knowledge, self-understanding and powers of discernment to be able to make those choices.

At any point in the process of becoming a digital musician, there will be many things you *could* know, a number of things you *should* know and several things you *must* know. Age is not a factor: it is a characteristic of this kind of music that even the most experienced practitioner in one aspect may be a beginner in another. Someone may be amazingly skilled at digital signal processing but cannot play an instrument, or an expert in sound recording but a beginner in computer programming, or work extremely well with sound alone but lack the technique to combine sound with visual imagery. Yet, a student of music technology is expected to have some ability in all of these. The digital musician is a 'jack of all trades' and a master of *some*.

■ Braun, H.-J. (2002) *Music and Technology in the Twentieth Century*. Baltimore, MD: Johns Hopkins University Press.
■ Cox, C. and Warner, D. (2006) *Audio Culture: Readings in Modern Music*. New York: Continuum.
■ Duckworth, W. (1995) *Talking Music*. New York: Schirmer.
■ Kahn, D. (2001) *Noise, Water, Meat: A History of Sound in the Arts*. Cambridge, MA: MIT Press.

- Negroponte, N. (1996) *Being Digital*. New York: First Vintage Books
- Prendergast, M. J. (2000) *The Ambient Century: From Mahler to Trance — The Evolution of Sound in the Electronic Age*. London: Bloomsbury Publishing.
- Seabrook, J. (2001) *Nobrow*. New York: Alfred A. Knopf.
- Swirski, P. (2005) *From Lowbrow to Nobrow*. Montreal: McGill-Queen's University Press.
- Tarkovsky, A. (1986, reprinted 1989) *Sculpting in Time*. Austin, TX: University of Texas Press.

Chapter 2

Aural awareness

> The entire music industry is deaf. Including journalists. And a lot of musicians.
>
> John Richards, conversation with the author, 2005

The ear is the most important attribute of the digital musician. The more music has become a matter of the manipulation of *sounds* rather than *notes*, the more central the aural aspects have also become. What musicians do with their ears, rather than their instruments, has been a relatively neglected aspect of musical training up until now. This is because the traditional aural skills (interval recognition, chord identification, aural transcription, score-reading, sight-singing, etc.) rely on *notation* as much as musical sound itself.

A small survey undertaken for this book asked fifteen leading academics in music technology the following questions. Should a digital musician be able to:

(a) distinguish between the sound of rain and the sound of fire? (This is not so easy as it might seem without a visual cue.)
(b) recognise a dominant seventh chord by ear? (This is a traditional 'aural skill' in music training.)

The answers to question (a) were unanimous: 'yes – that's essential'. The answers to question (b) were a lot less certain. There are obviously some situations where such a skill might be useful, but it could be preferable to be able to recognise the general characteristics of the interval of a seventh *wherever* they might occur. This would include many natural sounds and certain types of non-Western and folk music. The dominant seventh chord, in itself and accompanied by all the 'rules' of tonal harmony, is problematic: its harmonic function almost (but not quite) removes its status as a sound.[1]

These responses highlight the importance of the aural abilities of the digital musician: what matters most is *how they listen*. It is surprising how little this vitally important topic has been discussed in musical history. It is only during the twentieth century, with the advent of recording technologies, and, hence, the possibility of repeated listening, that 'aural awareness' seems to have become a recognised attribute. Even then, there have been relatively few attempts systematically to examine it with regard to musical concerns, outside the science of acoustics.

Listening

Listening is done for many different reasons and in many different ways. These are affected by the situation and motives of the listener at a given moment. The musician will often listen in a different way and with a different *purpose* to other people. Understanding this purpose is a crucial aspect of aural awareness. It begins with an awakening to the listening situation, both in a musical context and in daily life. This is followed by an increased sensitivity to the modes of listening, the ways in which one listens. Finally, 'active listening' summarises a state of heightened perceptive or receptive aural awareness that will be invaluable in most musical situations.

● Listen, listen

■ Mathieu, W. A. (1991) *Listening Book: Discovering Your Own Music.* San Francisco, CA: Shambhala Publications.
■ Schafer, R. Murray (1992) *A Sound Education: 100 Exercises in Listening and Sound-Making.* Ontario: Arcana Editions.

Listening situations

The composer John Cage declared: 'let sounds be themselves', and did so in the belief that *there is no such thing as silence*. He liked to tell this famous story of his visit to an anechoic chamber:[2]

> It was after I got to Boston that I went into the anechoic chamber at Harvard University. Anybody who knows me knows this story. I am constantly telling it. Anyway, in that silent room, I heard two sounds, one high and one low. Afterward I asked the engineer in charge why, if the room was so silent, I had heard two sounds. He said, 'Describe them'. I did. He said, 'The high one was your nervous system in operation. The low one was your blood in circulation.[3]

One outcome of this experience was Cage's notorious 'silent' piece: 4' 33". The point of this piece is, of course, that there is no silence, but that one should instead pay attention to the surrounding environmental sounds. Cage used the device of a musical time frame (usually presented by a performer making no sound in three distinct 'movements', the score showing *tacet* for each) to force our attention elsewhere. There is no need to witness a performance of this piece to learn the lesson: the environment can be listened to at any time.

Contrast this with a concert given in a blacked-out theatre or concert hall, through loudspeakers only. Because the loudspeakers fail to provide the listener with any visual indication of the sources of the sounds heard, the imagination of the listener may be thoroughly engaged. No musical performer, no visible sound source, just listening. This is an enforced listening situation that, once again, produces a state of heightened aural awareness.

In fact, despite their superficial differences, these two listening situations have a great deal in common. Both find ways of making the listener focus upon the sounds that surround them, and both structure and shape that experience to carry musical and artistic intentions. These two extreme examples are deliberately chosen to make a point about aural awareness. The reader's normal listening is likely to involve oscillations between various modes and states. The important thing is to be as aware as possible of listening at any given moment. This can be tested by listening to speech, to music, to nature, to machinery, to the body and noting what is heard in different listening states. Similar sounds can be heard differently in different situations and with a variety of meanings. Understanding these differences is the goal.

● Inner world, outer world

The soundscape

The general level of noise in the world around us has dramatically increased. Never has the contrast between the interior and exterior acoustic worlds, or sonic environments, been greater. In his book *Acoustic Communication*, Barry Truax observes:

> [Listening] is a set of sophisticated skills that appear to be deteriorating within the technologized urban environment, both because of noise exposure, which causes hearing loss and physiological stress, and because of the proliferation of low information, highly redundant and basically uninteresting sounds, which do not encourage sensitive listening.[4]

Truax identifies three levels of listening: *listening-in-search*, which is 'the ability to focus on one sound to the exclusion of others';[5] *listening-in-readiness*, which is the process whereby we can receive 'significant information, but where the focus of one's attention is probably directed elsewhere';[6] and *background-listening*, which is when the 'sound usually remains in the background of our attention'.[7]

Truax himself is part of a group of artists and scientists, musicians and composers, who are particularly interested in the sounds of the environment. The term 'soundscape' was coined by the Canadian, R. Murray Schafer to describe the acoustical environment. His book *The Soundscape: Our Sonic Environment and the Tuning of the World*, first published in 1977, significantly extends the notion of music to include *all* sounds and describes the cosmos as a continuously unfolding musical composition to which we are partial listeners.

Murray Schafer identifies *keynote sounds* (that are not heard consciously but give a 'tonality' to a soundscape), *signals* (foreground sounds that are listened to consciously) and *soundmarks* (specially noted sounds that function as acoustic landmarks). He also distinguishes between two different types of music: the Apollonian, which 'arises with the discovery of the sonic properties in the materials of the universe', and the Dionysian, which is 'an internal sound breaking forth from the human breast' and 'arises as a subjective emotion'.

Attracted by these ideas, but with her own 'take' on listening, the composer Katharine Norman defined it in 1996 as a 'complex, multi-layered activity' and observed (once again) three types: *referential* listening, which connects sounds to objects; *reflective* listening, which involves an enthusiastic appraisal of the sound for its acoustic properties; and *contextual* listening, which relates the sound to the context of the listener's individual history and memory.

Pauline Oliveros, on the other hand, writing in the 1960s for *Source* magazine, preferred not to theorise but simply to listen attentively, open herself up to, and describe, the sounds around her:

> The bulldozer starts again moving the air like an audible crooked staircase before reaching its full power. As I lean on my wooden table, my arm receives sympathetic vibrations from the low frequencies of the bulldozer, but hearing seems to take place in my stomach. A jet passes over. Some of its sound moves through my jawbone and out the back of my neck. It is dragging the earth with it.
>
> I would like to amplify my bowl of crackling, shaking jello. (Once in 1959 a bulldozer came through the side of my house while I was eating lunch. The driver looked at me, backed out, and continued to operate the bulldozer.)
>
> I would like to amplify the sound of a bull dozing.[8]

Notice how she makes connections between present sounds and imaginary or remembered sounds, even between materials (staircase/wood) and words (bulldozing/bull dozing).

Awareness of external sounds goes hand in hand with an increased concentration on internal sounds. The phenomenon of the in-ear listening system, for example, throws attention away from the environment to the sound world inside our own heads. The unique playlist, with its individually selected sounds, forms a kind of soundtrack to our lives, both blotting out the sonic environment and yet forcing us to engage with it in a different way. It throws us into a highly individualised state, each travelling around the environment in our own time and in our own sonic world.

This is a profound change from the world before recording technologies, when music was heard simultaneously by many people in a single hall and, generally, only once. Walter Benjamin's remarks about the emancipation of the work of art from its dependence on performance ritual is particularly exemplified by Muzak and other 'ambient' music which is created *not* to be listened to, but rather, in Brian Eno's words, to be 'a place, a feeling, an all-around tint to my sonic environment.'[9]

This artificial, or virtual, soundscape, created by oneself or others (or both in collaboration) fluctuates in its relationship to the 'natural' environment. In an extreme situation, such as the concert hall or the headphones, it overpowers it almost completely; at other times (in an airport, or a restaurant, perhaps), it drifts in and out of significance. 'Ambient Music' has, interestingly, made a transition from the kind of almost unnoticed aural wallpaper envisaged by Eno and others, to a distinctive musical genre in its own right, which exhibits different characteristics from other music and is designed to be listened to in a quite specific way. The 'chill-out' room is a good example, reinstating an element of ritual into ambience.

- Soundwalk
- Soundscape composition

■ Schafer, R. M. (1977, 1994) *The Soundscape: Our Sonic Environment and the Tuning of the World*. Rochester, VT: Destiny Books.
■ Truax, B. (ed.) (1999) *Handbook for Acoustic Ecology*, Vancouver: Cambridge St Publishing.
■ Truax, B. (2001) *Acoustic Communication*. Westport, CT: Ablex.

Listening modes

In 1966, the composer Pierre Schaeffer published probably the first serious musical study of listening.[10] He identified four *modes of listening*, defined by French words that have more shades of meaning than are available with English words:

1   *Écouter*, is 'listening to someone, to something; and through the intermediary of sound, aiming to identify the source, the event, the cause', thus 'treating the sound as a sign of this source, this event'.[11] Example: 'I hear the sound of a car and do not cross the street'.[12] This may also be called *causal* listening.
2   *Ouïr*, is 'perceiving by the ear, being struck by sounds'.[13] This is 'the crudest, most elementary level of perception; so we "hear", passively, lots of things which we are not trying to listen to or understand'.[14] Example: 'Traffic noise is continuous outside my window, but I am not aware of it.'[15]
3   *Entendre*, involves aural discrimination or, as Schaeffer puts it: 'showing an intention to listen [*écouter*], and choosing from what we hear [*ouïr*] what particularly interests us, thus "determining" what we hear'. Example: 'That sound has a texture which changes in a really interesting way'.[16]
4   *Comprendre*, is essentially *understanding*, or 'grasping a meaning, values, by treating the sound like a sign, referring to this meaning through a language, a code'. Example: 'That piece of music made real sense to me and I enjoyed it.' This may also be called *semantic* listening.

Schaeffer remarked: 'The four modes can be summed up more or less in this sentence: I heard (*ouïr*) you despite myself, although I did not listen (*écouter*) at the door, but I didn't understand (*comprendre*) what I heard (*entendre*).'[17] These thoughts led Schaeffer to his most famous notion: *reduced listening*. This means listening to a sound for its own sake, *in itself*, as what Schaeffer calls a 'sound object', by removing its real or supposed source and any meaning it may convey. A sound can have inherent value on its own and not just because of what it may appear to represent. Schaeffer recognised that this is different from ordinary listening and is, therefore, somewhat unnatural. The benefit of listening in this way is that we can understand sonic phenomena for themselves and in themselves.[18]

All these listening modes are interesting to the musician, but the most commonly used in musical situations are those which involve discrimination and understanding. Whereas sound *can* be used simply for information ('What is it? Who is it? What is happening?'), the musician often listens *past* the immediately obvious aspects of a sound and seeks to unlock something more from its sonic characteristics. As Schaeffer explained: a more sophisticated listener 'turns away (without ceasing to hear it) from the sound event and the circumstances which it reveals about its source and uses it as a means to grasp a message, a meaning, values'.[19]

Schaeffer's ideas have greatly influenced subsequent work on listening to music created with electronic technologies. In particular, the idea of 'reduced listening' has informed much electro-acoustic music created for an acousmatic listening situation, in which *only* audio information, without visual cues, is available to the ears. The word 'acousmatic' derives from an Ancient Greek practice attributed to Pythagoras (sixth century BC), of teaching from behind a curtain, so that students (called *akousmatikoi*, or 'listeners') would be forced to pay attention to what they heard, rather than being distracted by the physical presence of the teacher. The term was revived in 1955 by Jérôme Peignot and subsequently taken up by Schaeffer and others.

The 'sonic object' itself has become the focus of much musical attention, as artists and others seek new ways to discover and manipulate sonic material. Whereas tape and electronic media allowed some extraordinary manipulations, digital technologies have enabled the listener to 'enter' the sound to a level previously unimaginable, even to the point of being able to extract and edit the smallest constituents and sonic particles. This can, perhaps, go too far. The electro-acoustic composer Denis Smalley has identified what he calls 'technological' listening and observed that it has some dangers: 'Technological listening occurs when a listener "perceives" the technology or technique behind the music rather than the music itself, perhaps to such an extent that true musical meaning is blocked'.[20]

Another way of describing this is 'recipe listening', in other words, a tendency for the listener to be disproportionately interested in *how* something was made technically, rather than the musical or sonic outcomes. To listen well, then, requires not only an awareness of the modes, but also an ability to move between them and to discriminate appropriately at a given time, focusing upon the musical and sonic aspects as well as the technical processes that lie behind them, in a balanced way.

■ Schaeffer, P. and Chion, M. (1983) *Guide to Sound Objects* trans. J. Dack and C. North. To be published on the Electroacoustic Resource Site EARS: www.ears.dmu.ac.uk.
■ Chion, M. (1990) *Audio-Vision*. Trans. Claudia Gorbman. New York: Columbia University Press.
■ Smalley, D. (1995) 'The Listening Imagination: Listening in the Electroacoustic Era', *Contemporary Music Review: Live Electronics*, vol. 13, no. 2, pp. 77–107. Also published in J. Paynter *et al.* (eds) *Companion to Contemporary Musical Thought: Volume 1*. London: Routledge, pp. 514–554.

Active listening

For the *musician*, as opposed to the general listener, listening to music is a special activity, characterised by an interest not just in the superficial effects of the music but also in certain factors of relatively little importance to the non-musician, such as: Why was it made? How is it constructed? What does it resemble? Where does it come from? How much can I learn from it? and even, What does it mean? In his book, *When Music Resists Meaning*, Herbert Brün argues passionately for the possibility of a genius listener. He sees the experience of music being created mutually by the composer (who causes the music) and the listener (who causes the effect of the music). He says:

> There are three kinds of music for three kinds of listener.
>
> 1   First the music which reorganises already established music elements into new patterns. This is music for the listener who enjoys the status quo, to be looked at from different angles.
> 2   Second there is the music which enlivens old patterns with new musical elements. This is music for the connoisseurs, the listeners who enjoy looking at themselves from different angles.
> 3   And last, but not least, there is the music in which new musical elements create their new patterns. This is music for listeners who are still conscious of the fact that, after all, they had once created the need for music in their minds, and who now are happy and gratified if this need is met, in that at last they can hear what they never had heard before.[21]

Perhaps a less complicated way of saying the same thing is that there is a difference between the *active* and the *passive* listener. The active listener is curious and engages fully with the experience of the music by *seeking to understand*. Passive listeners are content merely to hear and pass on (possibly making a simple judgement about the quality of the experience as they do so). For the digital musician, active listening is essential. This is a hard lesson, because it might involve listening to things that are disliked. Why would anyone want to listen to something they do not like? Because this is part of the process of understanding that develops the individual's aural awareness. It may even lead to a reappraisal, a new appreciation, of the disliked music. At least, it will encourage an objective, impartial approach to the business of making judgements. This is not easily taught and is something for which the individual musician must take responsibility.

Active listening can take place when attending a concert or listening to a recording, but it is also a feature of both musical performance and musical creation. In the performance situation, responsiveness to other musicians is dependent upon active listening. This is especially true during improvisation, which is why that is such a useful practice for the digital musician. The ability to both hear accurately and understand the musical activities of others is essential to making your own contribution effective and relevant. In the creative or compositional situation, the technology allows the musician to listen and relisten time and again to the same material, which presents a uniquely active opportunity. Here, the aural awareness becomes highly focused until an extreme discrimination may be reached. This can lead to obsessive listening and often the key is to know when to *cease* listening and move on.

What all the above ideas have in common is that aural awareness is an invaluable skill for the musician who works with new technologies. In fact, without the ability to listen accurately and appropriately, the digital musician is almost useless. The good news is that these skills can be practised anywhere, any time. By getting into the habit of opening the ears to their surroundings, of hearing and listening to the world, the conscious process of *discrimination* that will be so crucial in more obviously musical situations, can be begun.

- Brün, H. (2004) *When Music Resists Meaning.* Middletown, CT: Wesleyan University Press.
- Cardew, C. (1974) *Scratch Music.* Cambridge, MA: MIT Press.
- Wishart, T. (1977) *Sounds Fun.* London: Universal Edition.

Hearing

Hearing is the means whereby we listen. The complexity of the act of hearing is best appreciated when taken out of the laboratory and analysed in the real world. The 'cocktail-party effect' is a good example: listening to a single person's speech in a room full of loud chatter or subconsciously monitoring the sounds around so that when someone mentions something significant the ear can immediately 'tune in' and listen. This is an example of *selective attention* and is normally done with relatively little apparent effort, but, in fact, it is a highly complex operation. First of all, the desired sounds must be separated from what is masking them.[22] This is achieved by using both ears together to discriminate. Second, the words must be connected into a perceptual stream. This is done using a process called *auditory scene analysis*, which groups together sounds that are similar in frequency, timbre, intensity and spatial or temporal proximity. The ears and the brain together act as a filter on the sound.

However, the ears are not the only way to register sound. In an essay on her website, the profoundly deaf percussionist Evelyn Glennie discusses how she hears:

> Hearing is basically a specialized form of touch. Sound is simply vibrating air which the ear picks up and converts to electrical signals, which are then interpreted by the brain. The sense of hearing is not the only sense that can do this, touch can do this too. If you are standing by the road and a large truck goes by, do you hear or feel the vibration? The answer is both. With very low frequency vibration the ear starts becoming inefficient and the rest of the body's sense of touch starts to take over. For some reason we tend to make a distinction between hearing a sound and feeling a vibration, in reality they are the same thing. [. . .] Deafness does not mean that you can't hear, only that there is something wrong with the ears. Even someone who is totally deaf can still hear/feel sounds.[23]

She goes on to explain that she can distinguish pitches and timbres using bodily sensation. This can be equally true when there is a direct connection to the human body. Antonio Meucci (1808–1889) was probably the first scientist to explore its sound-transmitting and -receiving properties, as part of his research into electromedical treatments. Meucci connected an electrode to a patient's mouth, then placed a similar device in his own mouth while standing in another room. When he passed a current through the two connected electrodes, his patient cried out in pain. This was unheard by Meucci's ears but, to his surprise, he 'heard' the sound through his tongue, in a so-called 'electrophonic' effect that he dubbed 'physiophony'.

Some digital musicians have taken this idea a stage further, to the extent of exploring the sonic properties of the human body itself. An extreme example is Stelarc, a performance artist whose work has included surgical interventions and body modification. His piece *pingbody* (1996) 'heard' electrical stimuli sent via the Internet which stimulated his wired muscles to involuntary motion. Part of his project to create a 'cyborged' body is focused on hearing, and he has explored the possibility of having an extra ear grafted onto the side of his face. The purpose of the extra ear is to emit sounds as well as to hear differently. He asks the question, 'Why an ear?' and answers, 'The ear is a beautiful and complex structure [. . .] it not only hears but is also the organ of balance. To have an extra ear points to more than visual and anatomical excess.'[24] Clearly, he sees the ear itself as an aesthetic object.

● Hearing fast

■ Martin, F. N. and Clark, J. (2003) *Introduction to Audiology*. Boston, MA: Allyn and Bacon.
■ Yost, W. (2000) *Fundamentals of Hearing: An Introduction*. San Diego, CA: Academic Press.

The ear–brain connection

The scientific study of hearing is called *audiology*, a field that has made great advances in recent years, especially with the advent of new technologies such as digital hearing aids. For musical purposes, an awareness of the basic aspects of hearing is usually sufficient, but a deeper investigation of the human auditory system can be inspiring and even technically useful. In particular, experiments with sound localisation and computer modelling of spatial effects derive to some extent from these understandings.

The mechanics of the ear are well known. It is divided into three sections: outer, middle and inner, as shown in Figure 2.1.

The outer ear comprises the external flap (*pinna*) with a central depression and the lobe. The various furrows and ridges in the outer ear help in identifying the location and frequency content[25] of incoming sounds, as can be verified by manipulating the ear while listening. This is further enhanced by the acoustic properties of the external canal (sometimes called the *auditory canal*), which leads through to the eardrum, and resonates at approximately 4 kilohertz (kHz). The final stage of the outer ear is the eardrum, which converts the variations in air pressure created by sound waves into vibrations that can be mechanically sensed by the middle ear.

The middle ear comprises three very small bones (the smallest in the human body), whose job is to transmit the vibrations to the inner ear. This contains various canals that are important for sensing balance and the *cochlea*, a spiral structure that registers sound. Within the cochlea lies the *organ of Corti*, the organ of hearing, which consists of four rows of tiny hair cells or *cilia* sitting along

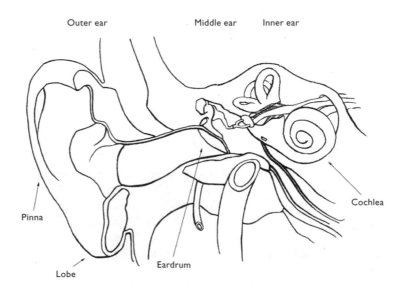

Figure 2.1 The human ear.

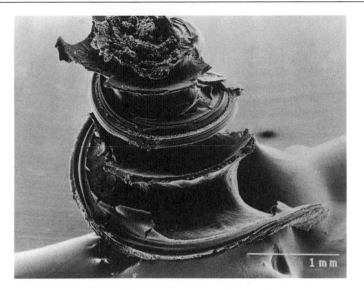

Figure 2.2 The (guinea pig) cochlea. (Photograph by Dr Spiro Comis/Wellcome Trust Medical Picture Library. Used with permission.)

the *basilar* membrane. Figure 2.2 shows the entire left cochlea of a guinea pig (magnification × 66), dissected free from surrounding bone. The basic design is the same as for humans. The organ of Corti sits along the outer spiral rim.

Figure 2.3 shows the sensory hair bundle of an inner hair cell from a guinea pig's hearing organ in the inner ear. There are three rows of outer hair cells (OHCs) and one row of inner hair cells (IHCs). The IHCs are sensory cells, converting motion into signals to the brain. The OHCs are more 'active', receiving neural inputs and converting them into motion. The relationship between the OHCs and the IHCs is a kind of feedback: an electromechanical loop that effectively amplifies the sound. Vibrations made by sound cause the hairs to be moved back and forth, alternately stimulating and inhibiting the cell. When the cell is stimulated, it causes nerve impulses to form in the auditory nerve, sending messages to the brain.

The cochlea has approximately 2.75 turns in its spiral and measures roughly 35 millimetres. It gradually narrows from a wide base (the end nearest the middle ear) to a thin apex (the furthest tip). High frequency responsiveness is located at the base of the cochlea and the low frequencies at the apex. Figure 2.4 represents this crudely, showing the spiral stretched out flat and its responses to high and low frequency inputs.

Studies[26] have shown that the regular spacing of the cilia and their responses to vibrations of the basilar membrane mean that a given frequency f and another frequency $f \times 2$ are heard to be an octave apart. Some of the most fundamental aspects of musical perception, such as pitch, tuning and even timbre, come down to this physical fact.

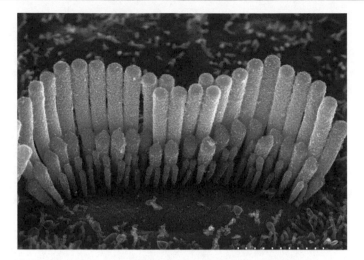

Figure 2.3 Hair cells, or 'cilia', in the inner ear (of a guinea pig). (Photograph by Dr David Furness/ Wellcome Trust Medical Picture Library. Used with permission.)

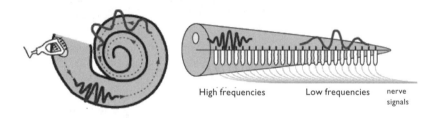

High frequencies   Low frequencies   nerve signals

Figure 2.4 Cochlea responses to frequencies.

The way in which the brain deals with the acoustical information transmitted from the ear is still not fully understood. The study of this part of the hearing process ranges across several disciplines, from psychology to neuroscience or, more precisely, *cognitive* neuroscience.[27] The latter uses biological findings to build a picture of the processes of the human brain, from the molecular and cellular levels through to that of whole systems. In practice, neuroscience and psychology are often combined and interlinked.

To simplify considerably, then: the cilia transmit information by sending signals to the *auditory cortex*, which lies in the lower middle area of the brain. Like the other parts of the cerebral cortex, the auditory cortex processes sensory information by organising its *neurons*, or nerve cells, into areas. Neurons are networked together and communicate with one another using chemical and electrical signals called *synapses*, which constantly fire during any brain process. Although the networks of neurons in the auditory cortex register and process sound itself, other

Figure 2.5 A network of neurons. (Image by Q.-L. Ying and A. Smith. Used with permission from the Wellcome Trust.)

parts of the brain contribute to deciding about characteristics such as its musical or aesthetic value. The nerve impulses are also important in determining the localisation of sound in space (see Figure 2.5).

Recent techniques such as PET scans[28] and Functional MRI scans[29] have enabled scientists to observe brain activity while hearing, seeing, smelling, tasting, touching. Figure 2.6 (overleaf) shows a three-dimensional (3-D) simplified model of the brain, in which the active areas associated with hearing are indicated. The locations of hearing and seeing activity, for example, are quite different, and in fact are even more complex than this implies, because different *types* of hearing stimulate different parts of the brain.

Figures 2.7–2.10, for comparison, show the areas of activity for the other senses.[30]

It is interesting to compare images of neural networks with maps of the Internet, such as those produced by the Opte Project.[31] While the Internet was not built to a model of a neural network, it is hard to resist drawing a parallel between the synaptic firings and communications traffic, the neurons and the individual processors connected by the data cables. Not surprisingly, dedicated research networks (sometimes called grids) have been created to study

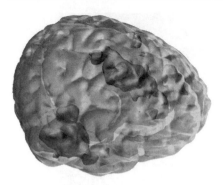

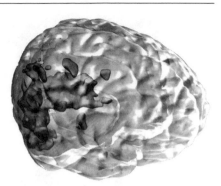

Figure 2.6 Hearing.

Figure 2.7 Seeing.

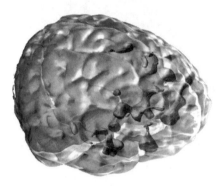

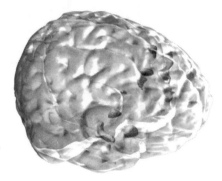

Figure 2.8 Smelling.

Figure 2.9 Tasting.

Figure 2.10 Touching.

(In Figures 2.6–2.10 the eyes look to the right. Images by Dr Morten Kringelbach. Used with permission.)

and develop artificial intelligence. This is highly demanding on computational power, and so uses parallel distributed processing (PDP) to make its models of human cognition.[32] The main use of such 'neural nets' is to identify patterns in vast and unstructured sets of data, such as weather forecasts, image and speech recognition and even in computer games. However, they have also been applied to perception of musical characteristics such as pitch, rhythm or melody, or for more intuitive human–computer interfaces, or to model the creative process itself. There has consequently been an awakening of interest in 'connectionist' models of music.

During the composition and realisation of their 2002 work *Construction 3*, for example, Tony Myatt and Peter Fluck used neural nets to map gestures by the performer onto the computer.[33] The work is an interactive multiple media composition for computer, computer-enhanced saxophone and computer graphics projected onto irregularly shaped screens. The work 'hears' the gestures made by the performer, although, as Myatt noted: 'The success of the technique relies upon a clear and appropriate attribution of meaning to each gesture and to generate information and an appropriate mapping of this generative data to musical parameters'.[34]

Figure 2.11 Performance configuration for *Construction 3* by Tony Myatt and Peter Fluck.

● Speech patterns

■ Bregman, A. S. (1990) *Auditory Scene Analysis: The Perceptual Organisation of Sound.* Cambridge, MA: MIT Press.
■ Denes, P. and Pinson, E. (1993) *The Speech Chain: The Physics and Biology of Spoken Language.* London: Worth Publishing.
■ Griffith, N. and Todd, P. (eds) (1997) *Musical Networks: Parallel Distributed Perception and Performance.* Cambridge, MA: MIT Press.
■ Hargreaves, D. and North, A. (eds) (1997) *The Social Psychology of Music.* Oxford: Oxford University Press.
■ Sloboda, J. (1986) *The Musical Mind.* Oxford: Oxford University Press.

The musician's ear

Given the delicacy and complexity of the human auditory system, and the importance of a 'good ear' to a musician, it pays to be aware of the potential risks to hearing. The main danger is excessively loud (or intense) sound. Digital musicians generally work with some kind of amplification and often explore unusual properties of sound, sometimes at extreme levels. Prolonged exposure to loud sounds can have the effect of flattening out the cilia in the organ of Corti. The consequences of this are a generalised hearing loss and, more damaging still for a musician, a loss of hearing *acuity*, which is the ability to distinguish different frequency bands. A third possible consequence is *tinnitus*, a disturbing and still insufficiently understood condition in which the cochlea generates noise. People often notice a ringing in the ears after a loud concert: this is tinnitus. For most young people, it will disappear after a time, but prolonged and repeated exposure to the source may lead to it becoming permanent.

A healthy young person can hear an average frequency range of between 20 Hertz (Hz) and 20 kHz. It is a fact of life that this range starts to diminish from the teenage years onwards. A typical 60-year-old may well have lost 12 kHz of hearing from the upper register. This is natural and to be expected, but prolonged exposure to loud sounds could accelerate the process, and hearing might be severely damaged without adequate protection. What constitutes a 'loud sound' is somewhat subjective and will vary from person to person and from situation to situation. When it senses loudness, however, the ear will attempt to protect itself against pain by using an acoustic reflex, which is an involuntary muscle contraction in the middle ear. This decreases the amount of vibration transmitted to the brain and can be felt quite clearly when a sudden loud or intense sound is heard. One unfortunate consequence for musicians is that they will often *increase* loudness levels in order to compensate and 'hear the sound better'.

Where the musician is in control of the sound levels (headphones, speakers, playing an instrument, and so on), then it is a good idea to be aware of the acoustic reflex. It is advisable to turn the volume level *down*, rather than up, in order to hear things more clearly. This might seem odd, but the result is that the acoustic reflex is disengaged, allowing closer listening. Where the musician is *not* in control of the levels, the only thing to do is to wear in-ear protection. Good quality earplugs will have a 'flat' attenuation, which will only reduce the overall level, without affecting the sound balance. These should be a standard item of personal equipment for digital musicians who are looking, above all, to control the sound they make.

These remarks should not, however, be allowed to prevent experimentation and exploration of the limits of sonic experience. With proper and appropriate safety measures and due consideration, some very extreme aspects of hearing can be creatively exploited. To give two examples, both *ultrasound* and *infrasound* have been used in musical situations. Ultrasound refers to sounds above the upper limit of normal human hearing and is used a great deal in medical sonography to produce images of foetuses in the womb, for example. Infrasound is the opposite, consisting of sounds below the normal range of human hearing.

In 2003, a team of researchers led by Sarah Angliss of the 'Soundless Music' project, and the pianist GéNIA, performed a concert at the Purcell Room, London, in which two pieces were 'laced' with infrasound (below 20 Hz). Audience questionnaires revealed a change in the musical experience when the infrasound was added. Up to 62 per cent of the audience reported having 'unusual experiences' and altered emotional states. The results were not completely conclusive, but there were strong indications that an unheard phenomenon could produce a different musical experience.[35] Ultrasound and, to a lesser extent, infrasound, have also been used in music-therapy treatments, with some success.

The musician will also need to be aware of a range of aural phenomena with musical applications. Take, for example, the phenomenon of *beats*, which has long been used to tune musical instruments. When two pitched notes are sounded together, a periodic and repeated fluctuation is heard in the intensity of the sound, resulting from interference between the two sound waves. Eliminating these beats will enable a piano tuner to tune a note to a unison. String players use a similar phenomenon to tune their strings to the interval of a fifth, where there is a clear mathematical relationship between the frequencies in the sound. Some composers have used this beating as the basis for their music, but mostly it is just a useful device for preparing to play. The digital musician has access to a wide range of similar sonic phenomena and aural illusions that can provide the basis for musical explorations. Some of these are embedded in software or take the form of plug-ins to modify the sound or create effects. Well-known examples, such as the *Doppler* effect[36] or *difference tone*,[37] can be used to add acoustic interest and excitement to a piece of digital music.

Aural phenomena normally exploit the natural tendency of the ear–brain connection to try to make sense of what it hears. This can give rise to convincing illusions based on patterns in which the listener fills in the gaps that apparently exist. The aural illusion of 'phantom words', for example, derives from the spatial locations of a collection of meaningless spoken fragments. After a while, listeners will naturally piece them together to hear words and phrases, in their own languages, that are not actually there. These illusions have been quite thoroughly researched,[38] and, interestingly, the results have tended to show that the ways the two hemispheres of the brain interact are a factor in their perception. In general, the left brain is logical, sequential, rational, analytical and objective and understands parts of things, whereas the right brain is random, intuitive, holistic, synthesising and subjective and understands wholes. Individuals tend to favour one side or another. The way in which certain patterns are perceived can therefore depend upon which side of the brain dominates or whether the individual is left- or right-handed, or even what language they speak.

One final aural illusion which may be regarded as a curiosity, but nevertheless a revealing one, is called the *Shepard tone* or *Shepard scale*, after the man who discovered it in 1964. This is one of those phenomena that are much harder to explain than to understand aurally. What is heard is a musical tone or scale that appears to continuously ascend or descend without ever actually getting higher or lower. The effect is achieved by superimposing tones with carefully controlled loudness levels to give the impression of continuous motion within an octave. Shepard tones have been creatively used by many artists, including the electroaccoustic composer Jean-Claude Risset, and the hip-hop musician Missy Elliott (in *Lose Control*).

To summarise: the digital musician's ear, like that of any musician, is a key attribute and needs nurturing and care. The kinds of aural phenomena and illusions that are familiar to most musicians are also important to the digital musician. Digital sound manipulation techniques, however, have opened up some new and potentially creative possibilities in this area, and the ear needs to develop in order to exploit those. In digital music, the ear has primacy and the subjective ability to be able to hear accurately and with awareness is crucial.

● Masking experiment

■ Deutsch, D. (ed.) (1999) *The Psychology of Music*. 2nd edition. San Diego, CA: Academic Press.

■ McAdams, S. (ed.) (1993) *Thinking in Sound*. Oxford: Oxford University Press.

▲ Diana Deutsch (2003) *Phantom Words and Other Curiosities*. Philomel Records, Philomel 02.

Chapter 3

Understanding sound

I was always into the theory of sound, even in the 6th form. The physics teacher refused to teach us acoustics but I studied it myself and did very well. It was always a mixture of the mathematical side and music.

Hutton, J. (2000) *Radiophonic Ladies: Delia Derbyshire* (interview). London: Sonic Arts Network.

Delia Derbyshire (1937–2001) worked at the BBC Radiophonic Workshop[1] and was famously responsible for the distinctive electronic arrangement of Ron Grainer's theme tune for the television series *Doctor Who*,[2] among many other things. She used tape loops, oscillators and early synthesisers to create music and soundtracks. She was a typical example of a technological musician, qualified in music but making 'special sounds' derived from an understanding of sound through the science of acoustics, combined with a belief in the supremacy of aural perception and the brain in shaping music.

Some of the basic elements of music are, traditionally: rhythm, pitch, dynamics and timbre. The basic elements of sound, on the other hand, include: duration, frequency, amplitude and spectrum. The two have much in common, of course, but the match is not exact. For example, rhythm in music is perceived in relation to pulse, beat or tempo, whereas the duration of a sound is usually measured in seconds, with little reference to its 'rhythmic' relationships. Likewise, 'pitch' arises from a subjective perception of the dominant frequency of a given sound, whereas 'frequency' is expressed in vibrations per second and is objectively measurable; 'dynamics' are relative, whereas 'amplitude' is fixed, and 'timbre' is the perceived quality of a sound, whereas 'spectrum' is a detailed account of its harmonic (or partial) components and their changing relationships.

The scientific study of sound takes in both *acoustics* and *psychoacoustics*. Where psychoacoustics concerns itself mainly with the human perception of sound, acoustics traditionally begins with the study of sound itself. Psychoacoustics is relatively new compared to acoustics, which is an established and vast field incorporating many sub-disciplines, such as:

- *aeroacoustics* (aerodynamic sound)
- *architectural* and *vibration* acoustics (how sound behaves in buildings and structures)
- *bioacoustics* (the use of sound by animals such as whales, dolphins and bats)
- *biomedical* acoustics (e.g., ultrasound)
- *speech* communication
- *underwater* acoustics
- *physical* acoustics, which explores the interaction of sound with materials and fluids, e.g., *sonoluminescence* (the emission of light by bubbles in a liquid excited by sound) and *thermoacoustics* (the interaction of sound and heat).

Some sub-disciplines of acoustics deal explicitly with musical concerns, including the study of the physics of musical instruments, and *acoustic engineering*, which investigates how sound is generated and measured by loudspeakers, microphones, sonar projectors, hydrophones, ultrasonic transducers, sensors and other electro-acoustical devices.

Acoustics has provided an objective, scientific, way of understanding sound, and most of the new technologies take that as their starting point. Some software may superimpose 'musical' characteristics to make the interface more acceptable to musicians, but the underlying processes remain mathematical. A computer is a number-crunching machine, which is very capable of extremely precise and sophisticated measurement and processing of the elements of sound. The kind of subjective perceptions and relative judgements required by 'music' represent an additional layer which may be built into the interface or software design.

What Delia Derbyshire and musicians like her represent is an embracing of the musical possibilities opened up by the scientific and acoustic principles that underlie the creative technologies. A good understanding of sound must be regarded as essential for the digital musician. Whereas musicians previously only needed to know how to get a good sound out of their instrument (which did not necessarily mean understanding sound itself nor even how the instrument produced its sound), the new technologies have expanded the sonic palette to include many more sounds. Nowadays, any music comes from an organisation of sound and, in order to be a successful musician, an understanding of whatever sounds are chosen for organisation is a first requirement. This chapter sets out some basic ideas, recommends reading for more detailed study and offers both examples and projects to further the musical understanding of sound.

- Backus, J. (1970) *The Acoustical Foundations of Music*. London: Murray.
- Benade, Arthur H. (1990) *Fundamentals of Musical Acoustics*. New York: Dover.
- Campbell, D. and Greated, C. (1987) *The Musicians Guide to Acoustics*. London: Dent.
- Cage, J. (1968) *Silence*. London: Marion Boyars.
- Howard, D. and Angus, J. (2001) *Acoustics and Psychoacoustics*. Oxford: Focal Press.
- Paynter, J. and Aston, P. (1970) *Sound and Silence*. Cambridge: Cambridge University Press.

■ Sethares, W. (2004) *Tuning, Timbre, Spectrum, Scale*. London: Springer-Verlag.
■ Sundberg, J. (1991) *The Science of Musical Sounds*. London: Academic Press.

Properties of sound

Sound is a disturbance in a medium such as air, water or even a solid, and it travels in waves. A sound wave has three main and related characteristics: frequency, amplitude and velocity. Velocity will depend on a number of factors, including the *density* and *elasticity* of the material through which the wave passes. Elasticity is the ability of a material to regain its shape after deformation from some force. The elasticity of steel and glass is much greater than that of water or air, so sound will travel faster through solids than through liquids or gases. The density of a material refers to its mass per unit volume.

Raising the temperature (which decreases its density) has the effect of increasing the velocity of sound through the medium. Sound travels through air at a rate of roughly 343 metres (1125 feet) per second (ms^{-1}) in a dry room at 20 °C (68 °F), but this figure will vary. At 0 °C (32 °F) in the same room, its speed will be roughly 331 ms^{-1} (1086 fs^{-1}), whereas in breath, which is not dry, at 25 °C (77 °F) it will travel at approximately 346 ms^{-1} (1135 fs^{-1}).

Amplitude is the measure of maximum disturbance in the medium during a single cycle. The amplitude of sound waves is normally measured in units of pressure called pascals (Pa).[3] Frequency is the rate of change in phase[4] of a wave and is equal to the velocity of the wave divided by its wavelength. The frequency of waves remains exactly the same when they pass through different media, and only their wavelength and velocity change. Frequency is measured in hertz,[5] which indicates the number of cycles (or periods) per second passing a fixed point. Figure 3.1 shows a typical wave form. The displacement of a particle in

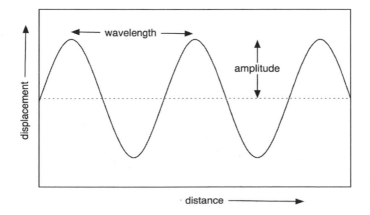

Figure 3.1 Wave diagram.

the medium is shown up the y-axis and the distance travelled by the wave along the x-axis.

Travelling waves are moving and make a disturbance that varies across distance and time. *Standing waves* result from the interference of two travelling waves and appear to stay in one place, e.g., the vibrations of a bass guitar string. *Longitudinal* sound waves vibrate directly along, or parallel to, their direction of travel, as opposed to a *transverse* wave, which oscillates perpendicular to its direction of travel. The vibrating bass guitar string is an example of a transverse wave, and a sound wave in a tube is an example of a longitudinal wave. One crude way to visualise the difference is to imagine a 'slinky' laid out on a table. If pushed back and forth from either end, a longitudinal wave is created. If moved from side to side, a transverse wave is the result.

A longitudinal wave compresses the air in between molecules, which then reacts by expanding according to the elasticity of the substance. This longitudinal motion generally happens in three dimensions, as unconstrained sound waves radiate in all directions in an expanding sphere. The wave form is, thus, a result of the displacement of particles in the medium (e.g., air molecules) as it moves from its state of rest. These variations in molecule displacement lead to related variations in pressure. The *wavelength* is the distance between any two equivalent points along a wave and is measured in metres, so audible sounds will have wavelengths of between about 1.7 centimetres (0.021 inches) and 17 metres (18.6 yards). The lower the pitch of a sound, the longer the wavelength.

● Sound types

Loudness

As was mentioned during the discussion of hearing in the previous chapter, loudness is somewhat subjective. Nevertheless, there are some commonly agreed perceptions, as was shown first by some famous research conducted[6] at the Bell Laboratories by Harvey Fletcher and W. S. Munson in 1933. They asked many people to judge when pure tones of different frequencies were the same loudness. The averaged results gave the 'equal loudness curves' (see Figure 3.2).

What these curves reveal is that, under laboratory conditions, the perceived loudness of a sound is, surprisingly, not directly equivalent to the amplitude of its pressure. This is because the sensitivity of human hearing varies according to the frequency of a sound wave. Each curve on the diagram represents equal loudness as perceived by the human ear, measured in units called 'phons'. The maximum sensitivity region of human hearing is shown to be around 3–4 kHz (3,000–4,000 Hz), consistent with the resonant frequency of the auditory canal.

Decibels are, thus, not a direct measure of the loudness of a sound, but are given relative to a zero level, which is (normally) the threshold of human hearing. This means, in practice, that doubling the decibels does not automatically result in a doubling of loudness. Loudness can, in fact, be measured in three dif-

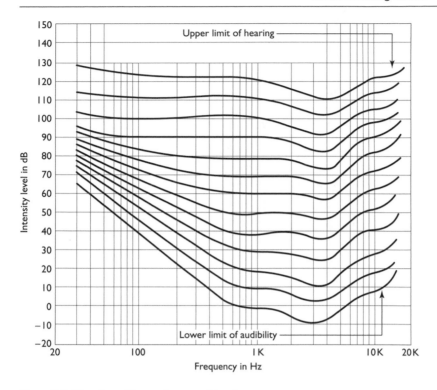

Intensity level in dB

Upper limit of hearing

Lower limit of audibility

Frequency in Hz

Figure 3.2 'Fletcher–Munson' or equal loudness curves.

ferent ways. The sound intensity level (SIL) is the flow of energy through a unit area in a particular direction, given in watts per square metre.[7] The sound pressure level (SPL) is the average pressure exerted by a sound at a particular point in space, given in pascals (where 20 micropascals (μPa), is the threshold of audibility and 20–30 Pa is roughly the pain threshold for most humans). The sound power level (SWL or PWL) is a theoretical total of acoustic power radiated in all directions calculated in comparison to a specified reference level (usually decibels relative to 1 watt, or dBW).

The decibel scale, sometimes abbreviated to dBSPL, is based on the fact that humans only register the SPL. Certain types of sound equipment, such as a sound level meter, use a 'weighting filter' to simulate the frequency response of the human ear. The calibration curves of loudspeakers and microphones are often compared to the equal-loudness curves. To give a sense of the scale, Table 3.1 (overleaf) is a chart of the relative decibel levels of various well-known sounds. Eighty-five dB is considered harmful, 120 dB is unsafe, and 150 dB will cause actual damage to the human body.

● Extreme quiet

Table 3.1 Chart of relative decibel levels.

dBSPL	Source (with distance)
180	Rocket engine at 30 m
150	Jet engine at 30 m
130	Threshold of pain
120	Rock concert; jet aircraft taking off at 100 m
110	Accelerating motorcycle at 5 m; chainsaw at 1 m
100	Pneumatic hammer at 2 m; inside disco
90	Loud factory, heavy truck at 1 m
80	Vacuum cleaner at 1 m, side of busy street
70	Busy traffic at 5 m
60	Office or restaurant inside
50	Quiet restaurant inside
40	Residential area at night
30	Theatre, no talking
20	Rustling of leaves
10	Human breathing at 3 m
0	Threshold of hearing (human with good ears)

Silence

In musical situations, sound is heard in relation to silence. A piece of music normally begins and ends with a notional 'silence' and may contain silences as formal devices, dramatic gestures, or moments of contrast. However, as Cage's visit to the anechoic chamber described in the last chapter makes clear, silence is only a relative concept, since there is always some environmental sound to be heard. *Digital* silence, though, is quite different from its acoustic equivalent, for two main reasons. First, an absence of data, or sound information, in a stream, represents a violent discontinuity: the contrast is abrupt and the silence absolute. Second, there is none of the noise, hiss, crackle and rumble produced by analogue equipment, which forms a sometimes-unwelcome backdrop to some recorded sound. A digital silence throws the listener suddenly out of the sound world of the machinery and into the natural world of the surrounding acoustic of the auditorium.

There have been many creative solutions to this 'problem' of digital silence, ranging from the addition of an 'ambient' resonance track to create an artificial acoustic within which the digital music can apparently reside, to the use of synthetic digital resonance to maintain the acoustic illusion. There is even software to produce artificial analogue hiss, crackle and so on. Some artists deliberately exploit the extreme contrast of digital silence and seem to relish the 'blackout' effect it produces. There are whole musical genres which set out to explore the extremes of quietness available to digital media.[8] The important point is that an absence of sound can be just as musically significant as the presence of sound, and this is heightened in digital music.

■ Cage, J. (1968) *Silence*. London: Marion Boyars.

Pitch

The role of pitch in music has changed. Traditional music gave primacy to pitch and the sounds called *notes* were defined first and foremost by their fundamental pitch. However, *all* sound, apart from certain types of noise, contains some pitch. What has changed in music made with new technology is that the pitch is no longer always the most important aspect of the sound. The pitch-based notation system and much of the music theory based on harmony have consequently become less relevant.

Pitch is very much a matter of human perception, based upon what is heard to be the dominant frequency in a given sound. As discussed in the previous chapter, this has a physical basis in the vibrations within the ear, but there is also a psychoacoustical aspect. Where the pitch perception is fairly unambiguous, the wave form is normally periodic; that is to say, it repeats in cycles per second (hertz) over time in a perfectly ordered way, producing a single pitch. An *aperiodic* wave, by contrast, never repeats itself but moves randomly (and noise is simply an unpitched aperiodic wave).

The resulting number corresponds to the pitch of the note, so the A above 'middle C' repeats at 440 Hz. A change in frequency normally means a perceptible change in pitch, but slight changes to the dominant frequency of a note (e.g., in vibrato) will not. The perception of pitch also depends partly on amplitude and other factors. When a given note is played on different instruments, the pitch may be recognisably the same, but the wave forms look quite unlike one another. This is because each instrument has its own distinct physical and acoustical properties which produce a unique timbre.

Tuning

The systematisation of pitch which is familiar in the Western world, comprising twelve equal steps to an octave, is by no means universal and is also somewhat controversial. It is a mathematical reinterpretation of the phenomenon of the *harmonic series* (see Figure 3.3), designed to create a workable system of tuning for keyboard instruments in particular. The discovery of the harmonic series is usually credited to Pythagoras, although there is evidence that the Chinese and other civilisations knew about it much earlier.

Pythagoras observed that a vibrating string touched exactly halfway down its

Figure 3.3 Harmonic series: musical notation.

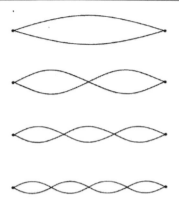

Figure 3.4 Vibrating monochord.

length produces a partial tone, which sounds similar to, but higher than, the one produced by the whole length of the untouched string. The point at which the string is touched is called a *node*, and the sound it produces is called a *harmonic*. Harmonics were historically known as *overtones*, and the open string vibration as the *fundamental*. Both terms are still used quite often today. It is the fact that a harmonic has a clear pitch that is crucial. An instrument such as a cymbal also generates many partial tones, but their lack of a whole number relationship makes them *inharmonic* rather than harmonic. Figure 3.4 shows a vibrating single string, or monochord, attached at both ends, with stationary points (nodes) at the ratios 1:1, 2:1, 3:2, 4:3. These nodes are distinct from the antinodes, or maximum moving points, between them.

This halfway division is in the ratio 2:1 and the resulting pitch is an 'octave' higher than the open string. The next sub-division that produces a clearly audible pitch is at 3:2, which sounds a 'fifth'. The one after that is in the ratio 4:3, then 5:4, 6:5, 7:6, and so on. The same phenomenon is equally apparent in a vibrating column of air. A flute, for example, is a vibrating column of air whose harmonic series is exploited by the flautist.

The fact that these ratios are whole numbers formed the basis of a great deal of Ancient Greek theory, not just in music, but also in architecture and astronomy, where they were seen as divine proportions. Their concept of *harmony* and even a harmonious universe is largely based on those theories, at least according to Renaissance theorists. The English philosopher Robert Fludd (1574–1637), for example, drew a 'Divine Monochord' (see Figure 3.5), with the hand of God turning the tuning peg, which linked the order of the universe to musical intervals, and the astronomer Johannes Kepler (1571–1630) also contemplated a 'music of the spheres' in which the orbits of the planets were derived from the same proportions.

Whatever theories the Greeks and others may have derived from these observations, the fact remains that the harmonic series exists as a phenomenon. The

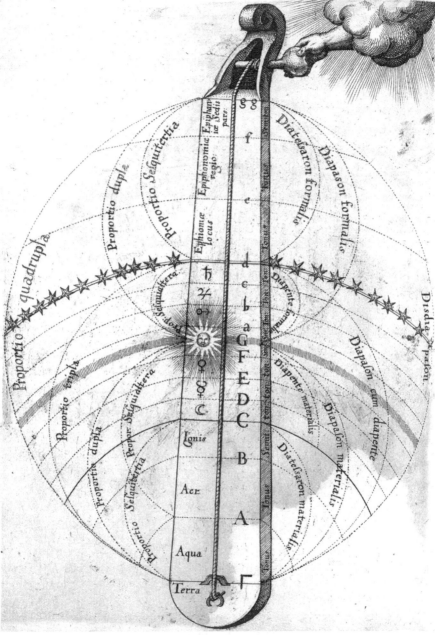

Figure 3.5 The Divine Monochord of Robert Fludd. From Fludd, R. (1617) *Utriusque Cosmi Maioris scilicet et Minoris Metaphysica* (History of the Macrocosm and Microcosm). Reproduced in Godwin, J. (1979) *Robert Fludd: Hermetic Philosopher and surveyor of two worlds.* London: Thames & Hudson, p. 45.

Table 3.2 The Pythagorean 'cycle' of 3:2s.

A0 = 27.5 Hz	'E1' (27.5 × 1.5) = 41.25 Hz	'B1' (41.25 × 1.5) = 61.875
'F#2' = 92.8125	'C#3' = 139.21875	'G#3' = 208.828125
'D#4' = 313.2421875	'A#4' = 'Bb' = 469.86328125	'F5' = 704.794921875
'C6' = 1057.1923828125	'G6' = 1585.78857421875	'D7' = 2378.68286133
'A7' = 3568.02429199 = 3568		

ability to recognise the harmonic make-up of a sound is an important aspect of aural awareness. The whole number ratios that produce the series of pitches are, in fact, *intervals* that get ever smaller. The resulting series describes a chord, which has a familiar appearance. All the pitches (apart from the fundamental and harmonic 2) are approximate in tuning to the notes indicated. Those with black noteheads are very significantly 'detuned'.

Pythagoras used this discovery to develop a tuning system. He made a nearly cyclical sequence of pitches, using the first ratio that was not an octave – the 3:2, or fifth. Starting at a fundamental pitch of 'A0' 27.5 Hz, for example, Pythagoras' system would repeatedly multiply by 1.5, or a ratio of 3:2. In Table 3.2, the pitches are named and numbered by octave, but these are given in inverted commas because the actual frequencies do not correspond to the notes on a standard keyboard.

Note, therefore, that the final 'A' is not actually the same frequency as A7 (which should be 3,520 Hz). Any interval can also be expressed in *cents*, which are hundredths of a semitone (thus there are 1,200 cents in an octave). A 3:2 ratio produces 702 cents (rather than 700): 702 + 702 + 702 + 702 + 702 + 702 + 702 + 702 + 702 + 702 + 702 + 702 = 8,424 cents. From this, it can be observed that Pythagoras' system delivers a final pitch that is noticeably 'out of tune' from the 8,400 cents that would be the product of seven octaves (2:1). This difference of nearly 24 cents, which is quite perceptible to the ear, is called the *Pythagorean Comma*.

Western civilisation made a decision, some time around the seventeenth century, to standardise its tunings by correcting this small but significant natural 'deficiency'. There were several reasons for this, not least the proliferation of various compromise tunings that made it difficult to predict the results when a piece of music was played on two different keyboards in two different cities. Some keyboards resolved the problem of the comma by combining whole number ratios ascending and descending (and then compressing the results into a single octave), whereas other systems tried to use 'just intonation' to keep the triads (the 2:1, the 3:2 and the 5:4) pure for chords built on the tonic (the 1:1), the dominant (the 3:2), and the sub-dominant (the 5:4). There were numerous variations on these systems, some involving split keys on the keyboards because *enharmonic* notes, such as D# and Eb, or G# and Ab, were not, in fact, the same pitch.

Equal temperament is, therefore, the name given to a tuning system in which the intervals between the twelve steps have been artificially retuned to be exactly equal. The numbers that result are anything but whole-number ratios; in fact, they are extremely complex. The frequency ratio of a semitone[9] in an equal tempered system is a number which, when multiplied by itself twelve times, equals 2. However, the benefit of equal temperament is it enables a piece of music to be played in any key and yet sound the same, which is perfect for a system built on diatonic harmony or tonality. The disadvantage is that the tuning system is never exactly in tune with nature, as anyone who has tried singing along to a piano will understand.

The intervals of the octave, perfect fifth, perfect fourth, major third, minor seventh, and the rest, as they appear on the piano keyboard, therefore correspond roughly, but *not* exactly, to the nearest relevant whole number ratios in a Pythagorean system. This detuning from nature begins with the so-called 'Perfect fifth', which is not *quite* a ratio of 3:2. (Note that in this list the intervals indicate the distance from the previous pitch.)

Fundamental (Harmonic 1) = Unison = 1:1
Harmonic 2 = Octave = 2:1
Harmonic 3 ≈ Perfect fifth ≈ 3:2
Harmonic 4 = Perfect fourth = 4:3
Harmonic 5 ≈ Major third (4 semitones) ≈ 5:4
Harmonic 6 ≈ Minor third (3 semitones) ≈ 6:5
Harmonic 7 ≈ Lowered (flattened) Minor third ≈ 7:6
Harmonic 8 ≈ Raised (sharp) Major second ≈ 8:7
Harmonic 9 ≈ Major whole tone (2 semitones) ≈ 9:8
Harmonic 10 ≈ Minor whole tone (1 semitone) ≈ 10:9.

In practice, it is fairly easy to hear up to Harmonic 6 in most sounds, and the seventh harmonic is particularly clear in highly resonant instruments or spaces.

Of course, there is no particular reason to subdivide the octave into twelve steps, and many cultures around the world use either many more subdivisions (Indian classical music, for example) or many fewer (Japanese folk music, for example). Nor is it necessary to have equal steps. By using just intonation (i.e., only whole number ratios), an octave containing over forty 'pure' yet uneven steps may readily be achieved. Nor is it necessary to be restricted to an octave: systems exist where the 2:1 is not the theoretical end of a given series of subdivisions. Even if the restriction of equal temperament is retained and only seven-step scales within an octave are used, there are still many alternative sequences to the one 'major' and two 'minor' used in traditional tonal music. Tuning systems, therefore, offer up a host of musical possibilities based on pitch alone.

● Exploring harmonics

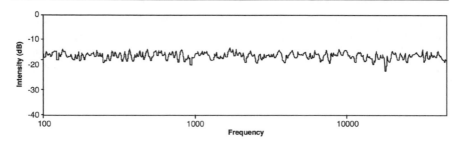

Figure 3.6 White noise.

Noise

The opposite of pitch is 'noise', a technical term referring to a signal without meaning or, in audio, a sound without pitch. 'White' noise sounds like the 'whoosh' of the sea (although without its fluctuations) and contains every frequency within human hearing (generally from 20 Hz to 20 kHz) to equal power over ranges of equal width. However, the human ear normally perceives this to have more high-frequency content than low. The range from 10–20 Hz is heard to be equivalent to the range from 100 to 200 Hz. White noise is, therefore, a random signal with a flat spectrum over a given frequency band (see Figure 3.6). To compensate for this uneven distribution of aural perception 'pink' or 1/f noise filters white noise by reducing the levels per octave.

> 1/f refers to the fact that the spectral falloff of such noise is 3 dB/octave, or a factor of 2 in power for every factor of 2 increase in frequency. Thus, the power in a frequency band is inversely proportional to its frequency.[10]

1/f noise occurs in nature, astronomy and even economic systems (see Figure 3.7).

Noise comes in several 'colours' (white noise is often compared with white light). 'Brown', or 'red', noise is the kind of signal produced by Brownian motion (the random motion of molecules) and is a more extreme version of pink noise

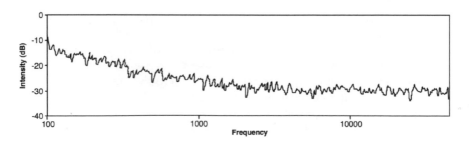

Figure 3.7 Pink noise.

that emphasises the lower octaves by reducing power octave by octave by 6 dB. The opposite of brown noise is 'purple' noise, which increases power per octave (also by 6 dB). 'Grey' noise exploits a psychoacoustic loudness curve to deliver a more accurate *perceptual* white noise to the listener. So-called 'black' noise has a power level of zero in all frequencies, apart from perhaps a few narrow bands or 'spikes'. Black noise is, technically, silence.

The pitch–noise relationship has become particularly relevant as sound synthesis techniques have developed. In *additive* synthesis, multiple sine waves are combined and shaped over time to produce either simulations of known sounds, or new 'electronic' sounds. *Subtractive* synthesis takes the opposite approach by applying time-varying filters to wide bandwidth noise or by removing partials or harmonics from wave forms. These began as analogue techniques, but have now transferred successfully into the digital domain. 'Noise music'[11] is, today, a substantial musical genre in its own right and will be discussed in more detail in a later chapter.

Timbre

Timbre is multi-dimensional and has no single definition, but may be summarised as the characteristics that allow us to distinguish one sound from another. In other words, its various dimensions add up to the perceived quality of a sound. One dimension of timbre is based on the observation that the physical properties of a sound-producing body give rise to 'formants', which help to shape the sound's spectrum. Formants are concentrations of acoustic energy or spectral strength within a particular invariant frequency range.

Continuous or transient noise is another dimension of timbre, which is also shaped by the *envelope* of a sound. The envelope is commonly described as having three stages:

- *attack* (initial or starting transient): the result of the means by which the sound was initiated
- *body* (continuant): how and whether the sound is sustained
- *decay:* the result of the damping in the system after any energy input has ceased.

Any sound has an overall envelope, and each and every partial tone also has its own envelope.

Where pitch predominates, the timbre of a sound may be varied as long as the pitch remains the same. Thus, a musically expressive 'note' may contain all sorts of variations in timbre and even some slight variations in pitch (such as vibrato), provided the fundamental pitch remains audible and dominant. However, if timbre replaces pitch as the dominant characteristic of a sound, such variations become less important.

The difficulty in making timbre the predominant characteristic of a sound is that it (timbre) usually changes over time. A complex sound, containing many competing partials (a bell, for example) is difficult to summarise, to hear accurately and to describe. How much easier it is to say 'that's an A on a piano' than 'that's a complex spectrum of shifting tones in which the fundamental appears to be around 440 Hz, but the sixth partial seems particularly strong after 10 milliseconds'. However, the difficulty of the challenge must not be allowed to deflect the digital musician, for whom an ability to hear spectral detail is essential.

The question posed earlier ('Is it necessary to be able to recognise a dominant seventh chord?') now comes to the fore. It *is* necessary to be able to recognise the 7th harmonic in the series, which gives an interval that is nearly (but not quite) a minor seventh above the octave above the fundamental. What's more, the intervening harmonics describe a kind of dominant seventh chord. Therefore, it is necessary to be able to recognise the characteristic sound of the seventh, because this is present in most sounds to some degree. The dominant seventh chord, on the other hand, has a functional value in a harmonic system, which may not always be relevant to the musical endeavour.

There are still further complexities here. The individual envelope of each partial (or harmonic) in a pitched sound may be analysed separately and, once again, there are changes over time. A sound may also contain components which are not whole-number multiples of a fundamental. Where the sound is periodic, and the wave repeats exactly, the spectrum is 'harmonic' (i.e., consists of true harmonics), but where a sound is aperiodic, the spectrum is 'inharmonic' (i.e., consists of inharmonic partials).

Pitch and noise, therefore, may be understood to represent opposite ends of a continuum.

Pitch ——————————————————————————— Noise

Every sound sits somewhere on this line, although often varying its position. Music technologies such as loudspeakers may be classified according to their responsiveness to points along this continuum. The extent to which the role of pitch has changed may be understood by comparing it with this continuum:

Music ——————————————————————————— Sound

Until fairly recently, it would have been assumed that the two lines were essentially the same, that 'music' was about 'pitch' and that 'sounds' were mostly 'noise' (in a musical context). Recent advances have blurred this distinction so that music, sound, pitch and noise all inhabit the same field, and artistic expression may exploit our appreciation of the qualities of all and the relationships between them, in a fluid way which nonetheless exploits contrasts when appropriate.

● Spectral study

Recording sound

- Bartlett, B. and Bartlett, J. (2002) *Practical Recording Techniques*. Oxford: Focal Press.
- Chanan, M. (2005) *Repeated Takes: A Short History of Recording and Its Effects on Music*. London: Verso.
- Hubner, D. and Runstein, R. (1997) *Modern Recording Techniques*. Oxford: Focal Press.
- Mellor, D. (1993) *Recording Techniques: For Small Studios*. London: PC Publishing.
- Rumsey, F. (2002) *Sound and Recording: An Introduction*. Oxford: Focal Press.

Recording sound is, of course, a lifetime's study in its own right, and many books have been written on specific aspects of its techniques. It is also a highly practical activity: doing is generally more useful than theorising. There are, however, certain key principles that need to be understood by the digital musician. Recording is about more than just achieving a convincing simulation of what is heard. The studio (of whatever kind) is a creative tool and a means of musical expression. When it is used as such, it has implications for both the form and content of the music itself.

There are three main situations in which sound recordings are made: the recording studio (a controlled environment); the location recording (a relatively uncontrolled environment); and field recording, which aims to capture environmental sound. These three types of recording are one of the basic means by which the digital musician accumulates sound information (another is through the use of prerecorded samples). It is assumed that at some time or other, the digital musician will want to make original sound recordings as part of the quest for a unique sound.

Appropriate microphone selection and placement, well-handled signal-to-noise ratio (S/N or SNR), well-judged mixing and mastering, are all desirable. An understanding of microphones is really a necessity and, although this information is readily available elsewhere, it would be wrong to omit a brief summary at this point.

Microphone choice

There are two common types of microphone: the *dynamic* and the *condenser*. Dynamic microphones contain a 'voice' coil of wire wrapped around (but not touching) a magnet. A diaphragm moves in response to changes in air pressure, consequently moving the coil and generating an output signal through electromagnetic induction. This is the 'moving-coil' microphone. This kind of microphone is regarded as highly reliable and generally useful. It does not require a power supply and is good for many live recording situations.

Sometimes, a thin foil is used in place of the more rigid coil, because the light weight and sensitivity of the foil gives a better frequency response. These 'ribbon' microphones have a relatively low output, so usually require some kind of transformer or amplifier, but they are excellent for detailed and delicate recordings.

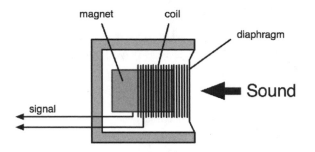

Figure 3.8 Cutaway of dynamic microphone's capsule.

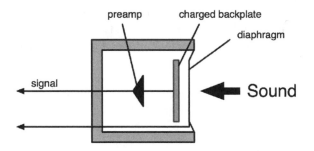

Figure 3.9 Cutaway of condenser microphone's capsule.

Condenser microphones are electrostatic, rather than electromagnetic; in other words, the head comprises two very thin plates, one of which can move, which make up a *capacitor* or *condenser*, capable of storing an electrical charge. This can be charged up using 48 volts DC of phantom power.[12] The moving plate functions as the diaphragm, and its changes in position vary the capacitance of the microphone, resulting in a change in output voltage. Because the output impedance is very high, this kind of microphone needs a pre-amplifier to give a useful signal, but the recording results are generally excellent, detailed and 'clean'.

There are certain types of condenser microphone that do not require phantom power, such as the *electret* microphones, which are permanently charged up during manufacture. These are generally used as small vocal microphones, or built-in microphones on cassettes, because the larger diaphragm required by the charge tends to compromise sound quality. However, there have been improvements in such microphones in recent years.

Various other microphones exist, including: carbon (carbon granules pressed between metal plates, often used in telephone handsets); various types of ceramic microphones; and the *piezo*, which uses a crystal called Rochelle salt that responds to pressure. A Lavalier microphone is a small dynamic microphone that is worn on the lapel for public speaking. A contact microphone picks up

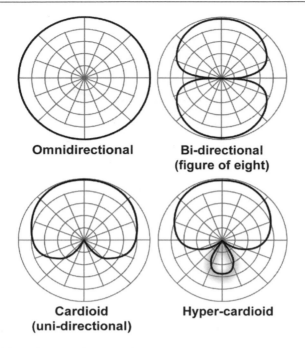

Omnidirectional   **Bi-directional**
                            (figure of eight)

Cardioid   **Hyper-cardioid**
(uni-directional)

Figure 3.10 Microphones – directional response patterns.

vibrations in a physical medium rather than air. A throat microphone may be attached directly to the front of the throat and will pick up even a whisper. These microphones are used by the military for communications, especially in noisy surroundings such as tanks and armoured vehicles. The funnel around the head of a parabolic microphone is designed to focus sound waves onto the receiver and is often used for field recordings.

Microphones are classified by their *directional* and *frequency* responses. The directional response is also called the *polar pattern* or *polar response*, and is represented by a 360-degree graphic depicting its sensitivity to frequencies from various directions. These are usually calculated in an anechoic chamber using pure sine waves, so are theoretical response diagrams only. Nevertheless, the directional response patterns are sufficient to be able to classify microphones into distinct groups (see Figure 3.10).

Omnidirectional microphones, as the name implies, pick up sound from any direction. Even so, the sounds that come into the 'back' of the microphone can seem duller than those at the front. This is because the body of the microphone itself will tend to diffract sounds coming from the rear, affecting higher frequencies to a greater extent, so the smaller the microphone, the better the frequency response.

Directional microphones pick up signals from a specific direction. Here, the

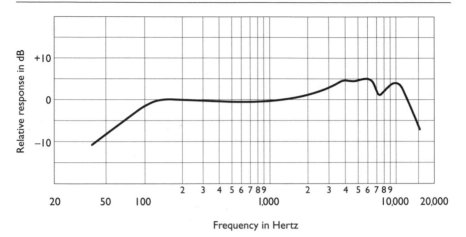

Figure 3.11 Shure SM58 frequency response.

range of possibilities is theoretically limitless, and different microphones will have different directional properties. However, the most commonly encountered patterns are the *cardioid* (heart-shaped), the *supercardioid* and the *hypercardioid*. The last two patterns are basically compromises on the cardioid model, allowing a certain amount of rear sound. These are therefore good for picking up reverberation from a space in which the recording is being made. Some condenser microphones can be electrically switched from one directional response to another to create various available supercardioid and hypercardioid patterns. Others, such as the *shotgun* microphone, are specifically designed for work outdoors, having a long and highly directional pick-up pattern designed to eliminate surrounding noise.

Frequency response is a measure of a microphone's output over the range of human hearing, usually given as dB against frequency. The limits of frequency response are defined as the points at which the response falls below −3dB. These are normally represented by a curve on a frequency response graph. An ideal microphone would have a *flat* frequency response or would respond equally well in all frequency bands. In practice, microphones are usually engineered to have better frequency responses in different areas of the spectrum. By way of illustration, Figure 3.11 shows the frequency response curve of the Shure SM58.

This illustration shows a boost between 2 kHz and 5 kHz, which means that this microphone will be particularly good for vocals, either sung or spoken, since its tailored frequency response enhances the effects of sibilants and consonants which generally sit between those frequencies.

However, the frequency response of a microphone is not the sole measure of its quality: its *transient* response is also important. This is the length of time it takes for the diaphragm to move in response to a signal. A transient is a short, relatively high amplitude signal; in other words, the initial characteristics of a sound that contribute to its timbre. Condenser microphones usually have an accurate transient response, which makes them especially useful for recording sounds with a high degree of transient detail such as percussion instruments. Moving-coil microphones generally have slower transient responses and therefore 'soften' the sound.

■ Nisbett, A. (1993) *The Use of Microphones*. Oxford: Focal Press.

Microphone placement

Whatever the frequency range and timbral characteristics of a given sound, *microphone placement* will be crucial to the recorded result. Since every microphone has its own individual characteristics, and most sounds also have their individual characteristics, establishing any hard and fast rule on this subject is difficult. There is no substitute for practice and experience. This is where the musician's creativity may come to the fore.

Distant microphone placement (i.e., more than a metre, or 1.09 yards) generally tries to deliver an overall impression of a sound, incorporating the acoustic properties of the space in which it is being made. Because this technique inevitably includes reflected waves, it can be subject to problems with out-of-phase sounds arriving at the microphone. Some special microphones, called *boundary* microphones, have been designed specifically to address the problem of reflective surfaces. Keeping the microphones close to floor level can also help to minimise the problem.

Close microphone placement will tend to exclude the acoustic environment. Where there are multiple sound sources in a studio situation, it is important to avoid leakage from one to another. Spreading the sound sources apart and using directional microphones will help, but it may also be necessary to interpose acoustic barriers between them. When close-miking the voice, a pop shield is also useful to avoid wind noise and distortion on certain consonants (e.g., 'p').

Spot, or *accent*, microphones are those placed somewhere in between the two described above to bring out certain features, such as a soloist in an orchestra. *Ambient* microphones are placed in a hall specifically to catch the resonant and acoustic properties of the space, rather than the 'musical' sounds being recorded in other ways.

One specific approach to microphone placement is called *stereo-miking* technique. This is a deliberate attempt to create a convincing stereo image through microphone placement rather than through mixing techniques. Here, the goal is to achieve an accurate sense of localisation and depth. The standard ways to achieve this are by using a *coincident pair*, a *spaced pair*, or a *near-coincident pair* of microphones.

A coincident pair of microphones have their capsules placed as close as possible to one another, so that there is no phase difference between them. The stereo image is thus created by amplitude alone, and because directional mikes detect more sound from the front than the sides, the centre of the angle between them will appear to be the centre of the stereo field. In an XY coincident pair, the angle between the two microphones is set at 90–135 degrees. The mikes can be cardioid, hypercardioid or supercardioid, but they must be the same.

One excellent type of coincident pair set-up uses two bi-directional cardioid microphones placed with their grilles nearly touching and diaphragms one above the other. This is known as the Blumlein array,[13] and the microphones are angled at 90 degrees apart and facing the left and right sides of the sound source. This reproduces very effectively the differences in amplitude levels used by stereo systems to create the illusion of localisation.

A spaced pair comprises two microphones placed several feet apart and directly facing the sound source. Omnidirectional microphones are often used for this technique. This uses the delay time between sound sources to give the illusion of localisation, but it is important not to place the microphones too far apart, otherwise an exaggerated delay (more than 1.5 milliseconds) will produce a ping-pong effect. Since it is often desirable to have these microphones wide apart, a common solution is to insert a third microphone between them to pick up signals from the middle of the sound source. The advantage of a spaced pair is that a good impression of the overall acoustic of the space can be achieved. The disadvantage is that time delays can produce unwanted effects.

A near-coincident pair comprises two directional microphones angled apart. Adjusting the angle of the spread adjusts the space in the stereo image. This method is routinely used by the French broadcasting organisation, the ORTF (Office de Radiodiffusion Television Française) and consists of two cardioids angled 110 degrees apart and spaced 17 centimetres (6.69 inches) apart horizontally. It produces very accurate spatialisation and gives a sense of 'air'.

Alongside these techniques, there are also stereo microphones, which contain two microphone capsules separated within a single head. The best stereo microphones allow you to vary the stereo field, and are excellent for field and location recording. However, they are often also extremely expensive. A similar kind of effect can be achieved by using two omni microphones separated by a baffle.

Binaural recordings are also easily achievable now that cheap in-ear microphones are available. These are particularly useful for field recording, since they resemble personal stereo earphones and therefore do not give away the fact that a recording is being made.[14] However, binaural recordings tend to sound better played back over headphones rather than through loudspeakers. There have also been some attempts to develop surround-sound recording devices, but the relative rarity and expense of these systems put them out of the reach of most musicians.

- Singing bowls

■ Bartlett, B. (1991) *Stereo Microphone Techniques.* Stoneham, MA: Butterworth-Heinemann.
■ Huber, D. (1999) *Professional Microphone Techniques.* Boston, MA: Artistpro.

Mixing

Mixing may be done using either a physical or a virtual mixing desk. The virtual desk usually mimics the structure of a physical desk, although the new generations of digital desks sometimes incorporate functions of which their analogue counterparts are incapable. Whether working on screen or at a desk, in a digital or analogue environment, it is from here that the musician will control the spatial positioning, blend, volume and general sound quality of the music. The mixer, therefore, has a role in both sound recording and live performance.

Traditionally, there are three main phases in the production of recorded music: recording, overdubbing and mix down. The mixer is central to all three. In the recording phase, the input signals are normally directed into an input strip on the mixer, or its digital equivalent. The gain of each input strip is set to a good level and the result is assigned to an output on the mixer. This output is then routed to a recording device such as tape or hard disk. Overdubbing, as the name implies, is a stage at which new material and tracks may be added, or corrections made to existing tracks. Many recording sessions build up layers in this way, overdubbing repeatedly to arrive at a finished result. Once again, there are different ways of achieving the same results when using digital technologies. In the mix down stage, the recorded material becomes the input, while levels, EQ, panning and effects are adjusted to achieve the desired result: the final mix. At all these stages, aural awareness is paramount, and this is far more than simply a technical exercise.

Although digital mixers are different from analogue mixers in a number of key respects, there are sufficient similarities to be able to usefully describe mixers in general, for the moment. Once a signal has reached the mixer, it must follow a path that is not always visible to the musician, because the connections are buried inside the desk. It is very important, therefore, to understand the flow within the desk. Each separate module in the console has its own input and output, or I/O, and is therefore 'chained' together. The links of this chain will trace the path of the signal. There are many variations in the configuration of modules in mixing desks and audio consoles, but the modules themselves are common to all and capable of being plugged in or bypassed as the situation requires. Typically, the chain will comprise a vertical strip containing several such modules, down which the signal flows. The most commonly found modules are as follows:

Channel input (microphone or line in)

Filters, gates and FX may also be inserted at this stage to remove unwanted noise or treat the sound.

EQ module (controls frequency bands)

This is sometimes preceded or followed by an *insert point* which enables the signal to be routed (sent and returned) through external devices, such as processors and effects boxes.

Auxiliary sends

Aux sends are probably the most useful section of the mixer for shaping sound. They enable the routing of the signal to external devices to create *sub-mixes*. The external devices may be an effects box, additional loudspeakers, headphones and so on. Each aux send can be handled separately, so different input signals can be sent to different destinations.

Dynamics

Various configurations of signal-processing devices, including: compressors, limiters, expanders, gating, EQ. The configuration and effectiveness of these elements varies considerably from mixer to mixer.

Monitor

Enables levels to be set in the control room rather than the recording device. Some mixing desks combine this with an I/O fader, which can be 'flipped' to assign either the monitoring mix or the 'tape' mix to the main faders or the monitoring faders. Other mixing desks take this one step further and have two entirely separate areas of the console for monitoring and tape return.

Channel matrix

Assigns the signal to a channel, normally using a matrix. Matrix design varies a great deal, sometimes comprising dual function 'pan-pot' type buttons to reduce the physical size, but they all enable the signal from one channel to be sent to another, which is especially useful in overdubbing.

Output fader

Includes a solo button to enable that channel to be monitored in isolation and a mute button to instantly silence the channel. Some mixers have a 'master cut' button to mute collections of channels. There will also be a pan pot, to place the signal to between the left and the right of the stereo field, and a volume fader.

The collective term for all these inserts, inputs and outputs, is *bus* or *buss*. On analogue desks, this is a copper wire that follows a route along the strip, possibly being diverted when the various junction points are reached. Although this is a feature of analogue desks, the same basic concept is retained in a digital desk, helping to understand the signal flow. Because the wiring set-up may be complex, studios will often use a *patch bay*, which has an input and output for every external device, to connect the various elements together. A connection is *normalled* when two of the sockets are connected without a patch cord. That connection is broken when plugs are inserted to connect two devices together. On some patch bays, an additional strip of sockets allows the user to 'take a sniff' of the signal without breaking the connections. Even a patch bay may be used creatively and musically.

The SNR is normally given in decibels and in relation to a reference level. The SNR is most useful in establishing the *dynamic range* of a unit or system, that is to say, the ratio of the loudest undistorted signal to the quietist, which is just above the *noise floor*. This is the sum of all the unwanted signals and low-level noise inherent in the circuitry of any particular device or devices. The 'high end' is where the signal level starts to distort, or clipping occurs. Heating, ventilation, air conditioning, audience noise, can all reduce the dynamic range of a system considerably in a live situation.

The SNR can be enhanced by a variety of signal-processing hardware devices which are often found in studios. *Expanders* are used to increase the dynamic range of a given signal, whereas a *compressor* does the reverse. A *noise gate* is a kind of expander with an infinite downward expansion ratio. This means that the user can set a *threshold* below which the *gain*, or amount of amplification, automatically drops the signal to zero. This is mainly used to remove unwanted noise generated by the equipment. A *limiter* is a kind of compressor that prevents a signal becoming any louder than a given value and is generally used to prevent overloads. Although these may seem like rather uninspiring devices, in fact they can be used creatively to make a distinctive sound in the studio.

There are many and various digital desks and control surfaces. Some link directly to, and are the physical expression of, software. Others are digitally controlled analogue desks, or self-contained digital desks. The advantage of digital desks is that they are generally smaller and that they offer great possibilities for automation. Fader motions, panning set-ups, effects inserts and the rest, can be stored as digital information and retrieved immediately at the start of the next session. Single buttons can be assigned multiple functions, and different states can be called up and manipulated easily and effectively. Furthermore, in the case of purely digital desks, the signal does not require constant digital to analogue (D to A) and analogue to digital (A to D) conversion. Despite these advantages, many users still prefer analogue mixing desks.

One final point is that monitoring in a studio situation can lead to hypercritical listening. This is partly due to changes in the ear, which perceives sound differently at different levels. When the sound is loud, the ear becomes sensitive to the extreme high and low frequencies. When the level is reduced, the ear loses interest in these frequencies. The result may be overcompensation in the mix. The only solution to this and all the other issues identified above is to try the music in a variety of different listening situations, and with both fresh and tired ears.

■ Misner, T. (1994) *Practical Studio Techniques: Recording and Mixdown*. Amsterdam: School of Audio Engineering.

Representing sound

One of the most significant changes brought about by electronic technologies is the general replacement of musical notation systems by the direct representation of sound itself. Electronic and digital technologies apparently represent sound analytically, that is to say, as 'neutral' information, divorced from a 'musical' context. In fact, as the means of representation has become more sophisticated, there has been an overlap between the use of visual images as a reference tool for editing, for example, and the visualisation of sound as a creative end in itself. The neutral layer of sound information representation has bled into the aesthetic layer of musical practice. The way in which a sound is presented on screen can give the impression that the musician can go 'inside' in ways that were not previously possible. Factual, scientific, representation is not as aesthetically neutral as might at first be thought. The process of representing sound leads on to the creative analysis of sound and, hence, to the manipulation of sonic artefacts, often in considerable detail and sometimes with astonishing breadth.

Wave forms

The basic representation of a sound is the *wave-form diagram*. Figure 3.12 is a simple flat wave-form diagram of a pure sine wave, a single harmonic, oscillating at a given amplitude and phase.[15] The lack of any additional harmonics means that the wave form is smooth and regular, and the resulting sound is extremely pure. The second image represents exactly the same sine wave but shows the harmonic spectrum, which in this case consists, predictably, of a single peak at the relevant frequency.

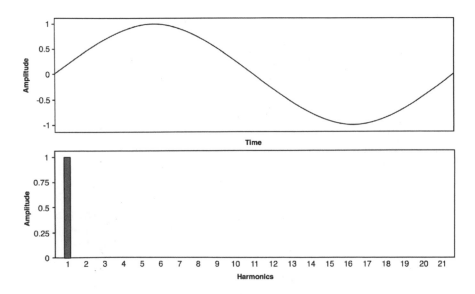

Figure 3.12 Sine wave.

The sine wave, or *sinusoid*, is most useful in synthesis, since it can readily be isolated or generated using electronic or digital equipment. However, synthesis does not normally restrict itself to pure sine waves but uses more complex variants, such as:

- *square waves* comprising the odd numbered harmonics of a fundamental
- *triangle waves* consisting of a fundamental frequency, with odd-numbered harmonics (these roll off in amplitude more quickly than in a square wave, producing a smoother sound)
- *sawtooth* waves, which normally ramp upwards over time, then sharply drop, although there are some which ramp downwards over time then sharply rise.

Notice how, in Figures 3.13, 3.14 and 3.15 the name of the wave form derives from its visual representation rather than from its sound. Already, even with such simple waves, the representation has become the way in which the sound is understood.

A more complex wave-form diagram, such as the one shown in Figure 3.16, gives a summary of the harmonic activity in a sound, resulting in a single line which uses a process called 'spectral averaging' to convey a certain amount of information about (among other things) periodicity, or lack of it. This is useful for getting a general impression of the timbral character and, especially, for identifying pitch, but what is needed for a more sophisticated understanding is detailed information about all the harmonics and their complex relationships over time, in other words, the *spectrum*. There are a number of solutions to this, but the most commonly encountered is the *spectrogram* (also sometimes called a *sonogram*).

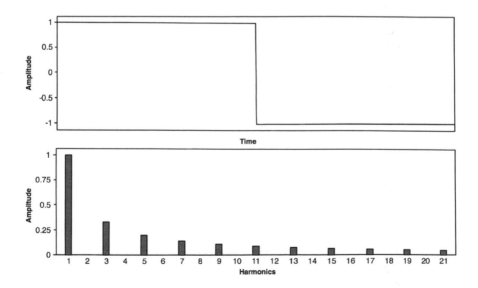

Figure 3.13 Square wave.

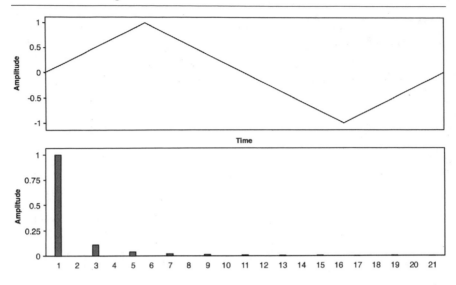

Figure 3.14 Triangle wave.

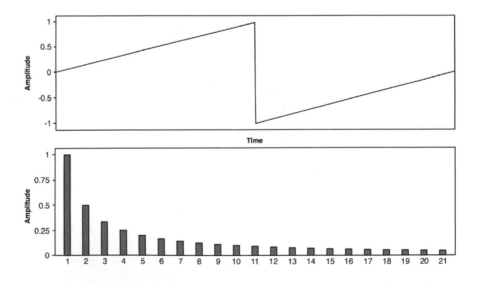

Figure 3.15 Sawtooth wave.

Spectrograms

In the digital realm, spectrograms (see Figure 3.16) are easy to produce and provide ready information about the spectrum of any sound. Some software enables audible spectrograms, so that the user may listen to an individual harmonic. A typical spectrogram represents time along the x-axis and frequency along the y-axis, but the most important and distinctive feature is the amplitude of the various harmonics, which are usually shown as striations of varying depths or intensity. These may be colour (rather like a weather map)[16] or monochrome, but in general the more dense or intense the striation, the stronger that particular harmonic will be in the spectrum. Figure 3.17 shows a two-dimensional (2-D) spectrogram of a piano playing a note, followed by another a fifth above. The harmonic series may be clearly seen.

Figure 3.18 shows a 3-D spectrogram of a sound showing the amplitude of each of its harmonics and their changing relationships over time, represented by the individual envelopes. Notice that the characteristics of the attack and decay of the sounds are as clear as the central continuant. This is a great advantage of spectrograms, whereas the conventional wave-form diagram is most useful in the continuant only. The perception of timbre is often located during the attack stage. There have been many psychoacoustical experiments to show that listeners cannot distinguish one musical instrument from another, for example, if the attack is removed and only the continuant is heard.

Figure 3.19 shows a 2-D spectrogram of the spoken word 'sound', showing frequency information represented vertically and time horizontally. Notice the higher frequencies are most dense during the sibilant 's' sound, whereas lower frequencies predominate during the rounded 'ound'.

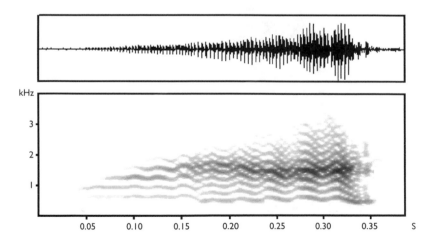

Figure 3.16 A simple wave-form diagram and a two-dimensional spectrogram of a frog call.

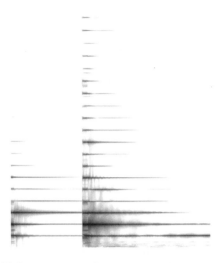

Figure 3.17 Spectrogram of piano notes.

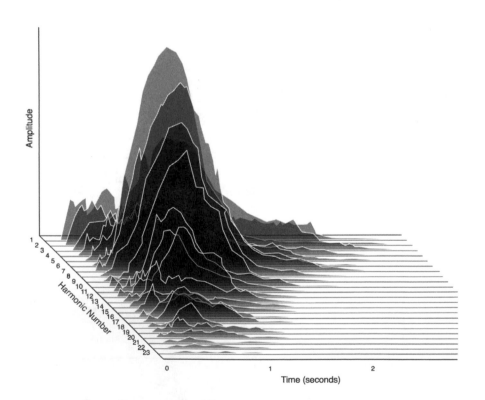

Figure 3.18 Three-dimensional spectrogram.

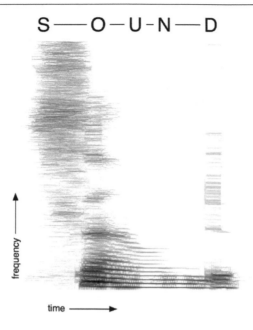

S——O–U-N——D

Figure 3.19 Spectrogram of the spoken word 'sound'.

Pictograms

Such scientific representations of sound do convey a large amount of useful information, but they also have drawbacks. From a musical point of view, they need to be decoded or 'read'. They have an inherent analytical quality which is excellent for understanding the detailed frequency content of a short sonic moment, for example, but less useful for revealing the musical function or context of that sound. A less accurate, but possibly more musical, way of representing sound, therefore, is the *pictogram*.

Pictography is a pictorial form of writing. Typical examples include hieroglyphs and cuneiform, a system of writing dating back to the Sumerian civilisation around 3000 BC. Pictograms resemble the thing they represent (as opposed to ideograms, which convey ideas) and many early cuneiform symbols had a phonetic value; in other words, they represented a vocal sound. A pictogram in a digital-music context may therefore be defined as *any* symbol or image which represents a given sound or collection of sounds. Music notation is one form of pictogram, but it is usually inadequate for digital sound. However, there is no generally agreed set of pictograms that is used to represent sounds, so individuals or groups will often devise their own. Three concentric circles might represent the sound of a raindrop, for example, but so might a dot, or a tick, or any other appropriate symbol.

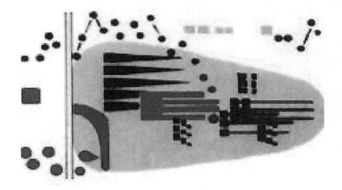

Figure 3.20 Excerpt from an 'aural score' by Rainer Wehinger of *Artikulation* (1958) by György Ligeti.

Despite this tendency to idiosyncrasy and imprecision, pictograms are actually often used in digital sound representation. They mainly appear in various kinds of 'aural score', in which graphical indications of sound location, musical gesture, frequency and amplitude content are useful for diffusion, synchronisation or analysis. One special case is the 'evocative transcription', in which a graphic representation of sounds and music is created mostly for analytical purposes. These pictograms may be subjectively designed but are nevertheless often quite clear as to their sonic and musical meanings. One classic example from an aural score is given in Figure 3.20, but both diffusion scores and evocative transcriptions will be discussed in much more detail later in this book, in relation to sound in space and musical analysis respectively.

Artikulation is a tape piece composed in 1958 by György Ligeti. Rainer Wehinger made his aural score with reference to Ligeti's compositional notes. The full score is in colour (see the book website for an excerpt), and the various symbols relate to aspects of the music. The dots represent filtered (pitched) or unfiltered impulses; the combs represent harmonic and sub-harmonic spectra; the thick lines and blocks are pitched sine tones (so the declining line near the start is a rapidly descending pitch); and the shaped background field indicates resonance. Time runs from left to right, and the higher the symbol on the page, the higher the pitch.

● Analysis-synthesis
● Visual score

■ Roads, C. (ed.) (1989) *The Music Machine*. Cambridge, MA: MIT Press.
■ Russ, M. (1996) *Sound Synthesis and Sampling.* Oxford: Focal Press.

Digitising sound

Most things that have so far been covered in this chapter apply equally to analogue and digital sound. It is only when the computer or other device converts or generates audio information in a digital format that the sound can be processed in ways that lead to the creation of new digital music. Digital signal processing (DSP) *is*, therefore, a defining characteristic of digital music. Once again, this book is primarily interested in the *why* and the *what* of digital music so gives only a brief summary of a subject that is treated in considerable depth by the numerous volumes on 'computer music', 'digital audio' and so on. For the musician, it is important to bear in mind that the following discussions have an effect not simply on sound-handling techniques, but also on the musical mindset that they produce.

Digital audio

It is first necessary to understand the distinction between analogue and digital sound. Loudspeakers, for example, are electromechanical devices, which use their physical characteristics to make an *analogy* of the variations in air pressure caused by sound waves or vibrations. All analogue devices do this, using a variable element, such as voltage (in the case of a microphone), or magnetism (in the case of tape), or deflections in the groove of an LP record. The variations in air pressure over time are translated into variations in voltage, magnetism, groove displacement and the rest, such that at any point there is a direct correlation between the variation in the recording medium and the original variation in the input signal. The only limits to the accuracy of these variations relate to the physical properties of the machinery itself.

Digital audio uses a quite different method to encode sound, by transforming it into numerical data. The word 'digital' derives from counting on the fingers, or digits. In most digital systems, counting is done using binary numbers. Binary is simply a way of representing more complex numbers using only two digits: 1 and 0. To do this, start by reading a sequence of decimal numbers from right to left, doubling each number in turn, as follows:

64	32	16	8	4	2	1

To represent the number 7 (for example) in binary, assign a 1 or a 0 to each decimal number, starting at the right-hand end and using the least possible number of digits, until decimal 7 is reached:

64	32	16	8	4	2	1
				1	1	1

Binary seven is therefore: 111

Binary nine would be 1001:

64	32	16	8	4	2	1
			1	0	0	1

The advantage of this method of counting is that it enables computers to translate 1s and 0s as 'on' or 'off' states at the machine level. Each 1 and 0 is called a binary digit, which contracts to 'bit', and a group of eight bits is called a 'byte' (by eight). There are several different ways of using binary counting to digitise sound, but the most common is called pulse code modulation, or PCM. This samples an analogue sound at a given rate over time: the *sampling rate* or *sampling frequency*. When the samples are played back in the correct order at the correct speed, an aurally convincing simulation of the original sound will be heard.

There are numerous sampling rates that are used in digital audio, depending on the quality of sound output required. The frequency of sampling is measured in hertz (Hz), where 1 Hz equals 1 sample per second, and 1 kilohertz (kHz) is 1,000 samples per second. Sampling rates are normally further constrained by the Nyquist criterion,[17] which states that a signal must be sampled at a rate which is at least twice the highest frequency component present in the signal to avoid the loss of information. If this criterion is not met, *aliasing* may occur, in which frequency components that do not exist in the original signal may appear, and the original signal itself cannot be recovered. Most systems have anti-aliasing filters, but oversampling (sampling with a higher frequency even than the Nyquist criterion requires) is also sometimes used to improve quality.

Each individual sample in a PCM file is, therefore, a separate step in a sequence, and its length is represented by a whole number. What results on playback is an approximation to the original sound itself but to such a level of detail that the amount of error becomes negligible. This assigning of numerical values is called *quantisation*, and its accuracy depends upon the resolution of the sampling process. Quantising is a way of expressing something that is infinitely variable as a series of discrete steps. A clock, for example, quantises time. In audio, the infinitely variable elements are the voltages coming from a sound source. The quantising steps may be of equal or unequal value, but the quantiser identifies them using a binary number. When that number is referenced, usually in a non-linear way, the numerical value at the centre of the quantising step is returned as a voltage. So, when the numerical value of a digital audio sample expresses its duration, and its magnitude is an expression of the changes in pressure on, say, a microphone, then the more samples per second and the wider the range, the greater the accuracy in both domains.

Quantising error can lead to distortion, however, in which unwanted harmonics (known as 'bird-singing') are generated. 'Distortion' is somewhat misleading as a term (although technically correct), because the acoustic result does not resemble the analogue phenomenon of overdrive such as might be heard in, say, rock guitar distortion. Instead, the unwanted sonic artefacts which are produced usually bear no timbral relationship to the original sound. In most systems, distortion is tackled using *dither*, which is essentially a way of introducing artificial noise into the signal in order to 'decorrelate' the relationship between the analogue input and the quantisation. The introduction of a random element makes the quantiser behave unpredictably, and the result is a reduction in distortion. The effective application of dither to quantisation is a technical study in its own right, but for the musician the main outcome is the availability of various algorithms that have been created to control digital distortion. Many exploit some kind of spectral processing techniques and may be grouped under the general heading of *constructive* distortion, or distortion that may be exploited musically.

In digital signals generally, the word 'bandwidth'[18] can refer to the amount of data that can pass through a given connection in a second. This is measured in kilobits per second or kbps.[19] So, the digital bandwidth is often called the *bit rate*. The bit rate indicates how many bits per second are used to represent the signal. Lower bit rates mean smaller file sizes but also poorer audio quality. Higher bit rates therefore give better quality, but the increase in numerical data means larger file sizes. The bit rate of uncompressed audio can always be calculated by multiplying the *resolution* by the number of channels (two for stereo) and the *sampling rate*.

The *resolution* is the number of bits per sample, that is to say, the precision with which each sample point is measured. The lower the resolution, the more numerical 'rounding' errors will occur, which will affect the perceived quality of the sound. A CD uses 16 bits per sample, whereas older computers used 8 bits per sample (just about good enough for speech). Twenty-four bits per sample is now seen as ideal, because it delivers more than the maximum perceived resolution. In other words, it offers a dynamic range[20] that exceeds the requirements of the human ear and brain to perceive the sound as completely authentic. Just like the 96 kHz sampling rate, 24 bits per sample is rapidly becoming a standard, although it places heavy demands on any A to D converter.

The two most frequently encountered sampling rates in digital audio are 44.1 kHz and 48 kHz. The first of these is the standard rate for CD recordings, and the second is most commonly used in digital video. The sampling rates which double these values, especially 96 kHz, are also increasingly encountered as digital audio artists try to overcome a perceived 'coldness' in 44.1 kHz sound. The results do indeed sound 'warmer' at 96 kHz, but this is not yet a generally standard sampling rate.

The digital method of using numbers to encode sound is efficient because it is not subject to the same kinds of errors introduced by the physical properties of the analogue medium. It is non-linear and, at least in theory, does not suffer degradation when identical copies are made (although a signal can sometimes be degraded at other stages in the process). This is the advantage of digital over analogue. However, whether a sound comes from an external source (such as an instrument, voice or any other acoustic sound) and whether the sound input is a microphone or a cable (line), it will at some point have to be converted into digital form to be handled by a computer or other digital device, and the same applies in reverse at the other end of the chain.

Digital audio uses an adjusted decibel scale whose highest possible level is 0 dB. This is obviously quite different from the analogue scale and is based upon the number of samples, rather than the *sound* as such. To exceed this level produces digital clipping which, unlike analogue distortion, gives a 'square wave'-type sound. It is generally a good idea to maintain a good headroom in the signal. Headroom is the gap between the highest peak in the sound and the point at which distortion begins to occur. A 6 dB headroom on the adjusted digital scale is a good level for which to aim.

A simple way to explore all the above ideas is to record an acoustic signal (a voice or musical instrument) with a good microphone plugged directly into the computer. By using software which allows for different settings of bit rate, sampling rate and resolution, the aural consequences of digitising sound can be investigated. Setting the level deliberately high will also give the clipping effect. Digital audio, like film, is an illusion. There is no actual sound in an individual sample but rather a set of values which, when correctly decoded by the technology, translates into a sounding result. Of course, analogue sound is also a kind of illusion, but its apparent physicality derives from the nature of the medium onto which it is literally written. The underlying reality of digital audio is mathematics, whereas the underlying reality of analogue audio is physics. This does not mean that the physical consequences of the digital manipulation of sound are any less, but the abstraction that sits at the heart of digital sound-processing also lies behind many attempts by instrument-makers and musicians to introduce more physicality and gesture into the act of performing digital music.

■ Moore, F. R. (1990) *Elements of Computer Music*. Englewood Cliff, NJ: Prentice-Hall.
■ Roads, C. (1996) *The Computer Music Tutorial*. Cambridge, MA: MIT Press..
■ Watkinson, J. (2001) *The Art of Digital Audio*. Oxford: Focal Press.

File formats

Digital audio is a collection of binary data. This data has to be organised in some way in order to be understood by anything other than the machine level of the computer. In addition, the sheer quantity of data in a typical audio file can be high. In order to maintain an aurally convincing illusion while being readable by software and, where appropriate, reducing the size of the file, the audio data is normally organised into a specific format. These file formats generally use some kind of compression, which comes in two forms: lossless and lossy.

Lossless compression does not sacrifice any audio information but still manages to reduce the amount of data in the raw file. Typical lossless file formats include .wav (wave-form audio format) on the PC, and .aiff (audio interchange file format) on the Mac.

A well-known example of lossy compression is the mp3, or, to give it its full title, MPEG audio layer 3, format. MPEG stands for 'Moving Pictures Experts Group', which is the body charged with setting standards for the encoding of audio and video. Mp3 is typical of lossy compression formats, in that it discards musical information that may be regarded as less important or even irrelevant to the listener, such as very quiet material simultaneous with or immediately following very loud material.

Lossy compression formats use various types of encryption, which produce generally better sounding results as the number of kilobits per second (kbps) is increased. For mp3 encoding, 128 kbps is generally considered the lowest rate to produce good quality, but this is a matter of opinion and will vary according to the music that is being encoded and the ears of the individual listener. Other examples of lossy compression include the successors to mp3, WMA (windows audio media), AAC (advanced audio compression) used by Apple for its iTunes and iPod products, and Ogg Vorbis, which is an open, patent-free compression.

File formats have become such a standard feature of the musical landscape today that there can be an assumption among musicians that they are a 'given', but there is in fact a big difference between, say, a vinyl LP and an audio file. Reformatting, resampling and editing techniques all allow for the digital sound itself to be modified. Furthermore, there is no appreciable loss in quality when multiple copies are made. The digital musician will want to ensure the best quality sound for the purpose in hand. Sometimes that will mean accepting the kind of data loss represented by lossy compression formats but, as a general rule, the closer the audio can get to an uncompressed PCM file, the better will be the result.

● File formats

Chapter 4

Organising sound

The raw material of music is sound. That is what the 'reverent approach' has made people forget – even composers. [. . .] As far back as the twenties, I decided to call my music 'organized sound' and myself, not a musician, but 'a worker in rhythms, frequencies, and intensities'. Indeed, to stubbornly conditioned ears, anything new in music has always been called noise. But after all what is music but organized noises? And a composer, like all artists, is an organizer of disparate elements.

Edgard Varèse, *The Liberation of Sound* (1936)

The digital musician is one who takes Varèse's visionary statement as fundamental. Indeed, he or she may decide to agree with Varèse completely and refuse the label 'musician', preferring 'sound artist', 'sonic artist' or even 'sound designer'.

Sound-art, sonic art and sound design

'Sound-art' and 'sonic art' have much in common, but there are also some cultural and artistic differences between them. 'Sound art' flourishes in many countries, and especially Germany, where it goes under the name of 'Klangkunst', which literally means 'noise art'. However, this word is more often translated as 'sound-art' and occasionally 'sonic art', which conveys the difficulty of giving a single clear definition of the term.[1] Sound-art is understood to emerge from a visual tradition in which sound is, unusually, the leading element of a work. This includes installations, mixed media works and even some types of radio art. Sound-art sometimes involves *recontextualisation*, which means taking something out of its familiar context and presenting it anew as an object of aesthetic contemplation.[2] A typical example of sound-art is Jem Finer's work *Longplayer*, installed in 2001 in Trinity Buoy Wharf Lighthouse in London's Docklands and made from recordings of Tibetan prayer bowls, looped and stretched by a computer for over 1,000 years' worth of combinations. Finer is also a banjo player with the rock band The Pogues. He commented in an interview:

I think [*Longplayer*] is definitely music, and if there's such a thing as sound art then it's certainly sound art as well. Sound is the consequence of an idea, and maybe that's sound art; and if you take that sound and make something else of it then maybe that's music.[3]

The phrase 'sonic art' seems to have come more from the tradition of electro-acoustic music that stretches back to the early days of music made using electronic technologies. At a recent meeting of the UK Sonic Arts Network, it was agreed that the phrase 'sonic art' has no single definition and is really an umbrella term which covers anything made with sound, including conventional music. The most celebrated account of sonic art appears in Trevor Wishart's book *On Sonic Art* (1996), and some of Wishart's own compositions, in particular the *Vox* cycle, may be regarded as classic sonic art works. These often explore sound morphing techniques, such as the '(super)human voice' used in *Vox 5* (1986), which transforms into various sounds, including bees and crowds.

'Sound design' has a less 'art-house', association. Sound designers work in film, television, theatre, new media and even museums and theme parks. The term probably originates in the tradition of separating the 'music' track from the 'sound' track in movies (although the most interesting film directors often blur that distinction). One of the most successful sound designers has been Walter Murch, who won one of his three Oscars for the sound-mixing on the film *Apocalypse Now* (1979, directed by Francis Ford Coppola). In an essay, Murch distinguishes between what he calls 'encoded' and 'embodied' sound in sound design:

> The clearest example of encoded sound is speech. The clearest example of embodied sound is music. [. . .]
>
> What lies between these outer limits? Just as every audible sound falls somewhere between the lower and upper limits of 20 and 20,000 cycles, so all sounds will be found somewhere on this conceptual spectrum from speech to music.
>
> Most sound effects, for instance, fall mid-way: like 'sound-centaurs', they are half language, half music. Since a sound effect usually refers to something specific – the steam engine of a train, the knocking at a door, the chirping of birds, the firing of a gun – it is not as 'pure' a sound as music. But on the other hand, the language of sound effects, if I may call it that, is more universally and immediately understood than any spoken language.[4]

These artists have much in common, despite the differences in their creative intentions and in the labels that are attached to them. They share a deep understanding of sound and how it behaves. The way in which they organise these behaviours is musical.

● Hearing hearing

■ Altman, R. (ed.) (1992) *Sound Theory/Sound Practice*. London: Routledge.

- ■ Kenny, T. (2000) *Sound for Picture: The Art of Sound Design in Film and Television.* Vallejo, CA: Mix Books
- ■ Sonnenshchein, D. (2001) *Sound Design: The Expressive Power of Music, Voice, and Sound Effects in Cinema.* Studio City, CA: Michael Wiese Productions.
- ■ Wishart, T. (1996) *On Sonic Art.* Amsterdam: Harwood Academic Publishers.

Sound in space

In practice, sound is always heard in some kind of space and is subject to various environmental conditions. The reality is that sound, like any other form of energy, decays and degenerates, a process which is hastened or affected by its surroundings. In an ideal world containing no friction, no energy would be lost. The potential, or stored, energy plus the kinetic, or motion, energy would be equal to the total energy input. However, the real world contains friction, and, consequently, energy is lost. The radiation of the sound, too, loses energy.

The creative possibilities opened up by the behaviour of sound in space are most evident in *sound diffusion*, where the source material may be sound produced by an instrument or instruments but also may be stereo or multi-channel recordings. Distance perception and a sense of spaciousness are often crucial to the subjective evaluation of the sound qualities of a given diffusion. To be enveloped by sound is often seen as valuable. Compare, for example, the experience of listening to a stereo system with listening to 'surround sound'. At its best, the surround-sound experience is richer because the sounds come from all directions simultaneously, not just in front of the listener. This resembles our experience of sound in nature, and the quality of naturalness seems to be very important. Surround sound tends to be less convincing when it appears too artificial or unnatural.

This raises an important point about both sound diffusion and, indeed, sound-recording: the human ear is the supreme judge of quality, rather than any objectively measurable, acoustical law. It may seem that a recording studio, for example, is where the most developed *technical* skills are required. A typical recording studio certainly conveys that impression, with its forbidding array of lights, buttons and equipment. But this is an illusion. The most important pieces of equipment in the recording studio are the ears of the people using it, and everything else should serve those. The recording studio is a temple to aural awareness, rather than technical skill. It is no accident that some of the most highly developed ears are those possessed by sound engineers. They are used to listening critically and carefully at all times.

In their book *The Musicians Guide to Acoustics*, Donald Campbell and Clive Greated give the following list of maxims that will serve the sound diffuser well in most spaces:

- Sound level should be adequate in all parts of the room
- Sound should be evenly distributed both in the audience and on stage

- Reverberation should be suitable for the particular application
- First reflections should not be excessively delayed.[5]

To develop the final point: one way in which the spatial location of a sound is understood by the listener is as a result of the phase differences, or timings, between the arrival of a signal at the two ears. (Other ways depend on frequency and amplitude.) The human ear can pinpoint the location of a sound with great accuracy up to a maximum phase difference of 0.65 milliseconds. If first reflections take longer than that to arrive, the localisation can become confused. This may be desirable in certain situations, but most of the time it is an unwelcome effect.

Behaviour of sound in space

Sound travels in three dimensions, which is often represented using a *wave-front diagram* (see Figure 4.1).

Here, the distance between the concentric circles gives the wavelength, and so the more tightly packed the circles, the higher the frequency. A *wave-ray* diagram, on the other hand, has the advantage that it shows the *path* of a single ray, but obviously lacks the detail of the total field (see Figure 4.2).

Parallels can be drawn between the behaviour of sound and the behaviour of light. Sound may be *refracted* (i.e., bent) by an object or by changes in temperature in the medium through which it passes. Diffraction occurs when the sound waves are obstructed or laterally restricted.[6] Sound may also be *reflected* from, or *absorbed* into, a surface. This will depend upon the rigidity, porosity and flexibility of the surface in question.

The sources of a sound are said to be *correlated* if they deliver the same signal (e.g., two loudspeakers) or if there is a single source but reflections off a wall or

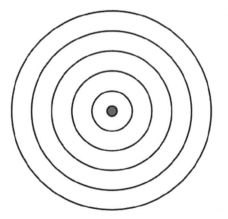

Figure 4.1 Wave-front diagram.

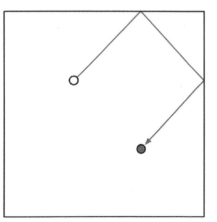

Figure 4.2 Wave-'ray' diagram.

other surface mean that more than one signal reaches the ear after a slight delay. *Uncorrelated* sound sources are those that deliver different signals (e.g., several different instruments spread around a room) or where the delay from reflections is so long as to cause an audible difference between signals.

Adding uncorrelated sources together is complicated, because the result does not depend upon the phases of the waves. It is the sound power level (SWL), rather than the sound pressure level (SPL), which is combined, resulting in a much lower increase in apparent loudness. In other words, two uncorrelated sources do not produce double the volume level. This can lead to confusion when using decibels to measure levels and becomes even more complicated and, hence, unpredictable depending on the type of space in which the sound is made.

An *echo* is a long-term reflection of a sound arriving at the ear of the listener a certain time (more than 50 milliseconds) after the sound itself. Echoes usually occur when the reflective surface is rigid, non-absorbent and inflexible. If a surface against which a sound bounces is not flat, then a *diffuse* reflection will have waves bouncing back in different directions. This can be a useful musical effect, and shaped surfaces are sometimes used for focus. Concave shapes, for example, bundle the sound waves together in a predictable way. Such shapes are often found in the construction of churches.

All these characteristics are factors in what is generally called *reverberation*. Studies of reverberation have been instrumental in informing the acoustic design of many halls and spaces. This field of research is in constant development, but there seems to be general agreement that the *early field*, or initial time delay gap (i.e., the time it takes the first reflection to reach the ear of the listener after the arrival of the direct sound) is crucial to the perception of acoustical presence. The arrival of bass sounds will condition the perception of qualities like 'warmth' and 'strength', and the *reverberant field* creates a perception of immersion in sound. Thus, an initial time-delay gap of between 8 and 25 milliseconds generally produces the best intimacy, or 75–300 milliseconds for the bass or 'warmth' field. As the waves get closer together and weaker, they form the characteristic reverberant *tail* of a sound in a given space. In general, the longer the delay between the arrival of a sound and the reverberant sounds, the more 'distant' the sound seems.

This wave-ray diagram (Figure 4.3) gives an impression of the collection of reflected sounds in a space that go to make up the reverberation. It is clear that factors such as the absorbency or reflection of the walls will affect the reverberation time.

Figure 4.4 represents the same information measured against time. The initial direct sound is followed by all the reflected sounds. The early reflected sounds will often be perceived to be more important than the later ones, but the overall reverberation time will normally be the most important characteristic. Space and time are inextricably linked, and separating them for discussion in this chapter has been done purely for convenience.

The reverberation time of a given space may be calculated using a formula[7]

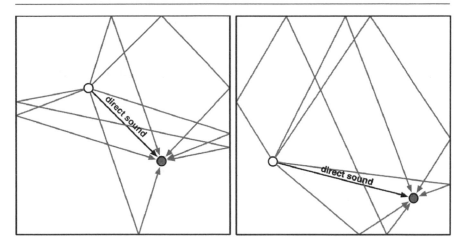

Figure 4.3 Reverberation.

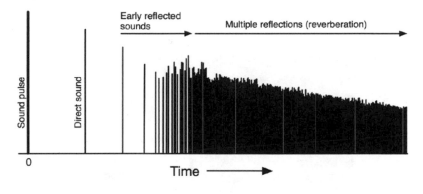

Figure 4.4 Reverberation time.

that measures the time taken for the SPL to drop to 60 dB below the level of the original signal. This drop of 60 dB is a somewhat arbitrary figure but works well in many practical situations. The loudest orchestral sound is about 100 dB, whereas the background noise in most auditoriums is about 40 dB.

The musical exploitation of reverberation and the behaviour of sound in space is a characteristic of more or less every live performance and can often be a crucial factor in its success. This is additionally important for digital musicians, whose ability to control the sound is central to their existence as artists. Given that digital musicians often perform in spaces which are not conventional concert halls, it is unsurprising that many site-specific works have been created to explore the resonant properties of spaces. One interesting recent example is the

Silophone (www.silophone.net) by [The User], a Montreal-based project begun in 2000, which:

> makes use of the incredible acoustics of Silo #5 by introducing sounds, collected from around the world using various communication technologies, into a physical space to create an instrument which blurs the boundaries between music, architecture and net art. Sounds arrive inside Silo #5 by telephone or internet. They are then broadcast into the vast concrete grain storage chambers inside the Silo. They are transformed, reverberated, and coloured by the remarkable acoustics of the structure, yielding a stunningly beautiful echo. This sound is captured by microphones and rebroadcast back to its sender, to other listeners and to a sound installation outside the building. Anyone may contribute material of their own, filling the instrument with increasingly varied sounds.

A somewhat different approach was adopted by Atau Tanaka, Kasper Toeplitz and their team for the *Global String* project begun in 1998 (Figure 4.5). This is an example of a conceptual mapping of the behaviour of sound in space which, nonetheless, has a physical equivalent in an installation. *Global String* is a physical string (12 millimetres diameter, 15 metres length) which is connected to the

Figure 4.5 Global String installation at DEAF2000, V2 Rotterdam.

Internet and treats the network itself as resonance. The artists explained: 'The concept is to create a musical string (like the string of a guitar or violin) that spans the world. Its resonance circles the globe, allowing musical communication and collaboration among the people at each site.'[8]

● Diffraction experiment

■ Blesser, B. and Salter, L.-R. (2007) *Spaces Speak, Are You Listening?: Exploring Aural Architecture.* Cambridge, MA: MIT Press.
■ Newell, P. (2001) *Recording Spaces.* Oxford: Focal Press.

Spatialisation

The artificial reproduction of the spatial characteristics of sound through loudspeakers is called *spatialisation*. Creating a convincing spatial representation, or *sound image*, is a feature of all sound recording and reproduction techniques; in fact, it is a key aspect of high-fidelity (or hi-fi) recording. The classic stereo system uses two channels of audio fed through two loudspeakers which are placed at an optimum angle of 60 or 30 degrees either side of a line drawn out from the listener's nose. To create a 'stereo image', either the amplitude or time difference between the two loudspeakers is used. In the case of amplitude difference, somewhere between 15 and 18 dB[9] is sufficient to create the illusion that a sound is *panned* hard left or hard right. The time-difference method is much more rare (although there is always *some* time delay between spaced pairs of microphones or loudspeakers), but a delay of between 0.5 and 1.5 milliseconds is sometimes sufficient to perceive a left–right distinction, depending on the frequency of the sound. Maintaining a convincing stereo image becomes problematic if the listener moves their head, and the location of the loudspeakers gives little scope for a more immersive experience. Stereo headphones are one solution, but there are other alternatives to conventional stereo.

Binaural stereo attempts to reproduce exactly the sound heard by the human ear. Binaural recordings, therefore, often use microphones placed in a dummy head or even worn in-ear. One consequence of this is that the sound is best heard through headphones, although in recent years convincing 'spatial equalisation' between loudspeakers in binaural systems has been achieved. Binaural stereo can give an excellent sense of 3-D, and is particularly useful in virtual-reality simulations and computer games, where the listener has an isolated acoustic experience. Algorithms for binaural sound-processing are built into a number of software packages and standard plug-ins, so the opportunity to manipulate sound in this way is readily available.

The 1970s saw an attempt to introduce a commercial four-channel system, known as 'quadraphony'. Although this format failed to achieve public acceptance, variations of one-channel per loudspeaker, or multi-channel systems, are still around. Eight-channel, or octophonic, systems are in frequent use for acousmatic and electro-acoustic concert music. There are many different configurations and speaker layouts used in such concerts.

A complex system might increase the number and variety of loudspeakers and include 'tweeter-trees', which resemble the hub and spokes of cartwheels with small speakers attached, suspended over the heads of the audience. This kind of system can achieve great accuracy in both localisation and spatialisation but is still something of a specialist set-up. A highly complex system might comprise an automated seventy-six-channel mixer feeding an array of fifty or more loudspeakers. However, it is not essential to work in such enormous surroundings to achieve good sound diffusion. A reasonably portable sound diffusion system can readily be assembled and configured to suit unusual spaces. This form of music-making is greatly on the increase as equipment falls in price and artists seek to take control of their own sound.

Figures 4.6, 4.7, 4.8 and 4.9 are some examples of typical spatialisation layouts.

A more familiar, and generally commercial, solution to spatialisation is offered by 5.1 (and more recently 6.1 and 7.1) *surround sound*, which is found in many cinemas and increasingly in the home. A typical 5.1 system has five channels playing back through five main speakers: three at the front (stereo left and right, plus centre mono), and two at the side or rear (stereo left and right); plus a subwoofer for bass sounds. The 7.1 system uses two more speakers, 6.1 one extra, and so on. The underlying concept of 5.1 surround is in fact 3.2 stereo, which means that the front three speakers are providing the stereo sound image, and the side/ back speakers are delivering ambient or supporting sounds. This can produce an unconvincing effect, most usually because the speaker placement is problematic

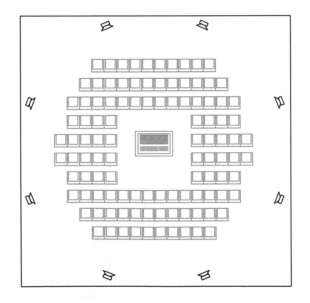

Figure 4.6 The 8-channel 'Stonehenge' layout.

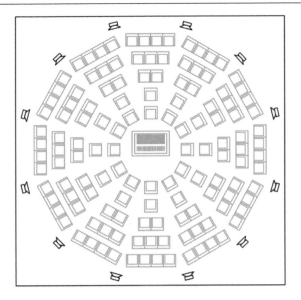

Figure 4.7 A 12-channel set-up.

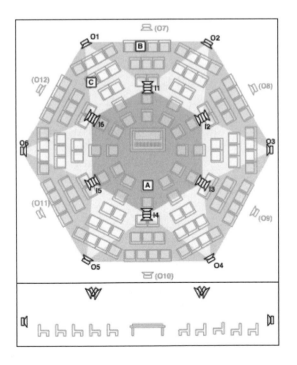

Figure 4.8 A set-up including overheads.

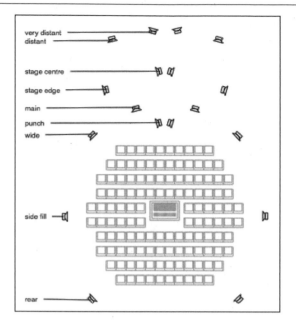

Figure 4.9 A 'theatrical' diffusion rig, designed to create a range of effects.[10]

and stereo signals delivered through three loudspeakers can be confusing. For 5.1 to work successfully, therefore, generally requires an acceptance of these limitations. If the effect desired is a true 360-degree surround, then these formats are not ideal. Note also that the subwoofer, or .1 loudspeaker, is optional and so should be treated as an additional effect. The 5.1 surround mix should work effectively *without* this speaker, which can only handle very low frequencies (generally below 120 Hz).

The design of loudspeakers has not fundamentally changed since 1925, but it is important to understand how different speaker types behave in different spaces. Certain sound fields can obscure the individual characteristics of a given speaker. This is especially relevant in live situations where there is an in-house PA (public address) system. Such systems often opt for a general, rather than characteristic, sound field, with sometimes fairly unpleasant results from a listener's perspective.

Small speakers ('tweeters') of 1.3–3.8 centimetres (0.5–1.5 inches) diameter are best for high sounds, medium-sized speakers (10–13 centimetres, 4–5 inches) are best for mid-range sounds, and large speakers (around 40 cm, 16 inches, diameter) best for bass. Very large dedicated bass-bins, or sub-woofers, are a feature of many sound systems, whereas tweeter trees are much less common. The overall balance and combination of speaker sizes will do a lot to configure the sound.

Where a speaker combines one or more sizes in a single box, a *crossover network* is used to ensure that the right frequencies are sent to the right speaker. Where this network is *active*, a smooth transition will be made between one speaker and another, by using separate power amplifiers for each speaker. Powered speakers, therefore, tend to give more consistent and controllable results than their unpowered counterparts. A pair of speakers is called *in-phase* when their speaker cones move in the same direction simultaneously in response to a given mono input signal. The audible result will be that the signal appears to come from a point between the speakers. *Out-of-phase* speakers do the opposite, and the audible result is a confused location for the signal. To correct the phase, simply reverse the leads on one of the loudspeakers.

Some other spatialisation techniques that are worth noting are *ambisonics* and *wave-field synthesis*. Ambisonics is an extremely thorough system that aims to provide a comprehensive solution to all aspects of directional sound, including recording, transmission and reproduction. It works by recording the loudness and spatial location of a signal onto separate channels and needs four or more loudspeakers and a decoder to achieve 'periphony'. Ambisonic sound recordings often use a special sound-field microphone that can record all the spatial information. There seems to be little doubt that this is the most effective surround-sound system in existence.

Wave-field synthesis is rare, although at the time of writing commercial companies are taking it up. It derives from the Huygens Principle,[11] which states that a sound wave front contains an infinite number of small sound sources that in turn form smaller waves that make up the next wave front. Since this process can be predicted, it is possible to synthesise the wave front such that a listener could not tell the difference between the real and synthetic waves. A large array of loudspeakers is required to convert this theory into a practical reality, but the possibilities it offers for precise localisation of sound are great.

As these descriptions demonstrate, one very practical problem with spatialisation is that it usually requires a quite specific or controlled listening environment. Even within standardised set-ups there can be considerable variation in listening experience, often based on the extent to which the listener's seating position varies from the 'sweet spot', the point of optimum listening. Given that the digital musician is seeking to create a unique sound, including its position (or apparent position) in space, this variability and lack of control of the listening situation can present a challenge. Many different solutions have been adopted, ranging from an extreme precision (fixed listening position) to an extreme lack of precision (the ambulant listener). It is an important aspect of any music-making that involves loudspeakers to consider the listening experience and, hence, the spatialisation.

The challenges of spatialisation have been a key focus of electro-acoustic music over many decades, and there have been numerous works designed for highly specific set-ups. The collapse of these pieces onto stereo CD can be damaging to the concept, and a live experience is preferable. The Canadian composer Robert Normandeau explicitly sets out to create what he calls 'cinema for the ears' in which the spatialisation is integral to both the sound quality and meaning of the music.

In his work *Clair de Terre* (1999), for example, the concept derives explicitly from photographic imagery of the Earth seen from outer space. Normandeau wrote:

> This work is divided into twelve movements that systematically explore elements of the grammar of cinematography that have been transposed into the language of electro-acoustics. Preceded by an overture — Ouverture — each of these twelve movements are composed of a soundscape, an object's sound, the sound of a musical instrument, and vocal onomatopoeias. All of these sound elements are drawn from the sound bank that I have built up over the last ten years.[12]

Normandeau has recently become interested in the possibilities offered by audio DVD formats, which allow multichannel control within a standard system.

● Composed space

■ Rumsey, F. (2001) *Spatial Audio*. Oxford: Focal Press.

Sound through time

Much of the previous discussion is equally relevant to the behaviour of sound through time. In fact, it is fairly meaningless to talk about sound *without* reference to time. The same is equally true of silence. As John Cage observed: the thing that both sound and silence have in common is *duration*.

There are only two ways of putting sounds together. The first is to hear them successively, one after another. This may be called *horizontal* composition, in the sense that time travels along an imaginary horizontal axis. The other is to combine them simultaneously, which may be called *vertical* composition. Most music mixes these approaches in some way.[13] It could be argued that even purely horizontal composition is in fact both horizontal *and* vertical, because music is a time-based art form and any one sound might be understood as a combination of many smaller sounds in varying relationships.

In a horizontal composition, layers of related sounds may develop in ways that the listener can perceive. In a vertical composition, the emphasis will generally be more upon overall texture. A composition need not restrict itself to one approach or the other, and often the musical interest derives from the interplay of the two. The drama of music comes from the way in which the various musical elements interact. Having a sense of how to handle these interactions is the mark of a good composer.

In digital music, the timing of sounds can be highly precise, even sometimes *over*-precise in the way that computationally exact processes tend to be. Part of the challenge facing the musician is to make digital processes *sound* natural – or sound characteristically unnatural if that is the aim of the composition. Much of this comes down to handling timings, and the listener will quickly perceive any inconsistency between the apparent aim of the composition and the sounding result as shortcomings.

Open form/closed form

One important aspect of all music concerns the creation of a sense of movement through time. In traditional composition this is achieved by phrasing, which is the shaping of smaller musical ideas into coherent, sentence-like, sequences. A group of phrases may then go on to form a larger structure, such as a melody, and so on. There is a link here to the duration of human breath and the structures of human speech. It is surprising how often this is still applicable, even in musical situations where the content is not pitch-focused. Every sound has its natural life span, and tends to 'breathe'. With machines, it is perfectly possible to work against this, and musical structures can be (and have been) devised to avoid an obvious sense of phrasing. But the absence or presence of a sense of motion through time is always a distinguishing compositional element.

Motion through time is a feature of 'closed-form' works, that is to say, works which are complete. Works in 'open' form are perpetually incomplete. This implies an ongoing experimental approach: one in which the *process* of creating the music, rather than the finished product, is important. This may have particular resonance in the age of digital music because, as Nicholas Negroponte points out: 'in the digital nothing is ever finished'.[14] Open form can seem more consistent with the handling of sound through time as a continuous data stream, which can be edited or modified in any way.

There are historical precedents for this in traditional music composition, with discontinuous forms of endless variation or mosaic-like constructions. A classic and very extreme example is *Vexations*, composed for piano in 1892 by Erik Satie, in which the same short musical idea is repeated 840 times. The piece can last around twenty-four hours, depending on how fast you play it. (Satie's directions are somewhat unclear.) Listening to (and performing) this piece is clearly an 'open form' experience, despite the repetition, because human memory changes over such a long time span.

There is a strong temptation to assume that this kind of music has no particular direction, or is arbitrary in its 'goal-orientation', but, in practice, there is often, paradoxically, *more* of a need to add a sense of motion through time. The absence of a clear start and end point risks losing the attention of the listener, so the composer must ensure sufficient dramatic interest. Part of the problem is the lack of opportunity in open form for musical development. This has become a central focus for certain types of computer composition, which uses evolutionary algorithms and other methods to simulate developmental processes.

To adopt open form can therefore be a risky strategy. There is the potential of losing musical identity, or the attention of the listener, and a possible surrender to the technology or the process involved. Nevertheless, as an experimental approach, or under the right situations, open form can produce worthwhile results. One interesting example is Peter M. Traub's *bits and pieces*, which is 'a continuous composition that gets its source sounds from the web. Every morning a special search process looks for web pages with links to sound files. If links are found, the sound files are downloaded. The day's "catch" is then used to create the pieces in "bits and pieces" for the next 24 hours'[15] This piece seems to succeed because the musical outcome maps the intention so well, and it fits with and reflects upon its context.

- ■ Eco, U. (1989) *The Open Work*. Cambridge, MA: Harvard University Press.
- ■ Peitgen, H.-O. (2004) *Chaos and Fractals*. New York: Springer.
- ▲ Peter Traub (1999) *bits and pieces*. Available at www.fictive.org/bits.

Duration

Digital techniques have opened up duration to a degree unimaginable before now. In his important book *Microsound* (2001), Curtis Roads identifies nine time scales of music, as follows:

1   *Infinite* The ideal time span of mathematical durations such as the infinite sine waves of classical Fourier analysis.

2   *Supra* A time scale beyond that of an individual composition and extending into months, years, decades and centuries.

3   *Macro* The time scale of overall musical architecture or form, measured in minutes or hours, or in extreme cases, days.

4   *Meso* Divisions of form. Groupings of sound objects into hierarchies of phrase structures of various sizes, measured in minutes or seconds.

5   *Sound object* A basic unit of musical structure, generalising the traditional concept of note to include complex and mutating sound events on a time scale ranging from a fraction of a second to several seconds.

6   *Micro* Sound particles on a time scale that extends down to the threshold of auditory perception (measured in thousandths of a second or milliseconds).

7   *Sample* The atomic level of digital audio systems: individual binary samples or numerical amplitude values, one following another at a fixed time interval. The period between samples is measured in millionths of a second (microseconds).

8   *Subsample* Fluctuations on a time scale too brief to be properly recorded or perceived, measured in billionths of a second (nanoseconds) or less.

9   *Infinitesimal* The ideal time span of mathematical functions such as the infinitely brief delta functions.[16]

With the exception of time scales 1 and 9, which are mathematical ideals, these are now all practically available to the digital musician. Roads develops an analogy with the science of matter by considering the properties of waves and particles, a debate that goes back to Ancient Greece and beyond and continues today in the field of quantum physics. He concludes with the comment: 'Sound can be seen [as] either wavelike or particle-like, depending upon the scale of measurement, the density of particles, and the type of operations we apply to it.'[17]

Many of the time-based modifications made to single sounds by digital technologies carry implications for longer-term musical structures. The action of digitally 'stretching' a sound, for example, simply fills the newly extended duration with additional data which may (or may not) give an aurally convincing impression of a stretch but nevertheless resembles the old data in that it consists of a certain number of samples per second. Each individual sample (or even smaller unit) contains a certain amount of frequency information, however imperceptible, which when added together over time creates the sonic effect.

The two best-known examples of such digital manipulations of sound through time are *pitch-shifting* and *time-stretching*. Although these are time-based effects, they may use fast-Fourier-transform algorithms (see p. 86). The latter affects the duration of a sound without changing its pitch, the former changes the pitch without altering duration. These techniques are often used in the recording studio to correct small errors of pitching or timing in human performance. However, their creative potential extends beyond mere error correction into sound transformation.

Both these techniques may be time-varying, that is to say, applied in varying amounts to portions of a sound file. Some software allows for hand-drawn or oscillator control or even control by dynamic envelopes extracted from the sound itself or from other sounds. The processes can be applied to any sounds or events or even to whole pieces of music. An amusing example of the latter is the *9 Beet Stretch* by Leaf Inge, in which Beethoven's Ninth Symphony is time-stretched to last twenty-four hours, with no pitch distortions.[18]

Duration is more than just a measurable time span. It is a perceptual consequence of the passage of time and is in many ways the stuff of music itself, since auditory events have an effect upon that perception. As sonic experiences constantly pass into memory, their remembered existence influences the perception of the present. The pace at which the present experience unfolds and the perceived relationships between that and other rates of change is largely responsible for excitement and interest in a piece of music. If a 'natural' duration is one in which the duration of the sound appears to be consistent with the nature of the sound source, then in digital music there is great potential for exploiting unnatural, even unfeasible, durations. A piece of music may even set up a counterpoint, or argument, between the 'natural' and the 'unnatural'. This has greatly expanded both the language of music itself and the dramaturgy available to musicians (where 'dramaturgy' refers to both the timing and character of the appearances of sounds within a composition).

● Extended duration

■ Roads, C. (2001) *Microsound.* Cambridge, MA: MIT Press.

Synchronisation

Digital audio may be transmitted in a number of different ways. The AES/EBU (Audio Engineering Society/European Broadcasting Union) protocol, for example, can carry two channels of interleaved (i.e., transmitted together) digital audio through a single, three-pin XLR[19] microphone cable. S/PDIF (Sony/Phillips Digital Interface) uses a similar principle but works through a phono (RCA) cable, although in both cases an optical cable may well be preferable for high speeds. It is possible to connect AES/EBU or S/PDIF devices together in a 'daisy chain' as long as some kind of synchronisation device is used. The digital signal may then flow on to any storage device or fixed medium. Various manufacturers of these devices will often insist on their own proprietary standards for their machines, including sample rates and even custom-made cables that only work with that particular device. To achieve accurate synchronisation, a detailed study of the equipment manuals is required.

Synchronisation uses time code. The first time code was introduced in 1967 by SMPTE, the Society of Motion Picture and Television Engineers. Pronounced 'simpty', it was designed to replace the old mechanical method of synchronisation used in movies (sprocket holes punched in film and related tape) with a binary code suitable for video (which of course has no sprocket holes). SMPTE divides up time using an eight-digit twenty-four hour clock, which shows: 0–59 seconds, 0–59 minutes and 0–23 hours. The seconds are then further divided into a number of frames. The exact number of frames varies according to the various frame-rates used around the world, of which there are four main standards:

1   SMPTE – 30 fps (frames per second) is generally used for audio work in the USA.
2   American Color Television Standard (USA, Japan, Asia), including NTSC – 29.97 fps (also known as '30 drop frame').
3   SMPTE/EBU (Europe/Australia), includes PAL and SECAM video – 25 fps.
4   SMPTE for film (not audio) – 24 fps.

SMPTE time code is, therefore, a stream of data, which comes in various forms, of which the most frequently encountered in audio work is LTC, or linear (longitudinal) time code. Here, the time code data is recorded as an audio signal (it sounds buzzy) which can be read by a wide range of devices. This time code is generally recorded as 'stripes' on to the digital storage medium.

MIDI time code (MTC) is a way of transforming SMPTE time code so that it can be transmitted and received along a MIDI chain. MIDI allows electronic instruments to communicate by using a standardised set of commands. These commands, collectively defined as the *MIDI protocol*, control various musical parameters and operations around the note-on and note-off commands. Because this is a standardised process, the various MIDI devices may all be synchronised to an absolute time code. The major application of MTC is in video, but it can also be useful in other situations to ensure absolute synchronisation to a single source. This method has the edge over conventional 'musical' synchronisation techniques in many situations.

MIDI also allows instruments to control one another. Thus there are: MIDI keyboards, wind instruments, guitars, drums, violins and the rest, which can all be programmed to trigger any kind of sampled sound (so a MIDI guitar can produce saxophone notes, for example). However, the content of the MIDI data stream can also be controlled by any varying modifiers, including: modulation and pitch bend wheels, sustain pedals, sliders, faders, switches, ribbon controllers, pan pots – in short, anything that is capable of altering the parameters of a signal, usually in real time. These controllers may stand alone, or be fitted on, or plugged into an instrument, depending on the manufacturer's specification. There are a total of 128 virtual MIDI ports available which can be assigned particular functions. Each port can transmit or receive messages which also carry one of sixteen channel identities. This channel information allows many instruments, or different parts of a multi-timbral instrument, to be controlled simultaneously through a single cable connection.

Alongside the channel information, a MIDI message may contain: note-on, note-off, pitch-bend, program change, aftertouch, channel pressure, system-related messages and continuous controller messages. In the interests of achieving a predictable outcome, there has been general agreement among manufacturers about which controller performs which function, but in practice these are often assigned differently under different circumstances. Computer-based MIDI sequencers take advantage of all this by enabling various kinds of MIDI data input from various kinds of devices and often act as central controller for all aspects of the performance.

MIDI is also found as a control device for various studio machines, where it is called MMC (MIDI machine control) and as a controller for lighting effects, pyrotechnics and other aspects of staging, where it is called MSC (MIDI show control). These observations give some idea of the protocol's versatility and it seems likely that it will survive for many years to come.

- Hill, B. (1994) *MIDI for Musicians*. Chicago, IL: A Cappella.
- Rumsey, F. (1994) *MIDI Systems and Control*. Oxford: Focal Press.

Sound manipulation

Whatever manipulations may be applied to a sound, be it digital already or the result of A to D conversion, one simple rule applies: 'garbage in, garbage out'. Computers are excellent at manipulating sounds, but if the original sound source is poor quality, it is likely to produce a poor-quality result. 'Poor quality' in this context is subjective. When working with material from a 1940s radio broadcast, for example, a limited bandwidth and extraneous noise is exactly what is required. But if there is a clear goal, and the initial sound, before manipulation or processing, contains unwanted material or is badly recorded, it is likely that the amount of time and effort expended in trying to correct the problems will be wasted. The resulting sound will probably either exaggerate the initial problem, or replace it with something that sounds too artificial to be usable.

Fourier transforms

Sound manipulation depends upon the computer's ability accurately to analyse the contents of a sound file. The most common method used for this is called a *Fourier transform* (FT).[20] A good way to envisage an FT is to imagine a spreadsheet containing a number of rows and columns of cells. The rows represent narrow bands of harmonics, grouped by frequency range, and are called *bins*. The columns contain single digital samples. At a sample rate of 44,100 Hz (CD quality), this means each column lasts 1/44,100ths of a second. Each cell, therefore, contains a tiny amount of information about a sample and its constituent frequencies. In other words, there is a very small amount of energy in a cell.

Now, in order to analyse a sound for longer than the duration of one sample, it is necessary to increase the number of columns in the imaginary spreadsheet. This is called the *buffer size*, *window length* or *window size* and typically increases by a factor of two, thus: 512 samples, 1024, 4096, etc. Raising the number of rows in the imaginary spreadsheet can similarly increase the frequency resolution. This has the effect of narrowing the frequency range of each bin. The size of the window, therefore, gives the frequency resolution and the time resolution. The buffer size divided by the sample rate gives the duration of the buffer in milliseconds. The sample rate divided by the buffer size gives the frequency range of each bin.

In practice, there is a trade-off between these two resolutions. A bigger buffer gives more accurate pitch definition but less accurate time definition. A smaller buffer gives less accurate pitch definition and more accurate time definition (see Table 4.1).

Figures 4.10, 4.11 and 4.12 show three sonograms of the same sound, of 3 seconds' duration, with increasing window sizes. Time is shown along the x-axis, frequency up the y-axis. Notice how the bins become smaller.

Table 4.1 Buffer sizes.

Buffer size	Frequency resolution (Hz)	Time resolution (milliseconds)
128	344.5	3
256	172.3	6
512	86.1	12
1024	43.0	23
2048	21.5	47
4096	10.7	93
8192	5.4	185

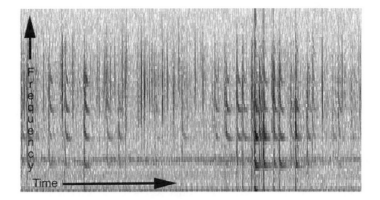

Figure 4.10 Sonogram – Window size: 64.

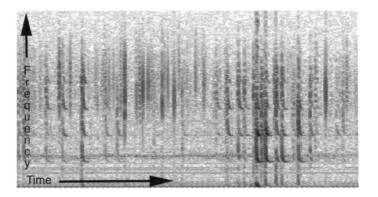

Figure 4.11 Sonogram – Window size: 256.

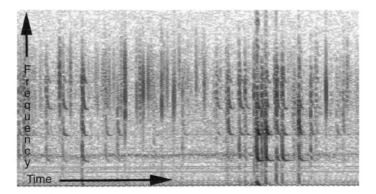

Figure 4.12 Sonogram – Window size: 1024.

An FT therefore, analyses the sound into a continuous spectrum of its constituent harmonics. It does this by calculating the frequency, amplitude and phase of the various sine waves within the given time frame. Because the amount of data produced by this process is large and the number of calculations per second can be prohibitively great, an algorithm[21] has been developed to enable FTs to be calculated quickly. This is called a fast Fourier transform, or FFT, and is the most common form of digitally processed sound. Input to an FFT is usually given an envelope whose shape can be chosen by the user. There are several of these window shapes, of which the best are: Hamming, Hanning and Blackman.[22]

Why is understanding such complex digital analysis so important? Because it provides the means by which musicians may shape and control their sound, which is one of the main goals. A thorough knowledge of the way digital sound is created, handled and manipulated is an essential skill. Furthermore, this knowledge and understanding will suggest creative possibilities. Consider the following example to illustrate the point.

The kind of errors thrown up in the timing processes of D to A conversion may be called *glitches*. However, a glitch is also just a fault in a system, such as an unwanted electrical pulse or a programming error. The idea could be extended to the surface noise on an LP, for example, or the accidental sound made by touching the tip of a jack plug before connecting it to an instrument. In the late 1990s, various artists and musicians became interested in these unwanted sounds and began using them, mainly in place of percussion. The result has been a burgeoning 'glitch' music genre, which operates on the margins of the techno scene. A survey of the Mille Plateaux record label's 'Clicks and Cuts' series will give an idea of the possibilities opened up by these artists. The best among them know what they are doing, just as surely as the best violinist knows how to get a good sound from the violin. These are not just arbitrary uses of digital artefacts: the digital musician combines engineering skills with artistic innovation.

FFT is not the only way to manipulate the spectral content of a sound. In the past decade or so, an alternative called the *wavelet transform* has begun to appear. These transforms parallel Heisenberg's Uncertainty Principle, which states that the momentum and position of a moving particle cannot be known simultaneously.[23] Whereas the FT works fine for stationary signals, that is to say, it renders the time and frequency information necessary for the spectrum of a sound to be understood discretely, as though it happened once and remained unchanged, the wavelet transform attempts to perform the same function for sounds whose spectra *vary over time*. Since Heisenberg's Uncertainty Principle excludes the possibility of complete knowledge of this, the Continuous Wavelet Transform (CWT) just gives as good a resolution as possible. The finer the resolution, the more computation required, with the result that the quality of CWT implementations, such as pitch-shifters and time-stretchers, in commercial software packages is variable.

● FFT processing

- Dodge, C. and Jerse, T. (1997) *Computer Music: Synthesis*, Composition, and Performance. London: Schirmer Books.

Granular synthesis

FTs are performed in the frequency domain, but it is also possible to manipulate sound through the time domain. The chopping up of a sound into small segments is called *brassage*, and is a common editing technique in digital music. *Granulation* takes this idea to an extreme. Each grain is an extremely brief, barely audible event, lasting typically between one thousandth and one tenth of a second and sounding like a tiny, faint, click. Despite its brevity, this sound event contains the conventional features: a wave form and an amplitude envelope. By combining many thousands of such grains, a larger, more extensive, sound may be made. In the illustration of a single grain (Figure 4.13), the upper sine wave is high frequency and the lower is low frequency, but both have the same duration.

Grains normally last less than 50 milliseconds and cannot be perceptually subdivided into smaller units. The characteristics of the wave forms of the individual grains affect the texture of a resulting sound when they are combined. The timbre of the outcome also depends upon grain size and the frequency of the resynthesis. Furthermore, these tiny waves can acquire the characteristics of the much larger waves: they can be fixed within the grain, or vary over time; they can be simple sine waves or samples of recorded sound or they can have several elements combined.

Granular synthesis, then, is based upon enveloped grains in high densities of hundreds or thousands per second, often formed into *streams* or *clouds*. Streams contain grains following one another at regular intervals but with tiny delays

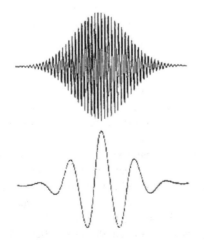

Figure 4.13 Image of two sine-wave grains.

between them. A good analogy for this process would be the relationship between individual hits in a continuous drum roll. The *density* of grains in a stream will appear to generate metrical rhythms up to a frequency of about twenty grains per second and continuous pitches beyond that. This emergence of pitch from rhythm is a fundamental idea in a great deal of electronic music,[24] and granular synthesis is an excellent way to understand the principles.

The perception of pitch in a granular stream, for example, will depend on a set of complex interactions between the frequency of wave forms, the grain envelopes and the grain densities. The synchronous nature of the grain *stream* allows these elements to be modified predictably over time. In the *cloud* model, however, the grains are randomly or chaotically distributed in time. Here, the density, duration, wave-form characteristics, amplitude envelopes and frequency bands may vary within the overall duration of the cloud.

● Brassage stew

▲ Curtis Roads (1980) *nscor*. Wergo 2010-50.
▲ Barry Truax (1986) *Riverrun*. Wergo 2017-50.
▲ Natasha Barrett (1997) 'Little Animals' on *Chillies & Shells*. Independent NB 980101M.
▲ Horatio Vaggione (1998) *Agon*, Mnemosyne MN314-2.

Effects and filters

Many standard sound manipulation effects are modelled upon their analogue counterparts. A typical case in point is *delay* applied to the signal. Digital delay includes the full range of traditional analogue delay techniques, but emulated in software. A software plug-in that handles delay might include classic 'ping-pong' effects, but also some of the frequency filtering, pitch flutter and saturation reminiscent of analogue delay. Larger digital delays are used in effects such as *cho-rusing* (in which many slightly pitch-transposed delays randomly spaced within a 30–40 millisecond time frame create the illusion of multiple voices from a single source) or *flanging* (which mimics the gradually shifting time delay of the typical filter sweep of the flanger).

Digital *loops* may also be used just like analogue loops to sustain sounds or to give the impression of a sound freezing in time. *Echo* effects are readily achieved by digital means, simulating the reflection of a sound off a surface. Sounds can be *reversed*, *inverted*, *repeated*, *spliced* and variously edited in apparently the same way as was possible with analogue tape, with the very remarkable difference that the processes take a matter of seconds or less to perform. Mastery of these techniques is made fairly straightforward by most software, but they are essential skills for the digital musician.

Filters of various kinds are found throughout digital audio, and their opera-tions correspond fairly well to their analogue counterparts, which tends to make understanding them relatively easy. A digital filter applies various processes to the samples which pass through it. A 'low-pass' filter, for example, allows low frequencies to pass through but blocks high frequencies, whereas a 'high-pass' filter does the reverse, and a 'band-pass' filter allows through frequencies within a given band. Digital filters are often specified in terms of their permitted variations in frequency response and can achieve a level of performance which far exceeds what is even theoretically possible with analogue filters. For example, a low-pass filter that blocks a 1001 Hz signal but allows through a 999 Hz signal can be achieved. Such minute differences are not possible with analogue filters.

As discussed earlier, digital audio time is measured in samples. Each sample is a discrete entity. A digital filter therefore operates at the level of the individual sample to reproduce the effect of an analogue filter. The digital filter may, for example, take an *impulse* and map it onto digital time. An impulse is a short signal comprising a single value followed by zeros. The nature of the filter's response, called the *impulse response*, will characterise the filter. The simplest form of filter is called a finite impulse response (FIR) filter, in which 'taps' are taken from successive samples, which are then multiplied by a coefficient (a multiplicative factor), and the results are added together to form the output of the filter. This is called 'finite' because there are a fixed number of taps.

An infinite impulse response (IIR) filter, by contrast, allows feedback between the output and the input, which can create some long-lasting results, including growth or decay over time. This is particularly useful for effects such as reverberation. Where the impulse response of a physical space may be recorded by, for example, firing a gun or bursting a balloon, the IIR filter may be used to model the same digitally. However, IIR filters are often unstable and somewhat inaccurate, owing to the complexity of their operation and can easily produce feedback and other such unwanted results. This makes digital reverberation one of the most difficult things to achieve successfully, and the range of commercially available solutions can be quite variable in quality.

Creative uses of such filters include: *interpolation*, in which sounds of two different types are apparently fused together over time; and *convolution*, which combines two sound files – an input and an impulse response – by multiplying their spectra together to produce a new sound file. Frequencies that are common to both sound files will tend to be reinforced and resonate together. The filter will try to match bin content across the two spectra. Where there is a match, the data is preserved. Where there is no match, it is discarded (or, strictly, multiplied by zero). Among other things, this enables the application of the reverberant properties of resonance to FFT windows over time and, thus, the superimposition of the reverberant characteristics of one sound upon another.

Where digital filters find the most direct parallel with analogue equipment is in the field of EQ, or equalisation. Both analogue and digital EQ are designed to make the final recorded sound *equal* to the original source, by correcting inadequacies of both equipment and the recording environment. However, it can also be a highly creative tool when used skilfully. EQ adjusts the quality of a given sound by attenuating or boosting certain parts of the audio spectrum or bands of frequencies.

Two well-known equalisers are the *parametric* and the *graphic*. The parametric equaliser adjusts the *gain* (output level), *bandwidth* (frequency range) and *Q* (the width) of a frequency envelope[25] around a centre frequency. The graphic equaliser normally has fixed frequency and Q values. A four-band graphic equaliser, for example, might comprise two central band-pass filters, each of which is assigned to a particular range of frequencies, and one low and one high shelf filter. Shelving allows frequencies up to a shelf point to be adjusted and leaves those above (or below) unchanged. In some equalisers, the shelf point is specified by the user and is called a shelf because the areas being cut or boosted are fairly flat. These shelves vary in accuracy and usually have a *slope* either side of the shelf point. Parametric equalisers have controls which can be tuned to the desired frequency ranges and levels and adjustable Q. They are therefore much more precise than graphic equalisers, but also harder to control.

A still more complex filter is called a *comb filter*. This adds a slightly delayed version of a signal to itself, and it is called a comb filter because its frequency response wave form looks like a series of spikes. Comb filtering is really a corrective device, using *phase cancellation*[26] to avoid unwanted phenomena, but it is also useful for creating echo effects. The effect of an echoing cylinder, for example, can be created readily using this method.[27]

The filters are useful for noise and feedback reduction, separating or positioning instrument sounds in a mix, or used more creatively to add pitch characteristics to noise, apply filter sweeps, add high, delicate content and even used to create musical structures. The digital musician would do well to become familiar with all of these filters and be able to handle their operation.

● Reverse EQ

■ Roads, C. (1996) *The Computer Music Tutorial.* Cambridge, MA: MIT Press.

Sound transformation

The transformation of sound is a highly important aspect of the creative manipulation of sound through time. Digital technologies have made many of the techniques described above quite commonplace. In a larger composition, those sound transformations can become a key formal or structural element of the overall drama of the work by producing sonic images that form the basis of the musical argument. In Trevor Wishart's piece *Red Bird* (1973–1977), for example, the transformation from vocal sounds to other sounds was the starting point for the form of the whole composition.[28]

There are many different ways to achieve sound transformations. Complex algorithms allow digital technologies to produce highly sophisticated results, but they are not always 'better' than their analogue counterparts. It all depends on the aesthetic intention of the artist. One crude example is the resampling of a signal at a different rate. This will produce an effect that resembles speeding up and slowing down a tape-recording: the pitch will get higher as the duration gets shorter, and vice versa. When this is done as a digital technique, the results can sound even stranger than the equivalent analogue manipulation, because the digital sound is not simply a transposed version of the original sound: it is a *brand new sound*, with its own features and characteristics.

Many sound-transformation techniques use a digital phase vocoder. Phase vocoding is not to be confused with analogue vocoding, which is a technique where the timbre of one signal is used to modify another, traditionally that of the voice applied to an instrument, hence 'voice coder'. Phase vocoding breaks the sound down into short chunks, applies some processing and then typically recombines the FFT with the resulting chunks in some way. This is quite effective for pitch-shifting and time-stretching, but the quality does vary depending upon the sophistication of the processes involved. It also requires a great deal of computational power.

Spectral *morphing* creates a seamless transition between two sounds by analysing their spectra and applying time-varying processes. These processes may include interpolation (where data from one file is inserted between data from the other) and concatenation (where the two sets of spectral data are combined in various ways). Often the most interesting part of a morphing process is the 'in-between' phase, and this can be further extracted and reprocessed. These kinds of processes: spectral analysis, resynthesis and cross-synthesis can all be undertaken live, in real time. Wave cycles or spectral windows may be shuffled, recombined and interpolated in numerous different ways. Pitch trace extraction and manipulation, transpositions and frequency shifts, retuning of individual harmonics, internal glissando effects and many more techniques are available in software packages. The quality of the results produced by such methods will depend upon the efficiency of the algorithm and the processing power of the computer.

■ Pellman, S. (1994) *An Introduction to the Creation of Electroacoustic Music.* Belmont, CA: Wadsworth Publishing Company.
■ Wishart, T. (1994) *Audible Design.* York: Orpheus the Pantomime Press.

Form and structure

Imagine a single sound. Its form will consist of the duration of the sound and the totality of what takes place within that duration. The content will be divisible into various elements, such as pitch, spectrum, rhythm, etc. The same can be said of an entire musical composition. In his book *Fundamentals of Musical Composition*, Arnold Schoenberg describes this interrelationship as *organisation*, in other words, the extent to which the combined components of the music resemble a living organism.

Used in the aesthetic sense, form means that a piece is *organised*; i.e. that it consists of elements functioning like those of a living *organism*. Without organisation, music would be an amorphous mass, as unintelligible as an essay without punctuation, or as disconnected as a conversation which leaps purposelessly from one subject to another.[29]

The 'form' of a piece of music is not the same as its 'structure'. The structure of a piece (e.g., the intro-verse-chorus-verse-chorus structure of many songs) is really a skeleton, while its form is like an entire body. Just as any two persons are different even though their skeletons are alike, so any two songs may have the same structure, but their form and content will be dissimilar. The assumptions that underpin these statements are collectively called 'formalism'. This implies that some kind of system may be used to organise music and that form is the sum total of a piece of music and the relationships of all its parts.

The organisation of sound may take a 'top-down' or 'bottom-up' approach to form and structure. A top-down approach would see the composition as a large-scale, or macro-structure (possibly subdivided into various sections) waiting to be filled with content, whereas the bottom-up approach will start from a sound or collection of sounds and try to evolve a larger-scale structure from them. In practice, composition is normally a combination of these two approaches. The composer's job is to develop form and content together so that they relate to one another successfully. The criteria for judgement described elsewhere in this book will determine to what extent success has been achieved.

In digital sound organisation, form and structure normally derive in some way from the editing process, in which the sounds are ordered into a desired sequence. The technology allows not just for linear sequencing (as in tape editing), but for non-linear and multi-tracked edits, or *montages*.[30] The structure of the resulting music is often called its 'architecture', a classical concept which has reappeared many times throughout history, most famously in Johann Wolfgang von Goethe's remark 'I call architecture frozen music'.[31] Sequencing, textures, and patterns therefore often provide the building-blocks of structure and the content of forms in such architecture.

As in all music, repetition and variation provide the basic ways in which a listener might orientate themselves within a piece, but in digital music the repetitions are often timbral and the variations come from sound manipulations. Musical *gesture* becomes an important device, not simply in terms of the physical motions of a performer, but within the sound organisation itself, as a way of moving on, of growing, developing and progressing *towards* something. This gesture will be the result of some *cause*, or perceived to be the consequence of some event or impulse. This provides the basic chain by which a musical 'argument' may be developed or a form evolved.[32]

There are many ways in which digital music may be organised into forms and structures. These will be considered in different contexts throughout this book, but a few summary examples will be useful at this point. It is always worth bearing in mind that the goal is to organise sound in a way that engages the listener, so it is not the means by which a sound is organised that creates musical interest, but how that organisation contributes to musical form, which develops in a meaningful way from its beginning to some kind of conclusion.

Many pieces of electro-acoustic music begin with an investigation into the acoustic properties of a sound which may be modelled or analysed in the computer. Various processes, including artificial intelligence, generative, evolutionary and genetic algorithms, may be applied to such material to develop the sound further. The human musician must decide in these cases to what extent to intervene, select or organise the resulting material. Again, the formal success of a piece may depend upon the organisational skill of the musician, in other words: a beautiful algorithm does not necessarily result in beautiful music.

Composers have explored both highly structured and highly chaotic approaches to organising sound. To give one influential example, Iannis Xenakis (1922–2001) used a strict mathematical approach to create *stochastic* music consisting of randomly generated elements. Stochasticism uses probability theory to model ways in which the individual elements within an extremely dense texture might behave. The paths of individual birds in a large flock weaving across the sky, or the many individual calls that make up the song of cicadas in a summer field, provide natural parallels. The complexity of these calculations were best suited to a computer, and, after some early orchestral pieces such as *Pithoprakta* (1956), which attempted to deliver stochastic music via traditional means, Xenakis moved on to computer-based composition. By 1979, he had devised a computer system called UPIC,[33] which could translate graphical images into musical results. Xenakis had originally trained as an architect, so some of his drawings, which he called 'arborescences', resembled both organic forms and architectural structures. Their many curves and lines translated into musical elements, such as pitches or melodic contours, which in turn contributed to the larger gestures that formed the architectural structures of the composition as a whole. The UPIC page from *Mycènes-Alpha* (*Mycenae-Alpha*) (1978) shown in Figure 4.14 lasts approximately one minute.

Other formal and organisational approaches to digital music are based on aleatoricism (chance) and chaos theory, on artificial intelligence and genetics, on tuning systems and musical grammars. All these will be considered at various points later in this book, but one organisational idea that has had a particular significance for a large number of digital musicians is *spectromorphology*. This will be examined in a bit more detail immediately.

■ Schoenberg, A. (1967) *Fundamentals of Musical Composition*. London: Faber and Faber.
■ Xenakis, I. (2001) *Formalized Music: Thought and Mathematics in Composition*. 2nd edition. New York: Pendragon.

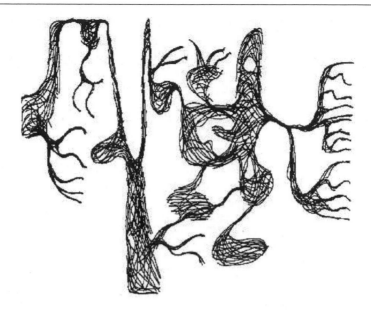

Figure 4.14 Iannis Xenakis, UPIC page from *Mycenae-Alpha* (1978).

Spectromorphology

This (rather cumbersome) term refers to an organisational approach based on inharmonics, where the individual digital sample represents a vertical snapshot of time-based relationships. The idea of the horizontal and the vertical in this situation can be extended both to the shortest possible sonic event and the largest musical structure. The word 'spectromorphology' therefore refers literally to the way sound spectra (spectro-) are shaped (-morphology) over time. It may be defined as 'an approach to sound materials and musical structures which concentrates on the spectrum of available pitches and their shaping in time'.[34]

Since sounds are the content of these shapes, and every sound must *have* a shape, it can be said that the two elements are indissolubly linked. The spectrum of a sound that lacks a fixed pitch changes so much over time that its morphology is often unstable and *dynamic*. The various elements are in transition, or moving. Most natural and environmental sounds fall into this category.

Sounds may be classified by their behaviour through time, as follows:

- *discrete* (single, short, separated)
- *iterative* (rapidly repeated, like a drum roll)
- *continuous* (sustained, continuations of sounds).

Musical situations often contain combinations of all three, but there is always motion from one type to the next. In his essay on spectromorphology, Denis

Smalley introduces a concept of *correspondence* to describe these moments of shift from one morphology to another. He describes an attack which:

> sets in motion a resonating spectrum which we might expect to decay gradually. The further away we travel from the attack point the more we may be coaxed into observing how the spectral components of the continuant phase proceed, and the less interested we shall be in the generic role of the initial impact. [35]

This example is typical of spectromorphological thinking, and Smalley goes on to elaborate how it might form a structuring principle for composition. Even at the relatively short-lived level of this example, a composer might use digital technology to manipulate, say, inharmonic elements of the decay, to begin its transformation into another sound type.

Just as the organisation of sound in space connects to its passage through time, so time-based manipulations reconnect to space. In his electro-acoustic piece *Valley Flow* (1992), Smalley explores this connection:

> The formal shaping and sound content of *Valley Flow* were influenced by the dramatic vistas of the Blow Valley in the Canadian Rockies. The work is founded on a basic flowing motion which is stretched or contracted to create floating and flying contours, panoramic sweeps, and the flinging out of textural materials. Special attention is paid to creating spatial perspectives – gazing out to the distinct horizon, looking down from a height, the impact of mountain bulks and the magnified details of organic activity.[36]

The result is a kind of sonic landscape which seems to link directly with a visual experience. The piece is layered and striated, just like the landscape it depicts, but also sweeps in a speeded-up version of the activity that formed the Blow Valley itself or the passage of the eye across its various features. The detailed manipulation of the sound through time, however, also creates a psychological effect that seems to correspond to the sense of awe experienced in the presence of such large geological formations.

● Sonic morph

▲ Denis Smalley (1992) *Valley Flow.* Empreintes Digitales, IMED-9209-CD, Montreal.

■ Emmerson, S. (1986) *The Language of Electroacoustic Music.* London: Macmillan.
■ Landy, L. (2007) *Understanding the Art of Sound Organization.* Cambridge, MA: MIT Press.

Chapter 5

Creating music

Music exists.

Howard Burrell, conversation with the author, 2005

The discussion of 'sound' in the preceding chapters became distinctly musical. The reverse will apply in this chapter, which will be concerned mainly with the aspects of 'music' that are relevant to technology-based music-making in the twenty-first century. This will involve ignoring or forgetting many musical 'givens'. Howard Burrell's comment serves as a reminder that, however much we may talk about sound, and to whatever extent we may use digital technologies, there always exists a vast body of music created in another way and at another time. This body of work casts a large shadow. A knowledge and understanding of past music will always benefit *any* musician, including a digital musician. Burrell's remark should be held as a warning to anyone who thinks that digital music renders all past endeavour obsolete and somehow negates the concept of music as it has been known. It will always have something to teach us.

The composer

The biggest change in music in the past thirty years or so has been in the role of the composer. To be the originator in Western classical music traditionally implies a hierarchy and one that is consolidated by copyright laws. This hierarchy is based on the idea that the composer is a figure of ultimate authority, underpinned by an assumption that the composer's ears are somehow better than those of a musician. The new technologies have somewhat challenged this hierarchy. First, they have placed all the tools for composing within reach: it is easy to create music. Second, they have enabled a degree of interaction with the music that can blur the distinction between the originator and the consumer. People can instantly remix, mash up, or otherwise recreate music. Third, they have transformed the act of performance into (potentially) an act of composition. People can record as they perform and make identical copies, which never degrade in quality. The separation that has grown up between composers and musicians is breaking down. The musician may be as much of an originator as the composer. In certain circumstances, the audience can become the originator.

Compare, for example, a violinist in an orchestra with a musician performing with a laptop computer. The violinist routinely copies the actions of his or her neighbour, following a precomposed score. The performance is essentially repetitious, and the function of an individual violin is to add to a collective sound produced by the whole violin section. The laptop musician, on the other hand, generally performs independently, relating to other musicians through choice. There is often no precomposed score, although there may be some plan, or some written notes. There is room for individual creativity in the laptop musician's performance.

In the case of the violinist, the composer is a remote figure (usually so remote as to be dead) and in any case mediated by the conductor. In the case of the laptop musician, the composer is probably the musician him or herself. If not, then there is often a living artist on hand to consult. There is not much distinction here between the act of composition and the act of performance.

The performance aspects of fixed medium works (tape, CD, etc.) are generally fairly irrelevant, except where there is live diffusion. But the nature of the medium implies a removal of the barrier of the performance ritual itself, so that the originator speaks directly to the consumer, because the originator is the musician. The traditional distinctions have, once again, broken down.

For many artists, the word 'composer' itself is problematic, conjuring up an image of a lone heroic genius or some historical character in a powdered wig. These artists do not call what they do 'composition', yet they are engaged in an activity which would undoubtedly be classed as such by most experts in the field, and they do it often with excellent results. The same issue arises in the case of sound designers and sonic artists, where the resistance to any kind of musical overtone to what is being done leads to a kind of horror at the idea of being classed as a 'composer'. The 'dots' composers, writing in the traditional way, would probably agree with that distinction. But the evidence tends to contradict them both.

'Composition' means, simply and literally, *putting things together*. The word crops up in contexts other than music, of course, including science, literature, even chess.[1] A musical composer, then, is simply someone who puts sounds together. The more conventional idea that a composer must write music notation and that others should be able to reproduce a given work in performance does not go far enough to cover electro-acoustic music, for example. To stretch the point, an improvising performer is also engaged in acts of instant composition. The education system complicates things further, by insisting that all students of both 'music' and 'music technology' engage in something called 'composition' which involves the origination of music. Today's musician is, to a great extent, a product of these developments. The digital musician is a composer.

Now, there is no reason to *insist* on someone who creatively puts sounds together using technology being called a 'composer' if neither the sonic artists (or whatever we call them) nor the 'real' composers want that. Except that, and it is a big point, there *is* a reason why traditional composers have evolved in the way they have: they understand composition. At the very least, the composers have something to teach the rest of us about composition. The study of existing music will always repay with dividends the effort expended, even if the music comes from a tradition that seems completely alien.

The major point here is that there is a blurring of roles in recent music-making and that a vastly increased number of people are today undertaking an activity that involves originating or combining sounds, often with musical intention or result. For the digital musician, engaged in such activity, developing a knowledge and understanding of composition may be regarded as highly beneficial, if not essential.

So, composition involves putting together sonic content so that it takes on some form or other. The new technologies make this easy, but the fact that it *can* be done does not mean it *should* be done. There has to be a reason to compose, especially if the composition is to be good. There has to be an intention behind the result. And the composer has to be able to judge the result when measured against the intention. The question now is no longer *whether* we can compose, nor even *what* to compose, but *why* compose?

Why compose?

One approach to this question is first to identify the purpose of the music, or (to answer a question with a question) what is the music *for?* We are no longer under the illusion that there is an objective purpose that can be ascribed to music, other than that which we ascribe. What are some of those purposes? If the brief is commercial, then more often than not the function of the music will be clearly defined (usually by someone else). However, not all music is commercial music. In fact, some would-be commercial music can turn out *not* to be commercial, and vice versa! But the purposes of music can extend far beyond the question of a commercial brief. Here are some musings on the question: what is music for?

- To explore and expand human experience.
- To awaken sensitivity to the divine.
- To mark something out as special.
- To facilitate social bonding.
- To exercise the choice of being creative.
- To extol, support, encourage.
- To provide therapy.
- To engage in a battle for supreme intellectual achievement.
- To evolve the human race and its social systems.
- To provoke questioning of the existing social order.
- To enact freedom.
- To calm the mind.
- To provide emotional catharsis.

- To encourage people to shop.
- To encourage people to march, celebrate, worship, kill . . .
- To encourage bodily health.
- To avoid thought.
- To seek answers to questions.
- To better understand oneself.
- To demonstrate to others how great you are.
- To pursue a fascination.
- To preserve a sonic environment.
- To tell stories.
- To avoid telling stories.
- To pass the time.
- To make a statement about self and/or group identity.
- To irritate the neighbours.
- To torture.
- To induce ecstasy.
- To pass a class.
- To entertain the family.
- To woo.
- To build one's career.
- To appear clever.
- To give theorists something to talk about.
- To make one feel [*fill in blank*].
- To experience pleasure or provide pleasure.
- 'Inner necessity'.
- Just because . . .[2]

What each of these has in common is an assumption that music is active, that it has a capacity to *do* or *say* something. In every sense, the music has an effect or a voice and, for many people, music has a *meaning*.

Academic discussions often focus upon an ancient debate about musical meaning. One camp argues that music resembles a language, with clear grammar and syntax and that, therefore, it is possible to ascribe meanings to, and even tell stories in, sound. The opposing camp argues that, in fact, music is 'absolute', that is to say, it has no meaning over and above the sounds that you hear and, as the composer Stravinsky famously, and provocatively, said: 'is incapable of expressing anything but itself'.[3] The debate becomes particularly heated when the subject of the way in which music expresses *emotions* arises.

Most people would agree that music can express, or at least *seem* to express, emotions. However, there is general disagreement about what those emotions may be in a particular case. Listeners' emotional states vary, and the responses they make also vary. A piece that seems sad to one audience may be amusing to another. There is nothing inherently *in the music* that makes this so, but, then again, without the music there would presumably be no such feeling at all.

This has implications for the composer or musician. Let's suppose you feel angry, and you want to create some music to express that anger. First, it is hard to create music when gripped by a powerful emotion such as anger. When you try it, the emotion itself gets in the way of the rational thought needed to organise materials and equipment, to structure and give form to the music. You may know what it is to feel anger, but what you want to do is to create some music *that evokes that feeling.* That is a very different statement, but it will probably be far more successful as an approach to achieving the expressive goal.

You may start to draw upon music's evocative power by exploring the ways in which anger may be expressed musically in your culture. At first, perhaps, you might think of loud, clashing, jarring material, which seems to draw a direct parallel with the emotion you felt. A more subtle approach might in fact avoid the obviously loud, clashing music in favour of a more 'internalised', 'tense', almost psychological evocation of anger. Whatever solution you adopt, the sheer compositional craft involved will tend to make the musical depiction of anger distanced, reflective. In other words, the expression of emotion in music is to a certain extent a matter of technique. This does not necessarily mean it lacks feeling, or is in some way 'cold and calculated'.

Musical expression depends a great deal upon *context.* To take some material that is 'sad' and place it in some new context it does not necessarily mean that the quality of sadness will also have transferred to the new situation. Since a great deal of contemporary music uses such recontextualisation, it is important to understand that any material, in any context, will have a relationship with its new context and its old context. The listeners' perceptions of this relationship will depend partly upon their knowledge of the two contexts and partly upon their abilities to deduce from the aural evidence. The fact that a composer knows both the origins and the destinations of recontextualised material does not guarantee that the listeners will share that understanding.

This can be extended to the question of intention and result. It is an unfortunate fact that whatever meanings you *intend* to communicate with your sounds, there is no guarantee that the listener will actually understand. Some recent research conducted by Robert Weale into the intention and reception of electro-acoustic music[4] tests this idea by playing various groups of listeners pieces of music with and without titles and additional information. Although there was some convergence in reaction, there were also differences in audience understanding *even when they had access to the composer's intentions.* Music as self-expression, then, seems, at best, an inaccurate weapon.

Despite this, the creation of music fulfils a need for such expression, and it is no accident that certain composers and musicians seem to communicate their ideas better than others. In some cases, this happens in spite of the composer. Stravinsky remarked, 'I was the vessel through which *Le Sacre du Printemps* passed'. On other occasions, the emotional involvement of the composer in his or her own music seems integral to its success (Beethoven is an obvious example).

There is no single answer to the question 'Why compose?' Each person should find his or her own reasons. There are plenty of reasons why *not* to compose, of which the most pressing is the sheer quantity of existing music. And yet, the desire to find a voice as an artist is so strong that many people feel impelled to do so. The wonderful thing about the new technologies is that they have enabled so many to produce good results and often with relatively little formal musical training or in unusual circumstances.

● Inspiration box

■ Miranda, E. R. (2001) *Composing Music with Computers*. Oxford: Focal Press.
■ Weintraub, L. *et al.* (1997) *Art on the Edge and Over: Searching for Art's Meaning in Contemporary Society 1970s–1990s*. New York: Art Insights.

Aural imagination

It is interesting to note how much the preceding discussion of musical meaning relates to the earlier discussion of Pierre Schaeffer's four modes of listening. The deeper understanding of the evocation of emotion, for example, corresponds to the deeper level of listening in modes 3 and 4, which relate to discrimination and understanding. The extent to which the musician succeeds in understanding the way in which music's evocative power may be harnessed is often the mark of a sophisticated and successful musical listener.

The emergence of an aural culture, working directly with sound itself, has certain consequences. One advantage of the notation-based system was that it forced composers in particular, but also musicians in general, to develop an aural imagination, often referred to as the 'inner ear'. This is the ability to hear accurately in the imagination, without reference to any actual sound. Often, this skill would be combined with score-reading, such that a skilled conductor, for example, would be able to 'read' a score off the page, hearing the music with the inner ear in the same way that one might read a book without speaking (or hearing spoken) the words.

The aural imagination has great creative potential, allowing musical forms and structures to be shaped by the individual before committing them to actual sound. It can also operate simultaneously with music-making, allowing the musician to imagine other ways to develop or manipulate the material as they do so. It is a means of experimentation, of creative play. It is, therefore, important to try to retain this as part of the 'hands-on', concrete, sculptural way of working encouraged by the new technologies.

Sculpture provides an interesting parallel to illustrate the role of the aural imagination. A sculptor may begin by seeing a pattern in nature or by observing an aspect of human existence. Or they may set out to make a reproduction of an existing object. Whatever their purpose, sculptors will often use their materials to make something that resembles their imagination. In doing so, they might reveal to the rest of us something not seen before, some truth. More often than not, there will be a single material, such as stone or wood. Sometimes, what is revealed is the inherent properties of the material itself, which nevertheless once again connects with the imagination: within this we might find *this* . . .

Sound and sonic exploration may be treated in very much the same way. The advantage of working in digital media is that the results can be constantly reviewed and repeated, just like a sculpture. In both cases, the role of the creator's imagination is crucial to the finished result. In the creation of any work, there is a three-stage process: the *intention* to create; the *result* of the act of creation; and the *reception* of the finished result. The imagination is relevant in all three stages but is most active in the gap between intention and result. It could be said that this is where the *art* resides.

● Sunset

■ Godøy, R. I. and Jørgensen, H. (eds) (2001) *Musical Imagery.* Lisse: Swets and Zeitlinger.
■ McAdams, S. (ed.) (1993) *Thinking in Sound.* Oxford: Oxford University Press.
■ Théberge, P. (1997) *Any Sound You Can Imagine.* Hanover, CT: Wesleyan University Press.

Intention and result

The criteria for judging the success of a piece may rest with a client or an audience, depending on the circumstances. For the artists themselves, however, the mapping of intention to result, coupled with a critical distance on the work, will be the main way such judgements are made. The ability to self-evaluate, to criticise one's own compositional work, is an important skill. There may be situations where indifference to the outcome of the work is part of the creative project itself, but this kind of situation needs considerable conceptual and artistic maturity to succeed. In general, the composer or artist will have some idea of what they want to achieve and some sense of whether they have achieved it.

Even in a situation where the computer is the composer, or an algorithm has been created which follows its own course regardless of human intervention, the initial intention to create such a musical situation must be there. The key to making good critical evaluations of one's own work lies in the ability to adapt mentally to the nature of the work itself. In other words, it is no good condemning an algorithmic piece for showing a lack of freedom from constraints or an improvisation for lacking sufficient pre-planning, any more than it is fair to criticise a lion for not being a tiger. The work should be evaluated on its own terms.

However, there are some criteria that will apply in any situation. A first, and obvious, one is: How well is the technology used? Notice this does not specify *which* technology. It is possible to create good music with limited equipment. However, an evident ability to handle the equipment is a prerequisite of a successful piece. Any sign of a shortcoming in this respect will reduce the effectiveness of the work. To take some typical and common examples: samples that end with clicks, timings that fail to synchronise, levels that are unbalanced, will all contribute to an impression of technical inadequacy. Of course, there are some situations in which clicks, lack of synchronisation and a lack of balance are precisely the intended effects, in which case the important thing is to ensure that the listener understands the intention. This is doubly hard to achieve.

The next criterion is *critical reflection*. The choices made in the creation of the piece tell the listener much about the intention of the artist. Sometimes, success is measured more by what is *not* done than by what *is* done. In any musical situation, there are always decisions to be made. The appropriateness and effectiveness of those decisions will be evident to the listener. They constitute a powerful indicator of the abilities of the artist and the success of the music. A bad decision will be one that contradicts the perceived intention of the work. Manipulating this perceived intention through the decisions made is the sign of consummate critical judgement.

The next criterion is evidence of *creativity*. Creativity is a broad and multifaceted concept. At its simplest level, any action that produces a result, in any sphere, is to some extent 'creative'. But the creation of good music implies something more: the generation of new ideas, the presence of some original thought, in other words: *inventiveness*. In 1961, Mel Rhodes conducted research into creativity that identified its three main aspects.[5] The first he called 'person', which refers to the skills, traits, motivation and abilities that make someone creative. The second was 'environment': the individual's physical and psychological surroundings that either enable or undermine creative thought. Third, he identified 'process', or the mental activities an individual (or a group) goes through to achieve a creative result. These three need to be in the right balance if a good outcome is to be achieved. The products of these (a piece of music, in this case) are merely the tips of a large iceberg. They are the evidence that creativity is present.

The final criterion is a sense of *purpose*. Even though, as has been said, the piece of music is inevitably the result of some kind of intention, there is nothing that reduces the effectiveness of a work more than purposelessness. Nor can purpose be easily introduced into something that has none. To be purposeful is not necessarily to be 'useful'. Art for art's sake can be purpose enough. The purposefulness of a piece is not linked to its function in the world but rather to its sense of its own right to exist. This comes from a combination of aesthetic or artistic intention with effective organisation of the materials. There should be purpose in the craft of composition as well as in the ideas that lie behind them. As before, this does not mean that a work cannot deliberately explore 'purposelessness' as an idea. That would be its purpose.

- Types of space
- Narrative

■ Norman, K. (2004) *Sounding Art: Eight Literary Excursions through Electronic Media.* London: Ashgate.

Structuring principles

Musical structure can range from the highly ordered to the chaotic, from the formulaic to the randomised. The job of the composer is to make decisions about the structuring principles in order to achieve an effective musical experience for the listener. The structuring principles can derive from the musical content of the sounds themselves or can be imposed upon them. For example, a digital sound may have a spatial dimension, as discussed in the previous chapter. This can become a structuring principle of the music by developing within the composition in ways which are distinctly perceptible by the listener. In this case, the spatial aspects become an active element within the composition, rather than simply the way in which the piece is presented.[6] Alternatively, the spatial distribution of sounds could be imposed as a structure in itself, independent of the actual sonic content of the music.

The key importance of a structuring principle is to engage the listener in a meaningful discourse which leads to some kind of perception of organisation. Sometimes, an extremely clear, even rigid, structure is the best means to achieve this, sometimes more 'organic' structures work well. Certain genres have given structures which represent a significant constraint for the composer. Working within these constraints can be beneficial for discipline and technical development. However, when approaching a free composition, some early decisions about structuring principles are normally necessary.

The best such pieces are those which convey a sense of an evolving argument or journey. Here, the structuring principle is based upon the idea that musical gestures can be developed beyond the point where they are simply a succession of more or less impressive effects. The tools for these developments in digital music lie in the effects and filters, sound transformations and time-based manipulations, described elsewhere in this book. Loudness and silence can be used formally as structuring principles. Dramatic contrasts, timbral changes and textural content are all capable of playing a structuring role, of forming key elements in a composition. From the listeners' viewpoint, the question will always be '*Why* has such-and-such an event taken place?'. The extent to which they can answer that question satisfactorily will determine the perceived success of the structuring principle that underlies the music.

● Sonic collage

■ Nyman, M. (1999) *Experimental Music: Cage and Beyond.* 2nd edition. Cambridge: Cambridge University Press.

Constraint

Musical creation may begin with freedom or may be highly constrained. It would be a mistake to assume that a free approach leads to freer composition. In fact, constraints can often be highly liberating. Adopting a deliberately restricted process or pattern can trigger ideas and inspiration and is usually a good way to start to make music. Having said that, there is nothing inherently wrong with a free approach, except that it can be difficult to do *anything* if all possibilities are open to the musician. In practice, most people end up submitting to self-imposed constraints, even if these are fairly underdeveloped (e.g., genre conventions or personal taste).

Some typical examples of constraints might include:

- material constraints, where restrictions are placed upon the quantity or nature of the sonic materials
- process-based constraints, where the musical process itself unfolds according to rules (e.g., algorithmic music)
- compositional constraints, placing constraints on the act of composition itself (e.g., making music in a particular *style* or using a particular technique for a particular purpose).

When working with constraint, it is important to bear in mind that the constraint itself is not the piece. An example from history will help to illustrate the point here.

In 1952, the composer Pierre Boulez published *Structures 1* for two pianos. This was an example of extreme compositional constraint. Every element of the piece (intervals, rhythms, dynamics, etc.) was subject to mathematical rules in which the individual units (notes, durations, dynamic markings, etc.) were ordered into series. The result, often called 'integral serialism', was a work that exhibits a startling apparent randomness in its surface, while being so tightly constrained behind the scenes as to lack much evidence of the composer's hand at work.

At the same time, John Cage was also composing a work for piano, also trying to remove evidence of the composer's hand but with a radically different compositional constraint. *Music of Changes* (1951) was created using chance procedures, in this case coin tosses, to decide the ordering of the musical elements. As Cage's fellow composer Earle Brown put it, Cage was 'beginning to consciously deal with the "given" material and, to varying degrees, liberate them from the inherited, functional aspects of control'.[7]

These two works were created very differently, yet the result is, to the ear, surprisingly similar. In fact, hearing one another's work made both composers reconsider their compositional approaches. Boulez gradually moved away from integral serialism, and Cage's chance procedures became more sophisticated and somewhat deterministic. Neither constraint has survived as a common working practice in music, and neither *Music of Changes* nor *Structures 1* finds a regular place on concert programmes.

This strange convergence of two extremely different, yet rigorously applied, constraints was a key moment in the evolution of music in the twentieth century. What they have in common is an obsession with control, either seeking to apply it thoroughly (in the case of Boulez) or to reject it utterly (in the case of Cage). What seems to have emerged is a realisation that, in applying their constraints so vigorously, the result was *musically* indistinct. For both composers, the solution was subsequently to address musical questions, where appropriate, at the expense of the constraints.

The message for the digital musician from this anecdote is: work with a constraint, by all means, but do not let it override the music. If the constraint produces unmusical outcomes, either change it, or ignore it, but do not fall back on the 'system made me do it' excuse. Of course, the word 'unmusical' itself implies a subjective judgement, which refers back to the criteria described earlier.

● Sudoku

■ Cope, D. (2000) *The Algorithmic Composer*. Madison, WI: A-R Editions.
■ Nattiez, J.-J. (ed.) (1993) *The Boulez–Cage Correspondence*. Cambridge: Cambridge University Press.

Modalities

The words 'mode' and 'mood' are closely related, and 'modality' was the word traditionally used to distinguish between 'modal' and 'tonal' music. Where tonal music has a 'key' which may change during a composition, modal music is defined by a set of relationships or intervals that make up the mode and often relates to a fixed element such as a drone. The modal tradition in Europe was superseded by tonality in the seventeenth century but has seen quite a revival in the past century. A great deal of popular music, particularly rock and pitch-based electronic dance music, is modal in a traditional sense. This partly derives from playing techniques, because modal patterns tend to fit neatly under the fingers on the guitar, and limited keyboard skills will often result in a white-notes-only playing style. White notes form the pitch sets of the so-called 'church modes'. However, modality is more than just a collection of pitch sets. A mode is essentially a repetition of patterns, which may be intervals,[8] but might also be rhythms, or resonances.

A great deal of music composed with new technology addresses the question of how a sound may be extended. This, as has been suggested already, involves analysing and modifying the spectrum. Any sound, apart from pure noise, will have an inherent modality, because its spectrum will contain some dominant pitches, a certain resonance, even repeating rhythms. Very short sounds, such as clicks or glitches, acquire a clear pitch when stretched. Extending sounds and their spectral characteristics will therefore tend to create a magnified modality.[9]

There are also various performance modalities, which have become compositional techniques in themselves. Apart from the drone (which may be a persistent rhythm instead of a pitch), performance techniques based on call and response, such as hocket (interpolation of individual sounds by different performers which, when combined, make up whole phrases) and antiphony (alternation between two blocks of sound, often spatially separated) are not only common in (early) modal music but also in music played through loudspeaker systems.

It is surprising how relevant these ideas of modality can prove to be, even in entirely noise-based music. Often a key compositional decision is whether to include an element that 'binds together' the whole piece. This, then, tends to function as a drone. Musical excitement and interest is often generated by listener perception of the relationships between the various sonic elements, which add up to a 'mood' picture. Performance techniques involving hocket and antiphony can often be the most musically engaging. Acousmatic music can sometimes exhibit a quite startling modality.

● Night piece

■ Roads, C. (ed.) (2004) *Composers and the Computer.* Madison, WI: A-R Editions.

Non-linear music

So far, what has been said on this subject applies to composition as practised by pre-digital and digital musicians alike. However there are two additional musical questions which tend to be peculiar to the digital musician. The first is to decide whether the form is to be *linear* or *non-linear*. Of course, the listener hears all music as linear in the sense that there is a succession of audio events passing through time, but from a compositional point of view there is a world of difference between writing a fixed, linear piece that has a beginning, middle and end, and writing non-linear music in which material is accessed using some kind of digital procedure that orders events or samples in a different way each time the music is experienced.

Non-linear composition is generally modelled on database structures and is typically driven by 'if . . . then . . .' coding, or looping and branching. Here, the drama of the piece is more to do with the way the listener or user interacts with the material than with any formal structuring. This leads on to the second distinctive question facing the digital musician: By what *agency* is the music to be made? If the answer is just an algorithm, then we are talking about a virtual agent. If the answer is through human interaction, then the virtual and the physical are combined.

This is sometimes called *adaptive* music, because it has to adapt in real time to a user's changing position in a given narrative or space. One way of achieving this is by varying the mix in a continuous set of loops. Although this presents considerable musical challenges, from a technical point of view it uses standard sequencing procedures. A more technically complex method is to shuffle precomposed segments of music into endlessly variable sequences.

However, the kind of 'Adaptive Music' first coined by Christopher Yavelow in 1997 works slightly differently. As he describes it:

adaptive music [. . .] relies on a continual feedback loop consisting of a user or users evaluating music generated by seed material provided by themselves (or itself generated). The software incorporates their preferences (opinions, tastes) into subsequent compositions by adapting the models it uses to compose in the future based upon this user feedback. Adaptive Music models are collections of compositional methods, rules, and constraints. The entire learning process allows the software to continually move closer to the ideal composition for an individual or collective group of users.[10]

Computer gamers who make choices that affect the behaviour of the music may be an accelerated version of this process. They can create original soundtracks and, indeed, whole movies by ignoring the objectives of the game itself and using the games engine creatively. At this point, the difference between the composer, the performer and the audience becomes so blurred as to be meaningless.

To summarise: just as a computer database sometimes organises its information in a hierarchical, tree-like structure, so event-driven software has been developed to allow musical components to be similarly organised. Very often, these will use some kind of algorithm to access musical elements, be they loops, individual sounds, sequences or whatever. The extent to which the algorithm is dictated by human choice or by the computer itself will determine the extent of the interactivity. An ability to manipulate sound design software is important in the development of interactive music skills for virtual environments.

■ Marks, A. (2001) *The Complete Guide to Game Audio*. Lawrence, KS: CMP Books.
■ Winkler, T. (2001) *Composing Interactive Music*. Cambridge, MA: MIT Press.

Originality and style

Who is the originator of a sample-based piece? The person who recorded the samples? The person who wrote the software that processes them? The person who diffuses the sound that results? Or is it, in fact, the person who takes all the decisions about these elements: the digital musician. The person who produces a recording, or creates the soundtrack for a computer game or makes a sound installation is a composer. Adaptive computer-game music pieces, or interactive sound installations, are not fixed objects in the manner of a notated score, and even a CD may be diffused by taking the stereo content and allocating it to multiple channels. What seems so fixed, so certain, is, in fact, highly mutable. The 'repeatability' of a 'performance' is by no means guaranteed. It is even a myth that a digital recording always sounds the same. In the hand of a good sound diffuser or performer, it *never* sounds the same.

The question of originality is, thus, a starting point for composition. To put it simply: To what extent should the composer use models or 'borrow' from other artists? Most music derives in some way or another from other music. However innovative a compositional idea or approach may be, it is practically certain that there will be some artistic connection with something already heard or known. This is not to deny the possibility of originality but simply to suggest that no music exists in a vacuum. For many young composers, the development and acquisition of technique is, in itself, sufficiently demanding, without having to create an entirely new musical language for themselves from the outset.

A traditional approach to this problem is to 'pastiche' known music. This crops up both in classical training (where stylistic exercises are commonplace) and band situations (in the form of the 'cover' song), but also a lot of multimedia and interdisciplinary work demands pastiche. Most Hollywood film music, for example, is almost entirely pastiche, generally of late nineteenth- and early twentieth-century classical orchestral music. Games soundtracks, too, can often call for film-like pastiche. Good pastiche of this kind is difficult to achieve and often requires a traditional training.

There is a less clearly established set of values regarding pastiche work available to the digital musician, because both the media and the musical forms that arise from them are so new. The sample-based culture is pervasive. Where the techniques are deployed in a recognisable sub-culture or genre, then a clear knowledge of the conventions of that culture are obviously required. But it is usually the case that the individual musician has to go beyond those conventions if they are to succeed in that culture.

The early stages of personal musical development may well involve pastiche work and, as the abilities improve, so the distinctive content in the work will evolve. Where the music itself is more experimental or less obviously genre-based, then pastiche may be less relevant. Either way, the practice of pastiche can be valuable to further an understanding of both compositional process and artistic intention, but it should be used with caution. If the goal is musical innovation, then over-reliance on pastiche work will get in the way. Having compositional models in mind is *not* the same as pastiche. This is the difference between showing a musical influence and simply aping somebody else's practice.

Musical style is often linked to genre classification as it implies the use of a certain basic 'language'. Reggae style, for example, seems quite different from country music, so at first glance this appears to be fairly uncontroversial. However, style has increasingly become linked to the need to pigeonhole musicians for commercial purposes. The musician John Zorn wrote:

> Jazz. Punk. Dada. Beat. These words and their longer cousins, the ism-family (surrealism, postmodernism, abstract expressionism, minimalism), are used to commodify and commercialize an artist's complex personal vision. This terminology is not about understanding. It never has been. It's about money. Once a group of artists, writers, or musicians has been packaged together under such a banner, it is not only easier for work to be marketed – it also becomes easier for the audience to 'buy it' and for the critic to respond with prepackaged opinions.[11]

It is clear from this that the self-conscious adoption of a musical style by a composer is risky if an individual voice or a 'complex personal vision' is the goal. However, it is equally very difficult, in fact impossible, to produce music that has *no* style. Once again, the use of critical reflection and judgement will be the guide for the digital musician. The important thing, when creating music, is the *music itself*, which will develop its own style. In the modern world, this may be influenced by just about anything, regardless of the maker's geographical location or personal background, so the sensitivity, integrity and awareness mentioned earlier are fundamental.

● Pastiche

■ Cope, D. (2001) *Virtual Music: Computer Synthesis of Musical Style.* Cambridge, MA: The MIT Press.
■ Zorn, J. (2000) *Arcana: Musicians on Music.* New York: Granary Books.

Chapter 6

Performing

> Music is a form of social communication; musical performance is a site of social intercourse, and a form of social dialogue [. . .] In surviving oral cultures, the relation between musical senders and musical receivers is much more fluid and symbiotic than in modern Western society. The anthropological evidence is unequivocal. There are no composers in such societies set apart from other musicians in a separate caste, and music is far from an exclusive activity of specialized performers.
>
> Chanan (1994)[1]

Performing and creating are practically indivisible activities for the digital musician. There is a historical basis for this. 'Performance Art', which has its own origins in the Happenings of the 1960s, successfully removed the work of art from an object in a gallery to an action in a particular space at a particular time. Much early experimentation with music technology was allied to similar experiments with performance ritual. Nowadays, performance need not even involve human performers. An installation can be performative, and an artificial intelligence may also perform. Locations may be physical or virtual, and time may not be fixed. Certain types of movies may be interactively performed rather than just 'shown', and gaming too offers performance opportunities. A good example is 'machinima' (machine cinema), in which people use game platforms to create original theatre featuring the avatars, or virtual characters, and settings of a computer game, without adherence to the goals of the game itself. Once again, the creator, the performer and the audience constantly shift roles.

At some point in history, music education decided to separate performing and creating. The conservatoires and other mainstream performing-arts institutions generally place more emphasis on creative *interpretation* than original creation. Composition is a specialist option, and the creators (composers, in this case) are not necessarily expected to perform. The classical system of notated music, supported by pedagogy and academic research, has reinforced the specialisation. This system is largely incompatible with digital music. The fact that the two activities are presented in different chapters in this book should not be understood as supporting their separation but rather as a matter of convenience for the organisation of certain ideas. The reader will quickly discover that the conventions are substantially criticised and reworked in the text that follows.

The projects given in this chapter are mostly designed to encourage group and ensemble work and so set themselves somewhat against the prevailing culture of individualism. The best way an individual can develop is in a group context. The absence of much recognised performance repertoire in this kind of music is also addressed, and this book contains a number of 'scores' for realisation in performance.

- Chanan, M. (1994) *Musica Practica: Social Practices of Western Music from Gregorian Chant to Post Modernism.* London: Verso.
- Goldberg, R. L. (1979, 2001) *Performance Art: From Futurism to the Present.* London: Thames and Hudson.

The performer

The performer, then, has changed almost as much as the composer. We may even speak of a 'digital performer'. This phrase implies a new performance mode, which is more than just a traditional concert performance executed on digital instruments. A pianist playing piano music on a digital piano is not really a digital performer. If the same pianist were to process or manipulate the sound of the piano in some way, then digital performance starts to appear. There are a number of distinctly different activities in which this new performer might engage, including sound diffusion and networked performance.

Sound diffusion

Sound diffusion is emerging as an important live performance technique. The organisation of sound in space has already been discussed. What is of interest here is the live performance situation. In the past, it has generally been assumed that the sound system for a concert is set up and controlled purely by engineers or technicians who would not themselves be classified as musicians. Given the level of control these people exercise over the sound heard by the audience, this is a rather astonishing attitude. In fact, sound diffusion is, or rather *can be*, just as musical an activity as playing the piano. It is certainly a form of musical interpretation. Digital musicians cannot place themselves at the mercy of sound engineers if they are to achieve an original sound. It is essential that they (the musicians) master sound-diffusion techniques to at least a basic level.

One of the performance challenges facing sound diffusers is the extent to which the audience can perceive what the performer is doing. The action of sliding faders on a mixing desk is quite uninformative compared to, say, the action of depressing a piano key. This becomes especially true when the fader motion controls parameters other than volume level, which it often does in live diffusion situations. The motion of sounds through space, the application of effects and processes, the grouping and assigning of a stereo source to various channels in a multichannel set-up may all be contained within a tiny hand motion which is, more often than not, invisible to the audience. For acousmatic situations, where the ideal is to remove visual distraction, this can be desirable, but in less refined circumstances it can lead to misunderstanding about the role of the diffuser.

The next major performance challenge, consequently, is the way in which musical gesture is interpreted through diffusion. There is an active debate about this. The premise is that the same types of gestures that are present in the shaping of the material that makes up electro-acoustic music should be reflected in its diffusion. Where sound is ascribed to channels and motion between channels is already built in to a composition, there is apparently little need to actively 'interpret' the result. The assumption is that the set-up itself will perform the diffusion. However, in practice, this is often not the case. A stereo piece played back over stereo speakers in a large concert hall will often lose the stereo image because of the size and reverberant characteristics of the space. A multichannel set-up is the solution, at which point the choices made during the diffusion become key performance decisions.

To be absolutely clear, then, sound diffusion is a *musical*, rather than a purely technical, activity. The diffusion should aim to reveal the formal nature of a work, its underlying structures as well as its local detail. The piece must be thoroughly rehearsed in advance of a performance and account taken of the characteristics of the space and set-up. Musical questions such as the rate at which diffusion changes take place and the kind of spatial motion that is introduced should be decided upon. Often, a form of notation called a 'diffusion score' can be used to aid this process. These can range from the highly technical to the lyrically interpretative, as may be seen in the following examples. Scott Wyatt's score (see Figure 6.1) shows time running vertically up the page and the eight channels, arranged in three stereo pairs plus two single channels for front and back centre speakers, are given vertically. Wyatt explains:

> Black graphic shapes indicate the amplitude contour information for each channel, the thicker the shape, the higher the amplitude and vice versa. Comments are often written in the vertical margins to alert the projectionist to specific cues or types of articulation.[2]

Claude Schryer's diffusion score for Francis Dhomont's *Chiaroscuro* (1987), on the other hand, shows time running from left to right across the page and gives almost no detailed information about the activities in the loudspeakers, preferring instead to use its imagery to evoke the character and gesture of the music itself (Figure 6.2).

■ White, P. (2005) *Live Sound (Performing Musicians)*. New York: Sanctuary.
■ Wyatt, S. *et al.* (2005) *Investigative Studies on Sound Diffuson/Projection at the University of Illinois: A Report on An Explorative Collaboration*. University of Illinois.

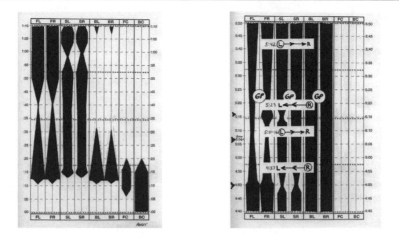

Figure 6.1 Two pages from the diffusion score for *Aftermath* (2005). © Scott A. Wyatt, 2005, reproduced with permission.

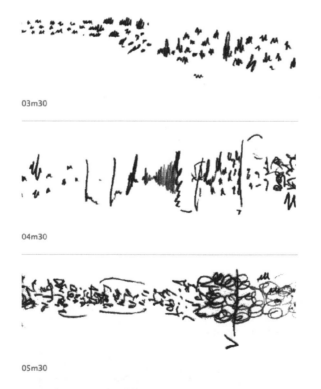

03m30

04m30

05m30

Figure 6.2 Excerpt from Claude Schryer's diffusion score for Francis Dhomont's *Chiaroscuro* (1987).

Networked performance

There are five main types of networked performance:

1   music that uses the network to connect physical spaces or instruments
2   music that is created or performed in virtual environments, or uses virtual instruments
3   music that translates into sound aspects of *the network itself*
4   music that uses the Internet to enable collaborative composition or performance
5   music that is delivered via the Internet, with varying degrees of user interactivity.

A typical situation might have a group of musicians sharing control of the parameters of a given sound file or collection of sound files. Modular software enables each individual to interact with the sound files in various ways while simultaneously communicating with one another. If the musicians are physically present in the same space, visual, verbal and textual clues may be exchanged, but the idea can be extended to remotely located musicians too. Telepresence is a relatively under explored aspect of this kind of music.

There are various kinds of network used in music, ranging from small local area networks (LANs) to wide area networks (WANs) that connect towns, cities and countries. The 'Internet' is a network of networks and is never used in its entirety, but 'net music' and 'Internet music' are terms that encompass music made on all kinds of network. The majority of such networks comprise nodes that are physically connected by cable, but, of course, there are also wireless networks and satellite networks, of which the best known are the mobile phone networks. All of these may be used in music-making.

The technical constraints that confront the musician on the network mainly relate to *latency* and *loss*. Latency is the amount of time required for a signal to traverse the network, and loss of data is partly a consequence of the bandwidth which, in networking terms, is the capacity or data rate of a link. To illustrate the scale of the challenge these create for music, consider this quotation from an article by Álvaro Barbosa:

> For the human ear to perceive two sounds as simultaneous, the sounds should not be displaced in time more than 20 msec, which means that for mutual awareness to be supported in a bilateral performance, the maximum threshold would be around 40 msec (the time it would take a performer to perceive a second performer's reaction to his or her action). It should be noted that the perception of two different sounds performed simultaneously is strongly dependent on sound characteristics (timbre, pitch and loudness), musical style and other types of feedback such as visual or physical stimuli. Nevertheless, a 20-msec threshold should be adequate. If we consider the smallest

possible peer-to-peer connection between two opposite points on the planet, we have an approximate distance of 20,004.5 km (half the distance of earth's perimeter: 40,009 km). Even with data transfer at the speed of light (approximately 300,000 km per sec) and unlimited bandwidth, bidirectional latency would reach approximately 133.4 msec, which is much higher than the tolerable threshold.[3]

Since unlimited bandwidth is a pipe dream, this problem is considerably magnified in many musical situations, and solutions usually concentrate on ways of accommodating the limitations of the network itself. Even quite small LANs can exhibit significant latency.

Network architecture is a vast study in its own right, but the two types of network that crop up repeatedly in relations to music are the traditional client/server network and peer-to-peer (p2p) networks. In the former, the server generally runs intensive software (e.g., databases, email, and so on) and the client usually consists of an interface that can request data from the server. P2p networks operate rather differently, each connected machine sharing its computing power and data with the others on the network, without using a central server.

Where interactivity in network music is the goal, various solutions have been developed using different programming languages. Here are a couple of examples: *JSyn*[4] ('Java Synthesis') uses the Java programming language to allow users to develop interactive applications such as synthesisers, audio playback routines and effects-processing algorithms; *Jade*,[5] on the other hand, takes a modular approach based on Max/MSP to allow multiple users to analyse, generate and process audio and video.

In recent years, making music in virtual worlds has become widespread, partly as a result of online gaming. The virtual worlds themselves are essentially object-oriented programming environments enriched with multimedia capability. These allow the users to build their own environment, to interact with other users, to create objects and so on. A virtual world is, therefore, made by its inhabitants according to their own imaginations, and in several such worlds[6] musical communities are developing formed entirely of virtual musicians. They build virtual instruments, which they sell or barter, and they perform virtual concerts or have virtual jam sessions.

Such new media represent more than just a technical development. They contain a fundamental cultural shift too. Now that non-linear music and network performance are a practical reality, numerous home-grown technical solutions to musical and multimedia problems are springing up. The digital musician may well contribute to these. It is not enough to use new media to disseminate music that could be heard equally well another way. Rather, the digital musician will seek to unlock the creative potential in networks, in multimedia, in sound design, sonic art and music.

- ping – hack – rom – seed
- Mobile phone piece

- Bailey, A. (2001) *Network Technology for Digital Audio.* Oxford: Focal Press.
- Gaye, L., Holmquist, L. E., Behrendt, F. and Tanaka, A. (2006) 'Mobile Music Technology: Report on Emerging Community', *Proceedings of the 2006 Conference on New Interfaces for Musical Expression* (NIME-06). Paris, France. pp. 22–25.
- Griffith, N. and Todd, P. (eds) (1997) *Musical Networks: Parallel Distributed Perception and Performance.* Cambridge, MA: MIT Press.
- Hugill, A. (ed.) (2005) 'Internet Music', *Contemporary Music Review*, vol. 24, no. 6. pp. 429–559.
- Jordà, S. (2002) 'FMOL: Toward User-Friendly, Sophisticated New Musical Instruments', *Computer Music Journal*, vol. 26, no. 3. pp. 23–39.
- Weinberg, G. (2005) 'Local Performance Networks: musical interdependency through gestures and controllers', *Organised Sound*, vol. 10, no. 3. pp. 255–266.

Being live

Whatever the situation, a common tendency these days is for the digital musician to work solo, whether diffusing sound or originating sound, or playing 'instruments' or a laptop. This is a reflection both of the developments in technology, which allow individual control of the sound, and the desire of the digital musician to produce an original sound. It is therefore understandable, but it is nevertheless potentially problematic.

One thing that has changed in digital performance is the notion of 'liveness'. In acoustic music, it is normally clear what is live and what is not. The human performer, sharing a space with the listener and making sound at that moment is performing live. There are some acceptable extensions to this concept: an offstage choir, an electronic relay from another building, even a simultaneous broadcast but, in general, being 'live' means *synchronous* musical activity.

For the digital performer, the situation is not always so straightforward. Performance across a network, sound installations, automated or algorithmic work, interactive music, may all be to some degree not synchronised, or *asynchronous*. Real-time performance is a network ideal, but is not always achievable, so the network latency becomes the equivalent to the resonant characteristics of a given space. Just as the synchronous musician must allow for acoustic delay, or reverberation, in a space (e.g., a church), the asynchronous musician must take into account the latency of the network.

In a sound installation, the human performer need not actually be simultaneously present with the audience for the performance to take place: a virtual presence may suffice. In some kinds of algorithmic music, as we have seen, the user *becomes* the performer, but unawares, using materials created in advance by another musician. In many such cases, the user is practically unaware of their role as performer.

For the digital musician to develop skills, it is very important to engage in collective performance activities as well as solo work. Eye contact, visual cues, verbal and non-verbal communication during performance are all musically important, but there is a larger ethical issue too: people *should* learn to work together. Physical gestures do more than simply ensure synchronisation between performers. They are part of the social exchange of performance.

Despite the importance of the technology and the development of interactive media, the human musician must develop in a human way. It may seem an obvious thing to say, but a human being is not the same as a machine. Artificial intelligence (AI) has developed considerably over the past few decades, but the average chicken is still far more intelligent than any robot. AI tends to focus on behaviours rather than the independent workings of the mind which, of course, are still little understood.

A fair proportion of AI is still mainly rooted in a branch of psychological research called 'behaviourism', which ignores mental states in order to enable an objective study only of people's behaviour. The computer scientist Alan Turing was responsible for creating tests to identify the differences between man and machine, to establish the moment at which artificial intelligence and human intelligence would no longer be distinguishable. In terms of behaviourism, we are already close to (or past) this point. However, despite their remarkable achievements, few AI scientists would claim to have replicated the human mind. Humans are more complicated than behaviourism would suggest.

So, the human performer must be at ease with the technology but must also be at ease with other humans who use technology. The latter is the greater challenge. Technology can extend human attributes, but an automaton still lacks a will of its own, it has no real freedom of choice. The human musician must make decisions, make choices, even if those choices are merely to initiate an algorithmic process. This implies a lack of indifference to the sounding result, in other words: *musicality*. The extent to which a performance is successful, therefore, is the result of a balance between the conceptual and the practical aspects, between right and left hemispheres of the brain. Virtuosity in performance comes from the audience's perception of this balance. Thus, we can admire the choices made by a DJ, the decisions made by a sound diffuser, the understanding shown by a multimedia artist. We trace the path made by these decisions through a field of possibilities. We appreciate the technical skill, the aural awareness and even the cultural knowledge that is shown in performance.

■ Emmerson, S. (2007) *Living Electronic Music*. Aldershot: Ashgate.
■ Landy, L. (1995) *Experimental Music Notebooks*. Newark, NJ: Harwood Academic.
■ Small, C. (1998) *Musicking*. Connecticut: Hanover, CT: Wesleyan University Press.

'Musicianship'

Technical skills, aural awareness and cultural knowledge, are all things that distinguish the digital musician, but they are not the things that make him or her a *musician*. A non-musician may equally well be computer literate, aurally aware and culturally knowledgeable. Here we reach a crucial part of this book, for if there is to be such a thing as a digital musician, that is distinct from other musicians, then it follows that their musical abilities will be substantially different yet identifiably 'musical'.

Traditionally, the attributes that constitute a musician are summed up by the word 'musicianship'. This word is problematic for the digital musician working with technology for two reasons: first, the word itself is so identified with traditional music-making that it seems to demand a particular frame of reference, and, second, some of the activities in which the digital musician may engage, such as sound design, sonic art and so on, do not sit comfortably with the word 'music', let alone 'musicianship'.

There is no new equivalent collective term for the totality of skills and expertise possessed by a digital musician. 'Digital musicianship' seems rather feeble and, in any case, as Barry Truax has remarked:

> 'Musicianship' is a traditional term and is always applied to instrumental music and is therefore irrelevant to digital music, sound art, new media. 'Musical value, quality and aesthetics' on the other hand are valid terms within the new media forms. So words like 'musicality', 'musical aesthetic', etc. *are* relevant.[7]

Nevertheless, there is clearly a need to summarise the things that constitute this unnameable 'musicianship' that has changed so much. This may involve saying what it is *not* as much as what it *is*. There are some musical skills that are irrelevant to it, some that are perhaps marginal, and some that are essential. There is no single path to success, no 'Gradus ad Parnassum' by which to measure progress.[8] Diversity, complexity and variability characterise this kind of music-making.

● . . . from scratch

■ Rowe, R. (2001) *Machine Musicianship*. Cambridge, MA: MIT Press.

Technological understanding

The first essential ability is an understanding of the technology that is used. This is somewhat different from the understanding of the piano shown by a pianist, for example. The digital musician will explore new technologies. In all probability, he or she will have a fascination with the market for second-hand equipment and will want to keep pace with new developments as they arise. This does not necessarily mean a rejection of old technology. In fact, innovative and unique music can be made just as well with old equipment as with new. To give one example, valves gave way to transistors back in the early days of radio, but recently people have realised that a valve can produce an attractively 'warm' sound in a way that a transistor cannot and so: valves are back. Music technology now is often digital, but not exclusively so.

The ability to be creative with technology, even to *abuse* the technology can be highly musical. Whole genres of music with quite distinct aesthetics have arisen from what might be termed the 'happy accident'. 'Glitch' has emerged from the unwanted noises produced by equipment. 'Circuit-bending' is a purposeful form of equipment abuse, rewiring and resoldering musical toys, speak-and-spell machines and early keyboards, in order to produce unexpected sounds and patterns. Even quite standard sounds can be made extraordinary with unfeasible pitch-shifting, time-stretching and other effects.

Whatever configuration of hardware and software is chosen affects the character of the music. Linearity or non-linearity of form and content, the degree of interactivity between humans and virtual agents, the sound qualities of the result, will all be dependent upon these choices. In general, what is wanted from the equipment is responsiveness and controllability. The interface is, therefore, crucial, and interfaces exist between human and computer, between computer and computer, between analogue and digital equipment, and even, in a performance situation, between performers and audience. Key decisions have to be made early on, therefore, about the types of interface to be used, about synchronisation and about how those map onto the sounds that will be produced.

These are all performative decisions, equivalent in significance and musical qualities to the traditional 'tone' that an instrumentalist might produce from their instrument. In other words, the technological set-up is not just a way of making an 'instrument' upon which to perform, it is integral to the nature of the sound that is produced, to the distinctive sound that makes the digital musician into the performer, to the musicianship itself. The musician's ability to handle the interface, or the controller, is a powerful indicator of the level of technological understanding.

■ Webster, P. and Williams, D. (1999) *Experiencing Music Technology: Software, Data, and Hardware.* Boston: Wadsworth.

Transliteracy

One major respect in which the digital musician can differ from a classically trained musician is the degree of 'musical literacy' they attain, in other words, the ability to read music notation. For the musician working with sounds, conventional music notation is apparently almost totally useless. It is usually inadequate to cover the complexities of timbre, timings, spectra and the rest, which are the elements of technological music-making. It carries cultural baggage that could be dropped: its scales and harmonies, its tuning system and crude rhythms, its 'period' detail and emphasis on the printable 'canon' of 'masterpieces'. It represents a musical practice, in which the musician abandons all pretence of an individual voice and slavishly treads the notated path trodden by countless thousands before, towards a performative result that is deemed to be 'musical' to the extent that it seems to resemble other efforts in the same direction. The point has been argued forcefully by Trevor Wishart[9] and many others that the 'pitch lattice' of five-line staff notation might as well be bars on the cage that imprisons music, so completely does it embody the hierarchies of an outmoded musical system. There seems to be a strong case for abandoning its use.

Music notation is really a set of instructions to *performers*, to make certain sounds at certain times. The fact that the music score has become an object of study, a 'readable' substitute for the act of music-making, is a by-product of the evolution of, variously, academic (i.e., conservatoires, universities, etc.) and commercial (i.e., music publishers) interests. The consequences have been profound. Christopher Small recounts[10] the story that the composer Brahms turned down an invitation to attend a performance of Mozart's *Don Giovanni* because he would rather stay at home and read the score. The implication is that a performance of a piece of music is a poor substitute for the 'object' that is represented in the score (and in the inner ear). Performance becomes reduction by definition.

This inversion of the natural order of things seems to go against the 'sculptural' approach of sonic manipulation driven by aural awareness. The supreme elements here are the sounds themselves, not any notated representation, let alone any instructions to the performers. Musical literacy may be replaced by *transliteracy*, which has been defined by Sue Thomas as follows:

> Transliteracy is a new term derived from the verb 'to transliterate', meaning to write or print a letter or word using the closest corresponding letters of a different alphabet or language. Today we extend the act of transliteration and apply it to the increasingly wide range of communication platforms and tools at our disposal. From early signing and orality through handwriting, print, TV and film to networked digital media, the concept of transliteracy provides a cohesion of communication modes relevant to reading, writing, interpretation and interaction.[11]

This term is equally relevant to music as to any other medium. The ability to 'read' *across* a range of software and tools, media and platforms and creative and performance situations is crucial. The digital musician must be able to adapt rapidly and comfortably to an increasingly varied world. This transliteracy might even, under the right circumstances, include an ability to read conventional music notation, in order to be ready for those situations in which the digital musician encounters other musicians who have that kind of literacy. In addition, there may be situations in which the production of some kind of 'score', be it graphical or textual, technical or conventionally musical, becomes necessary. The essence of transliteracy is that there are many musical situations in which various forms of 'notation' may be used and for which the digital musician should be prepared on a need-to-know basis.

■ Thomas, S. (2004) *Hello World: Travels in Virtuality*. York: Raw Nerve Books.

Interactivity

'Interactivity' is an important term but is also still the subject of much debate as to its precise meaning. Human communication is a traditional example of interactivity, but in the field of new media, the term refers to human–computer interaction or human–human interaction that is mediated by digital technology. A word processor might possibly be called interactive, since it involves the user in an interaction with the computer, whereas machine-level processes that do not respond to human input are not interactive. The level of interactivity on offer in a word processor, however, is fairly inadequate compared to that in a fully formed virtual environment (which might, in itself, be an inadequate version of reality, but that is another discussion). In such an environment, the human may move through and interact with objects, just as in the physical world. This means that the sound design has to take account of head movement, echoes and reverberations and the sonic properties of spaces and objects in general. It also has to process this information in real time.[12]

Performance interaction can be between musician and technology, musician and other musicians and even technology and technology. All, in some senses, represent aspects of being 'live'. That is to say, the extent of the musicianship will be the perceived success or otherwise of the interactions as they take place during a given time span. Technical questions can often dominate proceedings on these occasions, and they mainly concern the nature of the controllers. In theory, *anything* may be used as a controller: sound, gesture, touch, pressure, brainwaves, weather, data flow, motion and so on. It is simply a question of finding ways to translate these into digital data. In practice, this means that there is a vast array of more or less 'home-grown' interactive devices. An interactive device is anything that enables some form of communication between components, at least one of which can produce sound.

Haptic devices use touch, whereas *kinesthetic* systems use motion, but the two are closely related. In both cases, sensors register changes in state and convey information to the controller. The human body's motion through a space may be tracked by cameras and captured by a computer system. The resulting data stream outputs parameter messages that affect some aspect of the sound. A reciprocal relationship can also exist, where acoustic data is recorded and analysed to identify some characteristics, which then affect either the extended instrument or the nature of the sonic feedback. There comes a point in this process when the person who is triggering or influencing the sound *becomes* the musician. This person does not have to be a musician, nor even aware that they have become a musician! If well handled, the change in role can be attractively imperceptible. Whichever type of controller is used, the main technical challenges concern the design and build of the controller itself and how it maps its information onto sound. The musical success of the controller will often hinge upon these two elements.

A standard solution is to create a patch to map the human input onto some kind of sound-producing unit, often using MIDI as a trigger or to control parametric information. The computer will usually interpret the input in some way, often that relates the perceived expression inherent in a given gesture to some musical correlation (for example, a slowly raised hand might produce a sound that slowly rises in pitch, or gets louder). The decisions of the programmer of the controller, therefore, play a major role in determining the eventual outcome, so a mastery of at least some aspects of programming are more or less essential to success in this field.

In his interactive installations *MAP1* and *MAP2* (Figure 6.3), Garth Paine creates a space in which human movement controls sound synthesis. Using motion-sensing software, the mass, dynamic and direction of movement within predefined independent regions controls a real-time granular synthesis program to enable the user to manipulate sounds. The experience of figuring out and controlling the music through gesture and motion in space seems to reunite a form of dance and music. As Garth Paine puts it:

> The work explores the interaction between human movement and the creation of music. It attempts to create an environment in which people can consider the impact they make on their immediate environment and the causal loops that exist between behaviour and quality of environment. Personal aesthetic leads to decisions about preferential behaviour patterns and in turn preferential environment – one conditions the other.[13]

Where performance interaction is human–human, more traditional elements of musicianship apply. Good communication, sympathetic listening, timing are

Figure 6.3 Users exploring *MAP2* by Garth Paine.

all key factors. The importance of visual cues should not be underestimated. There is a tendency for digital musicians to hide, behind equipment, in the dark, from one another. On some occasions, the performance aesthetic demands this, but it is more often a result of poor performance skills. Finally, and in many ways most importantly, in a live situation, communication with the audience is a musical skill, which must be learnt. Knowing how to dramatise, to have stage presence, to signal the end of a piece, to be seen to respond, are all aspects of musicianship that have more to do with theatre than with sound production, but any great live musical performer will have these abilities.

Interactivity is an emerging area, and there are many unique and creative musical solutions. Indeed, there is little agreement about the precise definition of the word 'interactivity' itself. The following list of journal articles reflects the sheer range and diversity of approaches.

- Birchfield, D., Phillips, K., Kidané, A., Lorig, D. (2006) 'Interactive Public Sound Art: A Case Study', *Proceedings of the 2006 Conference on New Interfaces for Musical Expression (NIME-06)*. Paris, France. pp. 43–48.
- Blaine, T. (2005) 'The Convergence of Alternate Controllers and Musical Interfaces in Interactive Entertainment', *Proceedings of the 2005 International Conference on New Interfaces for Musical Expression (NIME-05)*. Vancouver, Canada. pp. 27–33.
- Blaine, T. and Fels, S. (2003) 'Collaborative Musical Experiences for Novices', *Journal of New Music Research*, vol. 32, no. 4, pp. 411–428.
- Chadabe, J. (1983) 'Interactive Composing: An Overview', *Proceedings of the 1983 International Computer Music Conference*, New York, pp. 298–306. Also published in *Computer Music Journal*, 8 (1): CA: People's Computer Company, pp. 22–27.
- Cook, P. (2001) 'Principles for Designing Computer Music Controllers', *Proceedings of the International Conference on New Interfaces for Musical Expression (NIME)*, Seattle, WA, USA. Available at http://www.nime.org/2001/program.html.
- Mandelis, J. and Husbands, P. (2003) 'Musical Interaction with Artificial Life Forms: Sound Synthesis and Performance Mappings', *Contemporary Music Review*, vol. 22, no. 3, pp. 57–67.
- Paine, G. (2004) 'Gesture and Musical Interaction: Interactive Engagement through Dynamic Morphology', *Proceedings of the 2004 International Conference on New Interfaces for Musical Expression (NIME-04)*. Hamamatsu, Japan, pp. 80–86.
- Pressing, J. (1990) 'Cybernetic Issues in Interactive Performance Systems', *Computer Music Journal*, vol. 14, no. 1, pp. 12–25.
- Wanderley, M. and Orio, N. (2002) 'Evaluation of Input Devices for Musical Expression: Borrowing Tools from HCI', *Computer Music Journal*, vol. 26, no. 3, pp. 62–76.
- Wessel, D. and Wright, M. (2002) 'Problems and Prospects for Intimate Musical Control of Computers', *Computer Music Journal*, vol. 26, no. 3, pp. 11–22. Also published in *Proceedings of the International Conference on New Interfaces for Musical Expression (NIME)*, Seattle, WA, USA. Available at http://www.nime.org/2001/program.html.
- Woolf, S. and Yee-King, M. (2003) 'Virtual and Physical Interfaces for Collaborative Evolution of Sound', *Contemporary Music Review*, vol. 22, no. 3, pp. 31–41.

Reflective practice

An understanding of the physical and technical aspects of musical performance is not the only significant factor in musicianship. The ability to critically reflect is key to improving both creativity and musicality. The goal of the digital musician is to develop a 'sound', in much the same way as a traditional instrumentalist. In many cases, it is the setting and refining of musical goals over many performances and the process of learning from experience that enables this development.[14]

Reflective practice is a circular activity: the musician will listen to a sound that is made, make another sound that in some way addresses the 'problem' posed by the first sound, then listen to that sound and so on. This process can take place almost instantly (in real time) or after some delay. It is a dialogue between the musician and the musical material he or she creates. The idea of reflective practice was first described by Donald Schön in his book *The Reflective Practitioner* (1983), in which he declared that: 'the knowledge inherent in practice is to be understood as artful doing'.[15] He identified two forms of reflective practice: reflection-in-action and reflection-on-action. Reflection-in-action is swift – thinking on your feet:

> The practitioner allows himself to experience surprise, puzzlement, or confusion in a situation which he finds uncertain or unique. He reflects on the phenomenon before him, and on the prior understandings which have been implicit in his behaviour. He carries out an experiment which serves to generate both a new understanding of the phenomenon and a change in the situation.[16]

Reflection on action takes place after the event, and in a musical context may be greatly helped by recording. Its purpose is to explore why and what was done. It may take the form of a private diary or log, or it may involve discussion with fellow performers or listeners. This process helps to build up a repertoire of ideas and actions upon which to draw on future occasions.

Critical reflection is relevant to any performer, but to the digital musician for whom creativity is so centrally important, it is indispensable. It is only through a reasonably objective appraisal of what is created that development and progress can be made.

● Sonic wiki

■ Schön, D. A. (1983) *The Reflective Practitioner: How Professionals Think in Action.* London: Temple Smith.

Virtuosity

A virtuoso digital musician, therefore, is one who demonstrates consummate abilities in handling technologies and interactions and is both musically transliterate and capable of advanced reflective practice. A virtuoso is able to both originate and develop successful musical materials and forms. A virtuoso will be someone whose evident accomplishment in these areas is so impressive as to leave no one in any doubt as to their expertise. Creativity and innovation will be the hallmarks of their virtuosity.

Instruments

The instrument they play traditionally defines musicians. A person is called a guitarist, or a pianist, or a sitar-player, before they are called a musician. A musician's instrument is usually considered to be an indispensable part of their musical identity and practice. In technology-based music, however, where the computer and other technological equipment is the means by which a musician performs, it is much more difficult to identify an instrument as such. Research conducted in 2006 by Thor Magnusson and Enrike Hurtado Mendieta highlights this problem.[17] Through more than 200 musicians' responses to a questionnaire, they were able to identify the following attitudes to digital and acoustic instruments (see Table 6.1).

The authors observe that for many people a crucial difference is the need to 'mould oneself' to an acoustic instrument, whereas a digital instrument can be created to suit the needs of the user. However, the mutability and lack of limitations of software can also be a weakness, because its short lifetime discourages the achievement of mastery. Technical problems such as latency (the delay between an action and the system's response) were also seen as problematic, but probably the most vexed issue was 'arbitrary mapping', or the fact that 'there are no "natural" mappings between the exertion of bodily energy and the resulting sound'[18] in digital music. One consequence of this is a difficulty in disengaging the brain and becoming 'one with the physical embodiment of performing'.[19]

Sound sources

In whatever kind of musical situation the digital musicians may find themselves, the question of sound sources is bound to arise. A sound source could be a recording, a live sound, an acoustic instrument, a synthesiser, the human body, etc. In fact, *any* sounding object can be a sound source, but there must *be* a sound source. The choice of sound source, as much as what is done to it during performance, defines the music. Some musicians take an inclusive approach, assembling as many sound sources as possible and offering the maximum range of choices at a given moment. Others are more exclusive, preferring to work with a limited set of sounds for a certain situation. Where the work is being done within a

Table 6.1 Survey of musicians' attitudes to digital and acoustic instruments, by Thor Magnusson and Enrike Hurtado Mendieta.[20]

Acoustic – positive	*Acoustic – negative*
Tactile feedback	Lacking in range
Limitations inspiring	No editing out of mistakes
Traditions and legacy	No memory or intelligence
Musician reaches depth	Prone to cliché playing
Instrument becomes second nature	Too much tradition/history
Each instrument is unique	No experimentation in design
No latency	Inflexible, no dialogue
Easier to express mood	No microtonality or tunings
Extrovert state when playing	No inharmonic spectra
Digital – positive	*Digital – negative*
Free from musical traditions	Lacking in substance
Experimental, explorative	No legacy or continuation
Any sound and any interface	No haptic feedback
Designed for specific needs	Lacking social conventions
Freedom in mapping	Latency frequently a problem
Automation, intelligence	Disembodied experience
Good for composing with	Slave to the historical/acoustic
Easier to get into	Imitation of the acoustic
Not as limited as tonal music	Introvert state when playing

known musical genre, the exclusive approach tends to predominate. There are fixed requirements for genre work, although the digital musician will always try to innovate even within the confines of genre practice. In other, perhaps more experimental, situations, a freer approach to sound sources will work best.

The idea of integrity is sometimes bound up in how sound sources are found or made. In an acousmatic music concert, for example, to use a sound downloaded from the Internet in preference to a sound you have recorded yourself could be seen to be lacking integrity. In a club gig, on the other hand, the idea of being over-fussy about recording your own sound sources may well be less important. Integrity here is often more to do with how you handle software.

The digital musician will constantly seek to explore the sonic properties of objects and spaces. Some kind of structured approach to, or self-devised classification system for, sound sources will probably be used as the sheer quantity of data increases, because it can become very hard to keep track of things. This is especially true once editing and processing the sounds begins. Documentation, backing up and systematic labelling are very important, in short: a database of sonic material stored on computer is usually created. In many software packages, the computer will automatically do a great deal of that work.

This is a distinguishing feature of the digital musician. Whereas a musician might work to extract good or interesting sounds from their instrument, the digital musician begins from a position of having unlimited sound sources. The processes of critical judgement, of cultural awareness, of musical intuition, may lead to a significant whittling away of extraneous material but, in theory, the digital musician *could* make any sound in any way and in any context. These sounds are then combined in such a way, or using such techniques, as to form an instrument. This new instrument resists easy classification and may even exist only for the duration of a performance.

■ Collins, N. (2006) *Handmade Electronic Music: The Art of Hardware Hacking.* New York: Routledge.

Organology

The study of musical-instrument technology is called *organology*. Up until fairly recently, to study music technology was in fact to study organology. Modern organology was first laid out by Curt Sachs in an influential text of 1913: the *Real-Lexicon der Musikinstrumente*. In 1914, he and Erich Moritz von Hornbostel developed this further with a classification system for musical instruments known as the Hornbostel-Sachs system. Although there have been changes and modifications to this system over the years, it remains the standard way of classifying musical instruments. They are grouped as follows:

1   *idiophones*, which produce sound by self-supporting vibration (e.g., the marimba, and the xylophone, although metal idiophones are generally called metallophones)
2   *membranophones*, which produce sound by a vibrating membrane (typically drums)
3   *chordophones*, which produce sound by vibrating strings (violin, guitar, etc.)
4   *aerophones*, which produce sound by vibrating volume of air (pipe organs, flutes, and so on).

Electrophones were added later. These are instruments such as theremins, which produce sound by electronic means.

A virtual instrument, capable of producing any sound and controlled by any means plainly resists organological classification. Conventional instruments that are technologically extended in some way might be easier to classify, but what value would this classification offer, given the likely mutability of the sound that results from the extension? And what about all those controllers – joysticks, light beams, sensor pads, motion trackers and the rest – that do not produce a sound in themselves but are essential to the music?

The point here is not to dismiss organology, which is in itself an important discipline, but to describe the vagueness and diversity of the situation that confronts the digital musician. To play a musical instrument, of whatever kind, will always be beneficial to a musician but, for the digital musician, there is no need to pursue this to a particularly high level of skill unless the emerging pattern of musical enquiry demands it. However, it is often the case in practice that digital musicians are also good instrumentalists.

● Infra-instrument

Voice and percussion

Each musical instrument requires a different technique, its own set of skills. It can help to have a working knowledge of as many of these as possible. But there are two instruments (or types of instrument) that *all* musicians would be well advised to know, to at least a moderate degree. The first is the voice. Vocal music is fundamental to music itself. The phrases and shapes of music, including music where there is no vocal component, may usually be traced back to speech, to articulation, to acoustic communication, or to singing. Not everybody is blessed with a good singing voice, but it is important to explore vocal capabilities even so. This can take the form of readings, of speaking (in a controlled way), of chanting, of ululating (howling or wailing), of droning on a single note, of singing either alone or in choirs. It need not be done in public, but it should be done.

After the voice, a working knowledge of *percussion* instruments will be a great advantage. Percussion includes such an array of pitched instruments (xylophones, vibraphones, tubular bells, timpani and so on) and unpitched instruments (drums, cymbals, tam-tams, woodblocks, etc.), that it still offers a superb resource for discovering and creating sounds. The basic techniques for many of these instruments are relatively simple, although, to be sure, it is possible to develop extraordinary virtuosity on even the simplest percussion instrument. Ensemble percussion work is probably the best musical training available, since it engages both the intellectual and visceral organs of the human body in a way that surpasses other instruments. A wealth of research into music therapy has revealed the health benefits of banging a drum, and in all probability it satisfies some deeply buried human instinct.[21] Beyond the voice and percussion, it is very much a matter of personal choice to what extent time is spent pursuing the study of an instrument: the time will not be wasted.

● Sound byte for voice or percussion

Extended instruments

If playing a conventional instrument proves musically fruitful, then it is possible to extend the capabilities of that instrument into the digital domain. This is a massively growing area of musical practice. However, it is also somewhat problematic, because the sheer quantity and variety of solutions available is bewildering and, more often than not, each of these solutions is unique. The best way forward is to make no attempt to survey the entire scene but to select an approach that appeals and work to develop within that.

MIT's *hyperinstruments* draw on existing musical techniques, but extend the playing actions such as touch and motion using sensors. The hyperviolin (see Figure 6.4) is a typical example of such *gesture mapping*.

The audio output from the electronic strings and the movements of the enhanced violin bow provide the raw material for real-time timbre and synthesis techniques, which analyse parameters such as pitch, loudness, brightness and spectrum. The controller here is as close as possible to the conventional instrument controller (a bow, in this case).

A different approach that does not alter the physical characteristics of the instrument itself, but processes the sound it makes, has been adopted by many artists. Kaffe Matthews,[22] for example, has extended her violin using LiSa (Live Sampling) software from STEIM (Studio for Electro-Instrument Music) in the Netherlands (Figure 6.5). STEIM 'promotes the idea that Touch is crucial in communicating with the new electronic performance art technologies' and that 'the intelligence of the body, for example: the knowledge of the fingers or lips, is considered musically as important as the "brain-knowledge"'.[23] LiSa allocates a large chunk of memory to certain 'zoned' functions, such as various forms of playback, recording, reading, saving and copying data, all in real time. So the controller in this case is computer software, physically external to the instrument itself.

Another approach is to invent a new instrument that exploits the capabilities of the controller, rather than the other way around. There are hundreds of such new interfaces for musical expression (NIME),[24] apparently limited only by the imagination of the inventors. One example is the 'Tooka', an intimate instrument

Figure 6.4 The hyperviolin (Tod Machover, Tristan Jehan, Diana Young).

Figure 6.5 Kaffe Matthews.

Figure 6.6 The Tooka (Sidney Fels, Florian Vogt).[25]

that uses two-person breath control (and some push buttons) to influence the music (Figure 6.6). Air pressure and flow, speed and direction, are mapped onto musical information (mainly pitch, in this case).

- Laubier, S. De (1998) 'The Meta-Instrument', *Computer Music Journal*, vol. 22, no. 1, pp. 25–29.
- Miranda, E. and Wanderley, M. (2004) *New Digital Musical Instruments: Control and Interaction Beyond the Keyboard*. Middleton, WI: A-R Editions.

Software instruments

The computer removes the need to use anything other than itself. Software instruments can be built which will do all the things (and more) that can be done by physical instruments. Here, the controller is simply the mouse or keyboard, or sometimes a joystick, graphics tablet or trackball device. The concept of a virtual instrument is already well established in commercial software, and emulation packages provide a graphical interface that gives the illusion of handling physical electronic equipment.

Modular software is currently setting the standard for software instrument-building. The advantage of these systems over more familiar commercial packages is that they are entirely user-designed. Many of the prepackaged software instruments presume some particular kind of musical outcome (often electronic dance music) and do their best to facilitate that. For the digital musician experimenting with software instrument-building, the possibility of realising an original idea is preferable. A typical environment includes MIDI, control, user interface and timing objects on top of which hundreds of objects can be built (generally called *patches*). Users of this kind of software have gathered together into online communities to share patches and discuss their use. This picture is replicated for other kinds of software and is a very effective way for musicians to communicate with one another.

There are many kinds of performance involving software instruments running on a laptop. One such is sometimes referred to as *electronica*. The origins of this term are unclear, but in the 1990s it came to refer to electronic dance music, and more recently that definition has widened to include more experimental electronic music. The cheapness and portability of laptop equipment have made this area of music an emergent and thriving cultural activity, based largely in clubs. It has even become something like a competitive sport. Here is a picture of the electronica musician Quantazelle performing in fancy dress at *The Thunderdome Matches*, a 'battle' of musicians, in a club in Chicago in 2003 (Figure 6.7). The audience played its part in the voting process, and innovation was a key element in judging the winners.

Figure 6.7 Quantazelle, performing in 2003.

● Restricted instruments

■ Jordà, S. (2005) 'Multi-user Instruments: Models, Examples and Promises', *Proceedings of the 2005 International Conference on New Interfaces for Musical Expression* (NIME-05). Vancouver, Canada, pp. 23–26.

■ Jordà, S. (2005) 'Digital Lutherie: Crafting Musical Computers for New Musics' Performance and Improvisation'. Unpublished PhD thesis. Departament de Tecnologia, Universitat Pompeu Fabra, Spain.

Improvisation

At some point in the history of Western classical music, improvisation was downgraded to the level of a frivolous activity. Somehow, just 'making it up as you go along' was deemed to be in no way equivalent to the more elevated activity of producing works that were fixed by notation. This is strange, because many of the great composers of history were in fact leading improvisers. Beethoven, for example, was most famous in his time as an improvising pianist, and several of his compositions are, in fact, written out improvisations. The same goes for Liszt. It is only church organists who seem to have retained improvisational skills. Many classical orchestral musicians asked to improvise today would find it immensely difficult to do so.

This is not the case in most other musical traditions. In much non-Western music, for example the Indian *raga*, improvisation is still part of the required skills of a successful musician. Jazz, of course, has also retained improvisation as a key element of performance. Here, the improvisation generally relates to a harmonic framework (the 'changes'), over which the improviser may develop melodic or rhythmic ideas. In practice, these tend to be built from motivic elements: short phrases containing characteristic melodic shapes, intervallic sequences or rhythmic patterns. In this respect, jazz improvisation resembles Indian *raga* or, indeed, Western classical music. What is distinctive is that it takes place in 'real time'.

Free improvisation

Free improvisation is probably the form of improvisation that is the most useful to the digital musician. Free improvisation is somewhat different from 'free jazz', which sets about removing the harmonic skeletons and familiar phrases of jazz in the interests of finding novel forms of expression. Free improvisation begins by trying to remove *all* traces of style or idiom from the music. In the words of its greatest theorist and practitioner, Derek Bailey, it is 'playing without memory'.[26] This can be extremely difficult to achieve in practice, but it is often a good starting point for musical creativity and works particularly well in technology-based performance, where a certain indifference to the cultural implications of the material can sometimes be an advantage.

What does quickly happen in free improvisation sessions is that the participants become aware of and responsive to the other members of the group. In fact, free improvisation is not really 'free' at all. It is highly constrained by the rules of social intercourse, rather than musical convention. For the digital musician to develop as a musician, interaction with other musicians is essential. If that interaction is to be just a question of finding other people to realise a single creative vision, then the interaction is limited. It is also unnecessary to use more than one person in the production of music. So, improvisation and, in particular, free improvisation, can open up dialogue and develop musical practice in unexpected and innovative ways.

This kind of improvisation can be useful in many different situations, particularly for developing a collaborative approach to music-making. Many rock bands use a similar process in the recording studio, just 'messing about' and collectively agreeing upon what does and does not 'work'. A more structured approach might have the musicians take individual responsibility for a particular aspect of the music by mutual agreement. So Musician 1 might handle the beat, Musician 2 the dynamics, Musician 3 the mix or texture, and so on.

Another useful approach that emphasises the drama of improvisation is to use a verbal score as a structure. There are a few examples of verbal scores, which deliberately set themselves up as structures for improvisation.[27] It is easy enough, however, to make one up. The advantage of a pre-agreed structure is that all the participants understand the relationships between the musical elements and 'characters', and the overall shape and process of the performance is to some extent predictable. Adopting a constraint-based approach to an improvisation can further develop this. Perhaps individuals are limited to a fixed number of sounds, a particular set of cues, a single effect, and so on. There may be even more rigidly imposed constraints about timing or level. Constraints in performance, paradoxically, do not necessarily mean a lack of freedom.

● Improvisation ensemble

■ Bailey, D. (1993) *Improvisation: Its Nature and Practice in Music.* New York: Da Capo Press.

■ Dean, R. (2003) *Hyperimprovisation: Computer Interactive Sound Improvisation.* Middleton, WI: A-R Editions.

Live coding

Live coding is a kind of improvisation that may also be one of the purest forms of digital music. Live coding is 'the art of programming a computer under concert conditions'[28] In other words, a live coder will write and edit the code that produces digital music in real time in front of an audience.[29] As a musical practice, live coding is currently in its infancy and has sparked some controversy, mainly because of its abstraction from the more familiar physical aspects of performance. There is animated discussion among live-coders about the best way to present

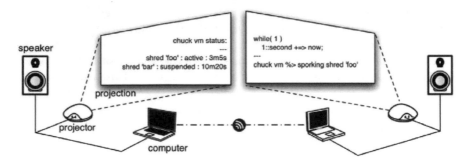

Figure 6.8 On-the-fly aesthetic.

this activity in a concert situation in order to avoid audience disaffection or to show the coding process and its effects upon what is heard. They (live coders) seem generally agreed that invisible typing is not a particularly engaging activity from an audience perspective. Most solutions therefore involve some kind of multimedia presentation or overhead display. Figure 6.8 shows one such set-up, created for an on-the-fly performance by Ge Wang and Perry R. Cook.[30]

It is also possible to use a more physical interface than just the computer keyboard. Amy Alexander's VJ tool *The Thingee* is a dance mat laid out with symbols,[31] and Dave Griffiths' *Betablocker* relies on joystick control.[32] Even the physical movements of the live coder at the computer may be readable as an input.

Live coding generally uses modular sections of code which can be edited separately. The coding needs to be concise, so that rapid changes can be made, and it needs to allow for precise synchronisation. In other words, the system has to be both flexible and manageable. TOPLAP[33] lists more than a dozen such systems on its website. In a recent article on the subject, the live coder Nick Collins draws a parallel between learning live-coding technique and the practice regimes of the nineteenth-century composer-pianists. He lists several exercises, including 'isolation exercises' such as algorithm composition and sound synthesis, and 'connectivity exercises' such as layering, mixing, enveloping and reacting to other code. TOPLAP have even suggested a system of 'grades' analogous to the traditional performance grades in music.

Live coding appeals both to musicians with programming skills and programmers with musical leanings. As a result, a number of competitive events and a sub-culture of live coders has grown up at the intersection of the two disciplines. Live-coding 'battles' are quite frequent, in which the artists challenge one another in various ways, such as: 'root wars', in which the hackers try to undermine each other's systems or to occupy areas of spectral information; or a 'Tetris challenge', in which each player presents the next with a chunk of code to use. A more cooperative activity is the combined reworking of code, sometimes using a tag team of coders, or in a laptop 'jam' session. It looks as though live coding could become a virtuosic activity in the right hands, but Collins is keen to downplay any arrogance at this early stage of its development:

> Right now, I think live coders are equivalent to potentially talented 11 year olds. Give us seven years of intensive practice and come to one of our gigs in 2014. [. . .] We currently have no master teachers to guide us, and must risk the possibility of ineffective practice whilst enjoying the sense of open discovery.[34]

- *music-is-life* (2006) by Rob Godman.
- *Hydroponics 1 for Laptop Orchestra* (2007) by Ambrose Field.

■ Andrews, R. (2006) 'Real DJs code live', *Wired: Technology News*, 6 July. www.wired.com/news/technology/0,71248-0.html.
■ Brown, A. R. (2006) 'Code jamming', *M/C Journal* vol. 89, no. 6. journal.media-culture.org.au/0612/03-brown.php.
■ Collins, N., McLean, A. and Rohrhuber, J. (2003) 'Live Coding in Laptop Performance', *Organised Sound*, vol. 8, no. 3, pp. 321–330.
■ Collins, N. (2007) 'Live Coding Practice'. Unpublished paper submitted to NIME.
■ Cook, P. R. and Wang, G. (2004) 'On-the-Fly Programming: Using Code as an Expressive Musical Instrument', *Proceedings of the 2004 International Conference on New Interfaces for Musical Expression (NIME)*, Hamamatsu, Japan, pp. 138–143.
■ McCartney, J. (2002) 'Rethinking the Computer Music Programming Language: SuperCollider', *Computer Music Journal*, vol. 26, no. 4, pp. 61–68.
■ McLean, A. (2004) *Hacking Perl in Nightclubs*. www.perl.com/pub/a/2004/08/31/livecode.html.
■ Oore, S. (2005) 'Learning Advanced Skills on New Instruments (or Practising Scales and Arpeggios on your NIME)', *Proceedings of the International Conference on New Interfaces for Musical Expression (NIME-05)*, Vancouver, Canada, pp. 60–65.
■ Rohrhuber, J., de Campo, A. and Wieser, R. (2005) 'Algorithms Today – Notes on Language Design for Just in Time Programming', *Proceedings of the International Computer Music Conference*, Barcelona, Spain, pp. 455–458.
■ Wang G. and Cook, P. R. (2003) 'ChucK: A Concurrent, On-the-fly Audio Programming Language', *Proceedings of International Computer Music Conference*, Singapore, pp. 219–226.
■ Ward, A., Rohrhuber, J., Olofsson, F., McLean, A., Griffiths, D., Collins, N. and Alexander, A. (2004) 'Live Algorithm Programming and a Temporary Organisation for Its Promotion', *Proceedings of the README Software Art Conference*, Aarhus, Denmark, pp. 242–261.

Chapter 7

Cultural context

The digital musician should start with the known and move into the unknown.[1]

Whatever becomes information, anyone can now store and reproduce, repackage and refashion to their own purposes without anyone's permission, without payment, and largely without detection. Hence the expanding domain of information threatens the principle of private property. . . .The results can be heard in the cacophony and confusion of contemporary music, which the recent introduction of synthesizers and samples has only increased. On the one hand, the technification of music has distorted the process of listening and damaged our hearing. On the other, it increasingly throws everything back into the arena, as the ease of reproduction allows the circulation of music to escape the control of the market and discover new forms. In short, the old hierarchies of aesthetic taste and judgement may have broken down, but music continues to breathe and to live according to its own immanent criteria.[2]

Michael Chanan was writing in 1994, just as the Internet began to take shape and the digital culture to form. The living and breathing music he predicted still finds its most vivid expression in performance situations, where many of his threats to private property pass through the momentary forms of samplings and borrowings, of mash-ups and remixes, of nods and homages, cut and paste. However, thanks to these technological developments, the 'immanent criteria' of today's music seem once again to have become those of the community.

The phrase 'cultural context' refers to the culture that surrounds the individual. A hundred years ago, this would have been conditioned to a great extent by geographical location. When Paul Gauguin relocated to Tahiti, he deliberately changed his cultural context, intoxicated by the 'exotic' world beyond Europe. This had an effect not just upon him as a person but also on the art he produced, as is clear from the painting on the cover of this book. But the 'cultural context' is not just one's immediate *physical* surroundings: it also refers to literature, art, social interaction, science and all other forms of human activity. Gauguin's initial ideas about Tahiti came largely from the writings of Europeans.

All artists, musicians included, make work that is to some extent a product of their cultural context. What has changed in recent years is the level of access to cultures beyond what may be thought to be 'one's own'. A knowledge of the cultural world around is, therefore, an important attribute for the digital musician. Given the sheer quantity of cultural activity, acquiring this 'cultural knowledge' is easy to find but difficult to absorb. To 'move into the unknown' can be both challenging and intimidating and requires considerable curiosity and engagement. This chapter first examines the digital culture and its effects on music, then looks at some ways in which digital musicians can learn from the music of diverse cultures and, finally, examines digital music itself from a cultural perspective. It also offers both creative and listening projects to stimulate cultural inquiry.

- Ayers, M. (ed.) (2006) *Cybersounds: Essays on Virtual Music Culture.* Ithaca, NY: Peter Lang.
- Berman, M. (1981) *The Reenchantment of the World.* New York: Cornell University Press.
- Bull, M. and Back, L. (2003) *The Auditory Culture Reader.* Oxford: Berg.
- Drobnick, J. (ed.) (2004) *Aural Cultures.* New York: YYZ Books.
- Franklin, M. (ed.) (2005) *Resounding International Relations: On Music, Culture and Politics.* London: Palgrave Macmillan.
- McLuhan, M. (1989) *The Global Village: Transformations in World Life and Media in the 21st Century.* Oxford: Oxford University Press.
- Duckworth, W. (2005) *Virtual Music: How the Web Got Wired for Sound.* New York: Routledge.
- Hafner, K. and Lyon, M. (1998) *Where Wizards Stay Up Late: The Origins of the Internet.* New York: Touchstone.
- Holtzman, S. R. (1994) *Digital Mantras: The Languages of Abstract and Virtual Worlds.* Cambridge, MA: MIT Press.
- Jacobson, L. (ed.) (1992) *Cyberarts: Exploring Art and Technology.* San Francisco, CA: Miller Freeman.
- LaBelle, B. (2006) *Background Noise: Perspectives on Sound Art.* New York: Continuum.
- Rheingold, H. (1993, revised 2000) *The Virtual Community.* Cambridge, MA: MIT Press.
- Rheingold, H. (2002) *Smart Mobs: The Next Social Revolution.* New York: Basic Books.

Digital culture

The cultural context for today's musician is very different from anything previously known. Digital technologies have not only made other cultures and their products more readily available, they have also presented and represented them in a different way. Our sense of cultural value has changed, as has our sense of ourselves. This affects music as much as anything else.

Consuming music

If we want to hear Tuvan throat-singing, or play a virtual bamboo xylophone, or examine a score by a contemporary composer, or buy and sell music technologies, we can readily do so with a decent broadband connection.[3] Each action takes a roughly equivalent amount of effort on our part. The only prerequisite is that we have to *want* to do those things in the first place.

But the influence of the new media goes far beyond a collection of interesting websites. Music itself is culturally present in a way that has never before been the case. Almost every cultural experience there is, from watching television to shopping, from having a meal in a restaurant to going to the movies, comes gift-wrapped in music. Then, we can further configure our musical landscape with personal stereos, mp3 players, CDs and the rest. We might even go to a concert now and then. Never has there been so much music.

Our listening choices have become markers of our personal and social attitudes. Music as lifestyle, or music expressing a tribal or communal identity, is commonplace. To be found listening to the right sort of music can become a badge of honour, and an entire industry exists to support and exploit this view. So, we are consumers of music, and the industry supplies huge quantities of the stuff, targeted with an ever-greater precision.

For a classical musician – say the violinists in the back row of the 'seconds' in an orchestra – all of this may appear to have no relevance at all. They continue to play their repertoire in the same way that they always have done. However, their *audience* has been changed immeasurably by CDs, in particular. The concert has to offer an experience that matches what can be heard, in comfort, at home. At recent classical music concerts, the audience has been invited to purchase a CD of what they just heard as they leave the concert hall. The message is clear: you *heard* the music, now *buy* it and take it home.

In pop music, this situation is often reversed. People attend a concert having become very familiar with the recording. The familiarity means that they are generally seeking some kind of added value from the live version, which nevertheless must match the quality of the recording. The most successful live acts are the ones whose performance skills are up to the task and who manage to avoid the obvious trap of over-long repetition of familiar patterns. Sometimes, the addition of visually or theatrically interesting material is used to help overcome any limitations in the musical content.

In either scenario, the influence of digital sound recording and manipulation techniques is strong. The perfectibility of the musical performance, the availability and transferability of the sound data, the slickness and style of the finished product are all things that have a cultural impact, which is not to diminish the importance of the 'liveness' of the live concert. That is what makes it distinctive, unique and worth attending. The orchestra sounds quite different live to a recording, and to actually witness a pop concert, surrounded by many thousands of fellow fans, is a thrilling experience. The point here is that the consumption of music stored in a digital format now greatly exceeds the consumption of live music. Since the digital form sounds so acceptable, this is a trend that seems set to continue.

● I hate . . .

■ Cook, N. (1992) *Music, Imagination and Culture.* Oxford: Clarendon.
■ Emmerson S. (ed.) (2000) *Music, Electronic Media and Culture.* Aldershot: Ashgate.
■ Frith, S. and Goodwin, A. (ed.) (1990) *On Record.* New York: Routledge.

The thinking musician

So where does all this leave digital musicians? Given the cultural landscape they inhabit, and given that they are intent on going beyond standard, known, musical practices, they *need* cultural knowledge. This knowledge will enable a greater understanding of cultural identity and, therefore, *integrity*. Without integrity, the digital musician is in danger of drowning in a sea of information, being swamped by a mud of culture, being lost in a forest of musics. The sense of identity begins with a search for certainties. Some certainties have acquired exceptional prominence in the digital age.

The first certainty is *change*. It is guaranteed that today's technologies, and the skills associated with them, will rapidly become obsolete. So, it is very important to be adaptable and open to new possibilities. Integrity means developing or creating something that is unique to the individual but not necessarily clinging to that thing in the face of a changing world. It also means having the skill and judgement to know when to move on, when to develop, when to diversify, and to what extent.

The second certainty is *diversity*. Wherever one may 'be', musically speaking, at a given moment, there is always something somewhere else, something different and even something unknown. Awareness and embracing of this diversity is vital. The philosopher Ludwig Wittgenstein suggested that a door might be defined by pointing to everything in the universe that is *not* a door. This might seem a laborious way to go about such an apparently simple task, but it can be advantageous to know what you are *not*, before deciding what you *are*.

The third certainty is a *context*. Whatever music is made will to some extent relate to the other things (not necessarily music) that surround it. The context for music now is multidisciplinary, because music is very often heard alongside other forms, whether they are visual, textual, or performative. It could be argued that music has *always* been this way, since the ritual of live performance is a kind of theatre in itself, but since the advent of recorded sound the live element has been capable of almost complete suppression; and the context for music is not simply 'musical', nor even 'artistic', but social.

The defining qualities of the digital musician, therefore, are: *open-mindedness* and *cultural curiosity*. In short, the digital musician is a *thinking musician*. This is the challenge: to go beyond the model of the unthinking musician who knows nothing other than their instrument and a tiny area of musical practice. It's not that such musicians are *bad* musicians, in their own terms, but they are *limited*. The digital musician, who is living in a digital culture, cannot afford to be limited to that extent.

The tools needed to overcome these limitations are: an awareness of other musics; an ability to listen critically, to analyse, and to form judgements based on more than instant, subjective reaction; historical knowledge and a sense of future possibilities, in particular where these concern developments in electronic or digital music and technologies.

Equally important is knowledge and awareness of developments and practices in other art forms, especially the visual and text-based arts. It is not enough to be *only* a musician, unable to converse with fellow artists or ordinary people about anything other than music. While to specialise is a likely consequence of audio manipulation techniques, this does not mean that it is beneficial to ignore developments elsewhere in the digital world. Ignorant musicians will be unsuccessful musicians in a culture that naturally and wholeheartedly embraces multimedia.

All this cultural knowledge, therefore, has a direct and practical application. You might be the best musician in the world, but if nobody knows of your existence, you might as well not be a musician at all. In order to advertise and promote your work, to disseminate and diffuse your practice, you will need an understanding of *networking*, including Internet and virtual interaction, and a knowledge of your own culture, as well as the music industry, its management and working practices.

- Cope, D. (2001) *New Directions in Music*. Prospect Heights, IL: Waveland Press.
- Eno, B. (1996) *A Year with Swollen Appendices*. London: Faber & Faber.
- Landy, L. (1991) *What's the Matter with Today's Experimental Music? Organized sound too Rarely Heard*. Philadelphia, PA: Harwood Academic.

Emergence

There is a paradox at the heart of this notion of a 'digital culture'. At its most fundamental level (that is, binary mathematics), the computer *lacks a context* whereas 'culture' is *all about context*. The juxtaposition of the two words is, therefore, an extreme expression of an apparent opposition between mathematical and organic realities. Yet, the two somehow seem connected enough that the phrase 'digital culture' has resonance and meaning.

In *The Language of New Media*, Lev Manovich identifies five principles which underlie a digitised culture:

- *numerical representation* (digital code), which allows programmability
- *modularity*, by which objects may be combined with other objects without losing their independent identity

- *automation*, by which the computer replaces certain types of human activity
- *variability*, in which numerous different variations can be generated, often automatically, from single originals (such as a database).
- *transcoding*, the process by which media is turned into computer data.[4]

Manovich makes a distinction between the 'cultural layer' and the 'computer layer'. In musical terms, this would be the difference between, for example, a song, and the computer processes that are used in the creation of the song.

For the digital musician, there is an indissoluble relationship between these two layers. Whether one is working to produce a CD or DVD, giving a live concert or making an installation, making music on the Internet or for a computer game, the computer layer has a profound effect on the cultural layer, and vice versa. However, music and musicians tend to flow best when the means of production present little apparent obstacle in practice to musical expression. It is increasingly the case that digital technology is so widely used, so unremarkable, that the fact that it is digital goes unnoticed. This is true of many consumer goods, such as fridges, cars and televisions, where a computer of some description is the heart of the machine. In music, too, digital technologies may be integrated with non-digital technologies, so that a seamless transition between, say, an obviously 'digital' and a clearly 'acoustic' sound can be heard on a CD, or played on a computer. In fact, both the digital and the acoustic sounds are really digital; it's just that the digitisation of acoustic sound is so commonplace that it seems natural.[5]

This is an evolving state of affairs, and its effects vary a great deal depending on the context. It may best be described as *emergent*. This is the technical term for work that is not entirely predesigned by an artist or composer but rather involves the conscious use of the shifting boundaries between the consumer and the maker. This label applies to many aspects of the digital culture and seems to encapsulate both the technological advances and the cultural changes that accompany them. Nowhere is this more consistently the case than in networking and communications technologies, and for the digital musician the ongoing emergence of Internet music is probably the most significant cultural development of recent times.

■ Manovich, L. (2001) *The Language of New Media*. Cambridge, MA: MIT Press.
■ Packer, R. and Jordan, K. (eds) (2001) *Multimedia: From Wagner to Virtual Reality*. New York: W. W. Norton.
■ Pratt, V. (1987) *Thinking Machines: The Evolution of Artificial Intelligence*. Oxford: Basil Blackwell.

Cultural diversity

This is an age of unprecedented access to the music of other cultures. The efforts of ethnomusicologists,[6] 'world music' scholars and enthusiasts and talented musicians who have been prepared to face the rigours of travel have opened up these possibilities. But even more significant than these has been, first, the availability of good quality recordings and then, more recently, the Internet. There are many general introductions to ethnomusicology, and two collections of essays which will be particularly useful are:

- Nettl, B. (2005) *The Study of Ethnomusicology: Thirty-One Issues and Concepts*. Urban, IL: University of Illinois Press.
- Shelemay, K. K. (1992) *Ethnomusicology: History, Definitions, and Scope: A Core Collection of Scholarly Articles*. New York: Routledge.

For a general bibliography of ethnomusicology, see:

- Post, J. C. (2003) *Ethnomusicology: A Research and Information Guide*. New York: Routledge.

A pioneering work of ethnomusicology was:

- Blacking, J. (1973) *How Musical Is Man?* Washington, DC: University of Washington Press.

In 1889, Claude Debussy was amazed to hear folk music from Indo-China at the Exposition Universelle in Paris. By 1999, it was possible to find whole online communities devoted to particular forms of folk music whose members had not necessarily even heard *live* versions of the music they gathered to explore. As the Internet continues to evolve, there is even talk of an ethnomusicology of cyberspace.

For a musician to adopt the musical language of a foreign culture without sufficient understanding can be a dangerous thing. It is also strictly impossible, because many of the folk musics are the result of centuries of cultural, even familial, evolution which is difficult to penetrate. At one end of the scale, therefore, lies *cultural imperialism*, which is the wholesale and unthinking 'lifting' of someone else's culture to suit one's own ends, while at the other end lies *cultural tourism*, where the culture itself is pre-packaged for the benefit of the outsider, often distorting its essential character in the process. Avoiding these two pitfalls is difficult. The goal is not so much to become a completely different musician as to establish a creative discourse with these other cultures, to learn from them and to absorb their influence.

Listening to, reading about and indeed, playing, other musics will have the benefit of opening up the ears to new possibilities. Through trying to engage seriously with other traditions and ideas, the digital musician may achieve a more profound understanding of the ways in which music may be structured or may function socially or culturally. These 'other' musics need not necessarily come from the other side of the world. They might, in fact, be examples of different musical practices within the musician's own culture. The point is that they present the musician with something unfamiliar, something new. They will all be examples of sub-cultures, in the sense that they are defined and particular areas within the broader culture called 'music'.

They may contain identifiably common elements, resonances with known music, revelatory ideas about musical practice, insights into the purpose and effects of music, and some practical ways in which these might be an influence. To illustrate these points, the following discussions examine three examples which are sufficiently well known to offer ready access to Western musicians but also sufficiently distinct to raise some important and interesting questions about digital music. They come with a word of warning: there is no way that a few paragraphs in a book of this size can do justice to the richness and complexity of these cultural traditions. The discussions should be treated merely as a 'pointer' to further lines of enquiry. To help this, each discussion comes with some recommendations for additional reading. The point of the discussions is merely to illustrate some of the potential benefits to the digital musician of looking at the music of other cultures.

- Greene, P. and Porcello, T. (eds) (2005) *Wired for Sound: Engineering and Technologies in Sonic Cultures*. Middletown, CT: Wesleyan University Press.
- Small, C. (1987) *Music of the Common Tongue*. London: Calder.

Gamelan

The traditional music of Java, Bali and a few other Indonesian islands seems to have absorbed early influences from India, China and even Europe and then evolved from about the ninth century AD into a distinctive music all its own. The Western world first became aware of this music in the nineteenth century, and it has had an influence on many composers and musicians ever since. Three books about *gamelan* that will be of particular use to the musician are:

- Brinner, B. (1995) *Knowing Music, Making Music: Javanese Gamelan and the Theory of Musical Competence and Interaction*. Chicago, IL: University of Chicago Press.
- Pickvance, R. (2006) *A Gamelan Manual: A Player's Guide to the Central Javanese Gamelan*. London: Jaman Mas Books.
- Spiller, H. (2004) *Gamelan: The Traditional Sounds of Indonesia*. Santa Barbara, CA: ABC-CLIO: Book and CD edition.

There is some difference in practice between Java and Bali, deriving from the fourteenth-century split of the two islands into Islamic Java and Hindu Bali. This resulted in a highly developed practice that occupied a unique position in both societies. *Gamelans* are often used to support shadow plays, puppet theatre and significant religious and social occasions. But the *gamelan* also forms a central part of village life, with the musicians often gathering after work to play. Everywhere you go in Java and Bali, *gamelan* music can be heard.

In the Western world, it is usual for musicians to specialise on a single instrument. Some musicians may play more than one but, with a few exceptions, would not normally do so during a single performance. It is also not necessary generally for the individual musician in an ensemble performance to understand the entire composition being played and their role in relation to the other musicians, other than on an occasional, local basis. Gamelan is quite different, because all the musicians in a gamelan orchestra are, in theory, capable of playing any of the instruments. This is in turn because all the musicians understand how the composition is structured, and what part each instrument has to play. Gamelan music is not improvised, yet has been described as a 'negotiation between musicians'.[7]

A typical gamelan orchestra consists mostly of percussion instruments, traditionally made from a single lump of bronze. The instruments are regarded as sacred: it is not permissible to step over them or move them without offering up a prayer, or apologising. The instruments have onomatopoeic names that resemble the sounds they make. The Gong Ageng ('gong' is in fact a Javanese word) is the largest instrument. Once struck, the gong is never damped. The Bonang are pot-shaped gongs, mounted in trays. They are often detuned slightly from one another, so that when they play their characteristic interlocking patterns, a shimmering effect is produced. They are never damped. The Kethuk are small, damped gongs. These produce a frog-like sound, which delineates the structure of the composition. The Saron are metal xylophones. The player damps the preceding note with one hand while playing the next note with the other, producing a smooth, seamless, melodic line.

Every gamelan instrument is duplicated: one with a five-note tuning system, and one with a seven-note tuning system. The five-note system, called slendro, is, in fact, an equal temperament system, but the division of the octave into five obviously means that the intervals between each step are relatively wide. Pelog, on the other hand, is an unevenly tuned system, with some intervals being very close together, and others spread wide apart. In fact, each gamelan has its own unique sound, because the tunings are always slightly different, based on the resonant properties of the instruments. Thus, a slendro gamelan will have five roughly equal steps to the octave.

Even with a limited number of notes per octave, gamelan tunes are highly selective about which notes are used, restricting themselves sometimes to only three or four, with an occasional colouristic extra note added to accentuate the contours of the melody. It is also not unusual for the same tune to be played successively in the two tuning systems. It is still reckoned to be the same tune, even though the tuning makes it sound quite different. The reason for this is that it has the same shape and number sequence (all gamelan music is played by memory using a system of numbers), and the structure remains the same.

Every gamelan composition is built around the central melody called the balungan (skeleton), which is played in unison by the mid-range instruments such as sarons. All the other instruments either decorate this melody, or delineate its structure. All the musicians in a gamelan performance know the melody, and know the way in which their particular instrument may treat the melody. *Gamelan* music is highly structured, with various gong strokes dividing up phrases into (usually) groups of four, eight, sixteen, etc. A drummer leads the orchestra and gives cues for changes of tempo. One of the most exciting things in *gamelan* music is the way in which the whole ensemble speeds up and slows down together. The interlocking patterns played by the smaller instruments change as the tempo reaches its highest speed. The effect is of shifting gradually to a new plateau.

If you play *gamelan* (and playing it is even more fun than listening to it), then you quickly learn to hear those around you very accurately. You listen for the drum cues, you move in time with your neighbour, and, at all times, you keep the *balungan* in mind. You experience a sense of the whole piece and of your role within it. This sense of wholeness also comes through when just listening. The music emerges from the initial big gong hit and dies away back into a gong hit at the end. The music changes speed and contains amazingly fast and intricate motion within it, but it does not appear to *go* anywhere. Despite all the activity, it is static, and a result is that attention shifts to the overall timbre of the sound, the tuning of the instruments, the attacks of the various hits.

There have been many examples of electronic and digital musicians who have absorbed the influence of *gamelan* by using similar structuring and techniques, either with actual *gamelan* instruments or applied to a variety of sonic objects. Some fairly recent examples include: Wendy Carlos's album *Beauty in the Beast*, which combines *gamelan* and Western orchestral sounds (among other things); Ensemble Robot, which has combined a *gamelan* orchestra with new technologies in pieces such as *Heavy Metal* (2006) by Christine Southworth,[8] for Balinese Gamelan Gong Kebyar, guitar, violin, bass, lyricon and robotic instruments; and even works which do not contain the actual sounds of *gamelan*, but are imbued with its spirit, such as the performance pieces of Augustinus Kus Windananto (aka Jompet), whose *Glorified* pieces from 2001, or the more recent *Ultraoutput* project, use the human body as a trigger for a '*gamelan*' of mechanical and electronic sound.

Indian classical music

To achieve a full understanding of Indian classical music would probably take a lifetime, or more. There is tremendous variety, from Hindustani music in the north to Carnatic music in the south and other types in between. What all the music has in common is a highly developed theoretical system based on an extreme refinement of the ear and a religious purpose that variously worships the Hindu Gods in all their manifestations. Whereas it is quite easy to learn to play *gamelan* music, it is less likely that a Western musician will play Indian classical music, because of the prohibitive length of time it takes to absorb both its musical and devotional aspects. Even to play the drone, the simplest element, requires considerable technique.

Indian classical music has been extensively studied, both from a practical and a theoretical viewpoint. A useful text which contains profiles and interviews with many leading musicians is:

■ Qureshi, R. B. (2007) *Master Musicians of India: Hereditary Sarangi Players Speak*. New York: Routledge.

Two good recent general guides are:

■ Chib, S. K. S. (2004) *Companion to North Indian Classical Music*. Delhi: Munshiram Manoharlal.
■ Pesch. L. (1999) *An Illustrated Companion to South Indian Classical Music*. Oxford: Oxford University Press.

At the heart of the music is the *raga*. This is a single melody, but it is also a collection of pitches and gestures, of intonations and inflections, of musical rules and shared cultural understandings. Each element of the *raga* and each *raga* itself is highly expressive and detailed, although it is hard to define in words precisely what the expression may be. *Ragas* may be performed on specific days or at specific occasions, even at appropriate times of the day.

A *raga* must contain at least five notes, of which one is the *Sa*, the tonic, or the 1:1, and another must be either the fourth or fifth. A *raga* is characterised by the pattern of ascent and descent (*aroha-avaroha*) from the low to the high *Sa*, a pattern which may well omit certain notes in either direction, or flatten or sharpen notes. These small variations in pitch or interval are called *sruti* and allow much of the expressive abilities of the performer to come through. In addition to the tuning, the way in which a note is approached and left, whether by a slide or a step, and the ways in which certain notes are emphasised or weakened, gives much of the character to a particular performance. The musician will often work with small groups of note patterns, forming distinctive shapes and patterns within the overall melody of the *raga*, thus allowing performances to last half an hour or more.

The *raga* may be accompanied by rhythmic patterns played on *tabla*. The rhythmic patterns are called *tala* and are no less precise and structured than the *ragas* themselves. Time is divided up into a fixed number of counts, which then repeat in cyclical fashion, as in the following patterns: *dadra* (3 + 3); *rupak* (3 + 2 + 2); *kaharva* (4 + 4); *jhaptal* (2 + 3 + 2 + 3); *ektal* and *chautal* (2 + 2 + 2 + 2 + 2 + 2); *dhamar* (5 + 2 + 3 + 4); *dipchandi* (3 + 4 + 3 + 4); *addha tintal/sitarkhani* (4 + 4 + 4 + 4). Rhythmic variations are introduced as the tempo changes, so the playing may get faster and faster, producing some very rapid hand motions. The patterns are memorised using vocal syllables, which may actually be spoken by the musician during the performance, and quite often a pattern will be repeated three times in succession to bring a *raga* to a close.

The melodic aspects of the *raga* may be sung or played on instruments such as the well-known *sitar* but also a host of other plucked and bowed string instruments, wind instruments and keyboards. In a typical performance, the *raga* emerges freely and gradually in an opening section called the *alap* or *alapana*. A faster section follows, with the entry of the *tabla*, and generally the music becomes faster and tighter. There will be ornamentations and interactions between the main soloist and the percussionist. The performance may well end with a restatement of the main *raga* theme itself, but it should always be remembered that *ragas* are dynamic and the forms are not precisely fixed. The word *raga* means 'colour', and the essence of the *raga* is a colouristic expression of emotion.

The influence of Indian classical music on Western music has been lasting and profound, from Ravi Shankar's famous performances with The Beatles, especially George Harrison, in the 1960s and 1970s, to jazz artists such as Miles Davis and John McLaughlin, and experimentalists such as La Monte Young and Terry Riley. Indian film music and popular forms such as *bhangra* have retained some links with the classical tradition, and this comes through even in their fusion with genres such as hip-hop.

Given the emphasis placed upon the *instrument* and its traditions in Indian classical music, it is no surprise to find that, beyond the use of drones, samples and perhaps rhythmic patterns, digital music has had to grapple with some difficult challenges to absorb the finer nuances of the music but, even so, attempts have been made. In 2003, a live collaborative music performance entitled 'Giga-Pop Ritual'[9] took place simultaneously at McGill University in Canada and Princeton in the USA, based on two *ragas*: Raga Jog and Jai Jai Vanti. The performers were linked via a bi-directional high-speed network, and the instruments included an *eDholak* (electronic Dholak), an *RBow* (a violin bow extended with motion sensors), and a *DigitalDoo* (an electronically extended digeridoo), alongside conventional instruments such as sitar and tabla.

In his essay 'Bézier Spline Modeling of Pitch-Continuous Melodic Expression and Ornamentation', Bret Battey describes a technique he has devised for 'analysis and computer rendering of melodies such as those found in Indian classical music, in which subtle control of the continuum between scale steps is fundamental to expression'.[10] He has subsequently used this technique in a number of works, including his audiovision piece from 2005, *Autarkeia Aggregatum*.[11] As he succinctly puts it: 'I spend my life trying to make my computer sing.'[12]

West African drumming

Rhythmic patterns are mathematical subdivisions of time. This makes them fairly easy to create using digital equipment, and much of the abundant cross-fertilisation between different types of rhythm-based music from around the world has been greatly facilitated by this fact. More or less any non-Western percussion-based music will, therefore, be of interest to the digital musician. West African drumming is here chosen partly because it has particular social characteristics and partly because its influence is still being explored in many educational establishments and by many musicians. Of special interest is the extent to which a very local tradition, with considerable meaning to a specific group, is capable of making a transition to a wider public without losing its significance.

For a very detailed account of this music which reveals the subtlety of meaning in local variations, see:

■ Charry, E. (2000) *Mande Music: Traditional and Modern Music of the Maninka and Mandinka of Western Africa.* Chicago, IL: University of Chicago Press.

A more general introduction is:

■ Stone, R. M. (1999, 2nd edition 2008) *The Garland Handbook of African Music.* New York: Routledge.

For practical interest and an enjoyable way to study basic techniques for *djembe*:

■ Dworsky, A. (2000) *How to Play Djembe: West African Rhythms for Beginners.* Minnetonka, MN: Dancing Hands Music (book with CD).

West African drumming, like Indian *raga*, is a form of music that is usually performed on special occasions and for specific functions. The drummers form a circle and play a variety of drums made from animal skins stretched over hollowed-out logs. The drums may have various pitches, depending upon their size and head tension, or even contain more than one pitch in a single drum. The 'talking drum' has leather thongs connecting a skin at either end. When the drummer squeezes the thongs, the resulting change in tension 'bends' the pitch of the drum, which is played with an L-shaped stick. In addition to the drums, a variety of bells, rattles and whistles are used, along with a chesty, rasping singing voice that makes much of swooping, glissando sounds. Vocal lines are often sung by more than one singer, harmonising in parallel intervals such as thirds and sixths.

The drum music is constructed from many overlapping rhythmic patterns, set against a constant timeline laid down by bells. A master drummer will also improvise solos over the top of the patterns and will generally lead the ensemble. This kind of music exists in various forms in the West African countries of Senegal, Gambia, Guinea Bissau, Guinea, Sierra Leone, Liberia, Ivory Coast, Ghana, Togo, Benin, Nigeria and Cameroon, and inland to Burkina Faso and parts of Mali, Niger and Chad. However, the regional variations are enormous, and rhythmic patterns that are common in one country, or region, or even village, may be unknown elsewhere in West Africa.

The attraction of this music beyond the region may be exemplified by the surge in popularity of the *jembe*, or *djembe*, ever since the world tours of Les Ballets Africains (led by Fodeba Keita of Guinea) in the 1950s. The *djembe* offers several different tones, including a deep bass note made by striking the centre, a slap made by slapping the rim, and a tone note, also made at the rim. Using only these sounds, very complicated and yet rhythmically precise patterns can be achieved, which when combined produce thrilling polyrhythms. Because the drum rhythms are literally understood to 'talk', and what they say is peculiar to a small, localised community, the assembly of larger regional, national, or even 'West African' ensembles for a European audience has led to some curious combinations of apparently unrelated rhythmic patterns.

Djembe music has quickly spread across the world. A quick Internet search on the word will reveal large resources and a thriving culture devoted to all aspects of the music. To take part in a *djembe* ensemble can be a thrilling experience: apart from the sheer excitement and energy of the music, the structuring of the patterns and the way they interconnect is highly intriguing. For the digital musician, what may be learnt from this is the importance of communal or social interaction. Rhythmic ensemble work like this is an excellent way to quickly achieve mutual understanding among a group of musicians. The connection with dancing, and physical motion generally, is an important reminder of the physicality of performance, given that digital music can often require little or no performance motion. Also, the social context for the music can be very different from the formality of a Western concert hall.

The influence of West African drumming on music created with new technologies is probably best exemplified by the work of Steve Reich, whose most recent multimedia and digital pieces still show evidence of the pattern-based processes he first exploited following time spent studying with a master drummer in Ghana in the early 1970s. He explains:

> I became aware of African music via a composers' conference that was held in 1962 in Ojai, California, when I was still a student of [Luciano] Berio's at Mills College. [. . .] Although I had heard African music before – I'd heard records, I knew that it swung, I knew you made it with drums, I knew it was very rhythmic – I hadn't the faintest idea of how it was made; how it was put together.[13]

The most immediate influence of the drumming techniques was on his 90-minute work for percussion ensemble with female voices and piccolo, *Drumming* (1970–1971). However, this instrumental piece is itself an example of a synthesis of technology-based processes with drumming techniques, because of the inclusion of 'phasing', discovered by Reich in the mid-1960s, when he played two tape loops simultaneously and used varispeed gradually to adjust their synchronisation. Applying this technique to instrumental music enabled a variation on traditional drumming which lacked none of its rigour and fascination. Although he rarely uses phasing as a technique today, Reich has continued to draw upon his studies of West African drumming. Digital works such as *The Cave* (1993/2003), for amplified voices and ensemble, use the rhythms and inflections of speech to generate musical patterns and melodies that overlay video images, in an echo of the 'talking drum' tradition.

Another digital musician who has worked in West Africa is Lukas Ligeti, whose *Beta Foley* ensemble includes performers from the Republic of Guinea, Ivory Coast and Burkina Faso. The band works with many conventional African instruments, including *wassamba*, *kora*, *balafon* and *djembe*, along with computer and an assortment of MIDI controllers. Ligeti describes the purpose of his first visit to Africa thus:

> I felt that an interesting premise for this voyage would be for me not to attempt to play African music, and not to ask the African musicians to play in a European style, but to construct a 'third plane' on which we could meet and interact, exploring the creative possibilities of musical electronics.[14]

Cultural translations

This listening list explores some aspects of cultural diversity in electronic and electro-acoustic music. It is worth preceding the project by listening to examples of Javanese *gamelan*, Indian *raga* and African drumming, in order to get a fix on some of the models.

The list should illustrate the benefits of an approach to the music of other cultures which has integrity and depth. There are some fairly obvious superficial musical characteristics that can readily be heard in these musics. A more detailed understanding might explore the sonorities and timings of *gamelan*, the gestures and modal nuances of Indian classical music, the rhythms and physicality of West African drumming. But to recognise the significance of these musics to sufficient depth to do them justice requires critical judgement (discussed in the next chapter) and a degree of self-awareness. In other words, an attitude that absorbs the cultural as well as musical lessons that these musics can give, but also deepens its understanding of its own position and cultural context.

The major questions to be asked while listening are: to what extents do Western and non-Western musical cultures become apparent during these pieces? What are their major features? Is the translation from one culture to another successful? How do these pieces reflect their non-Western models?

▲ Steve Reich (1965) *It's Gonna Rain*. Elektra Nonesuch 79169-2. This tape piece is the first example of Reich's phasing technique, and predates his study of West African drumming, and yet it already shows an interest in the detail of patterns emerging from the layering of rhythmic material (in this case, speech).

▲ John Hassell/Brian Eno (1980) *Fourth World, Vol. I – Possible Musics*. Editions EG Records B000003S2B. 'Fourth World music is a unified primitive/futuristic sound combining features of world ethnic styles with advanced electronic techniques' (Jon Hassell, writing in the 1970s).

▲ Wendy Carlos (1986) *Beauty in the Beast*. East Street Digital ESD 81552. 'I've taken ideas from many disparate cultures, heeding Debussy's dictum: "whatever pleases my ear," and filtered it through all the wonderful new musical means at my disposal and through my decidedly Euro-American post symphonic composorial skills' (Wendy Carlos, sleevenotes for *Beauty in the Beast*).

▲ Alejandro Viñao (1991) *Chant d'Ailleurs (Song from Elsewhere)*. Track 1 on the CD *Hildegard's Dream*, Musidisc MU 244942. In *Chant d'Ailleurs* the human voice is taken on an imaginary journey through an imaginary culture.

▲ Lukas Ligeti and Beta Foley (1997) *Lukas Ligeti and Beta Foley*. Intuition Music and Media INT 3216 2. The members of Beta Foley have included: Yero Bobo Bah, wassambe, vocals; Lamine Baldé, acoustic guitar, vocals; Wendé K. Blass, electric guitar; Kurt Dahlke, electronics; Sylvain Dando Paré, bass guitar; Mamadou Dao, soku, kora, guitar and vocals; Babagalé Kanté, pastoral flute; Tchemsé Kanté, bolon, vocals; Aly Keïta, balafon; Lassiné Koné, djembe; Lukas Ligeti, drums, electronic drums; Maï Lingani, vocals; Amadou Leye M'Baye, sabar.

▲ Bent Leather Band: Joanne Cannon and Stuart Favilla (2004) *The Other Side of Nostalgia*. CMF007. Live processing of adapted instruments (including LightHarp and Serpentine Bassoon) infused with microtonal tunings and musical material that refers to many cultures both past and present.

Digital music

In his book *Music, Society, Education* (1977), the musicologist Christopher Small suggested that consumerism has led to music in the West (and increasingly in India, Indochina, Africa and everywhere else) becoming a *product* rather than a *process*. In the following passage, he discusses the effects of Western consumerism on traditional Balinese virtues of valuing the moment, collectivism and spontaneity. The same points may be made about African music too.

> I must emphasize again that since the end of the second world war these values have become severely eroded as western commercial values and consumerism take over; the change from artistic creation as a process involving the whole community to art as a commodity made for sale by a few professional artists has happened here, as throughout the non-European world, staggeringly quickly.[15]

Small could not have foreseen the emergence of digital culture, nor the extent to which the 'erosion' to which he refers would itself become eroded. Today, there is, once again, a community based culture, collective and spontaneous, sharing in artistic creation. The rise of a social Internet, which increasingly configures itself to suit the individual user, has enabled this development. Blogs[16] and wikis,[17] user groups, forums and 'myspace', mp3-sharing and individual playlists. In short, everything that personalises cyberspace[18] means that the consumer culture is increasingly morphing into an online culture. To be sure, commercialism is always present, and the commodity merchants are always busy trying to figure out how to exploit the new digital culture. Meanwhile, people interact and share online, grouping around common interests and passions, around ideas and sounds. The major difference, of course, is that geographical location is no longer the defining characteristic of this community.

What is fascinating about the changes brought about by digital music is the extent to which, once again, we are building an aural tradition based on this communal understanding, on shared tools and practices and, to some extent, on regional variation. It is true that there is a great deal of *production* and especially commercial production in digital music, but the 'product' itself is also seen as part of a process. In fact, the phrase 'music production' increasingly refers to the process of creating music, rather than a layer of polish applied to a finished artefact. Perhaps the digital musician is making a new kind of music, and the musical situation is, once again, coming to resemble the informal, process-based, communal activity of some parts of the non-Western world.

In order to apply the same kind of ethnomusicological approach that has already been used to consider *gamelan*, Indian classical music and African drumming to digital music, some attempt to identify its key characteristics must be made. This is not easy, because the phrase 'digital music' covers such a potentially vast range of types, categories and genres that a purely musical system of classification rapidly becomes unworkable. A more fruitful way of approaching the problem might be to consider the role of the *musician*. This is a method that also fits well with the central theme of this book. By using a human-centred classification system, the vast and messy field of digital music may be organised into three broad types: audience or user-controlled music, computer-controlled music, and composer/performer-controlled music.

- Collins, N. and d'Escriván, J. (2007) *The Cambridge Companion to Electronic Music*. Cambridge: Cambridge University Press.
- Lysloff, R and Gay, L. (eds) (2003) *Music and Technoculture*. Middletown, CT: Wesleyan University Press.
- Taylor, T. (2001) *Strange Sounds: Music, Technology and Culture*. New York: Routledge.

Audience or user-controlled music

Here, the person who receives the music may determine when it begins and ends and, to a greater or lesser extent, what happens in between. The musician (and possibly the computer) has a hand in creating prime content, and possibly in the context within which the music appears, but no more.

Musical attention in this category usually focuses on the nature and extent of the interaction. In adaptive music, for example, the sounds (whether obviously 'musical' or not) that accompany computer games are capable of combination and recombination in many different ways. This is event-driven music and is shaped by the user's decisions in the context of the game. The sounds are created so as to enable the user to seamlessly make a transition from one into another.

This process can even be extended to user-made adaptive compositions in which the choices made in some way condition subsequent outcomes.

A different kind of user-control is encountered in sound installations, which may range from public sculptures, to interactive stands in museums or attractions, to art-gallery pieces. Here, the interaction is usually physical rather than virtual, and often the user's own actions will change the nature of the sonic activity. However, this might also include all kinds of ambient music designed to enhance a given location, including Muzak. Sound environments are also relevant here, because, once again, the user is placed at the hub of the musical activity, usually with a decisive role. An immersive environment is a virtual reality in which the user can interact with objects and experience sounds within a digitally fabricated world. In the physical world, a soundscape may be created (such as through a soundwalk, as described earlier), which has its users interact meaningfully with the sounds around them.

What all these have in common is some degree of interactivity, which means that they tend to beg the question: who is the artist or, in the context of this book, who is the musician? If the users control their experience, then in a very real sense they become the composer and the performer in that situation, and the role of the originator of the prime material, which they are manipulating, is relatively diminished.

■ Toop, D. (1995, 2001) *Ocean of Sound: Aether Talk, Ambient Sound and Imaginary Worlds.* London: Serpent's Tail.

Computer-controlled music

Here, both the listener/user and the musician are subject to some process that is undertaken by the computer. This is generally algorithmic music, since the computer must use rules to run the process. Algorithmic music has included systems based on: chance, randomness and stochasticism; number series, sets and fractals;[19] evolution, genetics and L-systems;[20] network information, statistics and magnetic fields; and so on. In fact, any organisational system may provide useful algorithms.[21] Such 'machine music' is often a product of music analysis, so the computer can control things in such a way as to produce stylistically convincing results. There are numerous examples of machine music that produce pastiche composition or can successfully accompany human musicians within a known genre. It is the way in which the algorithm is mapped onto musical information that distinguishes the sounding result.

Once again, this begs the question: *who* is the musician? Does the computer compose and perform the music, or does the person who programmed the computer take the credit? It is certainly possible to speak of a 'computer composition' and 'machine creativity'. This may be aesthetically desirable where the removal of the human hand is the artistic goal. However, no computer begins an algorithm of its own volition, so at some level there is some kind of human intention.

The tendency for the human to erase him or herself from the creative process is the subject of some discussion in the next chapter, but may be summarised as an aspect of a certain mistrust of the notion of a single authorial figure that is a defining characteristic of contemporary digital culture.

- Schwanauer, S. and Levitt, D. (eds) (1993) *Machine Models of Music*. Cambridge, MA: MIT Press.
- Willcock, I. (2007) 'Composing without Composers' in C.-S. Mahnkopf, F. Cox and W. Schurig (eds) (2007) *Electronics in New Music*. Berlin: Wolke Verlag, pp. 221–235.

Composer/performer-controlled music

This is the largest category, because it includes the traditional mode of musical delivery and reception and presents relatively few conceptual difficulties. Here, the musician originates or produces the sound, and the listener/user simply receives the result. However, the size of the category does not make it more significant in the field of digital music, and it has some distinctive features. First, the role of the composer/performer has become substantially blurred, as has been mentioned before. Second, the assumption of passivity on the part of the listener is risky, because the many different ways of listening to digital music, from in-ear headphones to concert halls, can make this a more active process than might previously have been imagined. Third, the possibilities opened up by digital technologies have led in some instances to an unusual performance and listening state, as, for example, in the kind of loudspeaker orchestra situation found in some acousmatic music in which the sources of the sounds are not evident to the listener.

There are some overlaps between the three categories outlined above, but not so much as to destroy completely the distinctions between them. Consider, for example, the case of *radiophonics*: the experimental use of sound in radio. Here, the listener does have ultimate on/off control and a great deal of flexibility in how they listen, but it is still the radiophonic artists who are really controlling the musical experience. The main point of these classifications is to show that a musician may have multiple and changing roles during a given musical experience and that the consumers of music are not completely passive.

The lessons of *gamelan*, Indian classical music and African drumming can equally well be applied in digital music. There is now a new listening context for music, which may fluctuate from headphone space to club space, from concert hall to studio. What defines all these arenas is the extent to which the listener, the user, is in control. The user's playlist itself becomes a kind of digital composition. The DJ becomes a super-listener and a musician. The 'mash-up' and the remix constantly explore a plurality of unexpected associations. The studio engineer becomes the 'producer' who actually *makes* the music. Even in the classical concert hall, the audience expresses its preferences by its attendance, influencing the development of the music through its sheer economic will. Where all this leads is to increased user satisfaction through the creation and evolution of a multitude of *genres*.

● Mood music

■ Kahn, D. and Whitehead, G. (1992) *Wireless Imagination: Sound, Radio and the Avant-Garde.* Cambridge, MA: MIT Press.

Genre

'Genre' was a relatively little-used term until fairly recently. Music might be divided into 'classical' and 'popular', or 'jazz' and 'folk', but not much beyond that outside of the specialists. Music-lovers who knew 'folk' music, for example, might recognise a distinction between, say, Celtic and Gaelic music, but these terms in themselves would not necessarily constitute a genre, but rather a *style* of music within the larger genre category of 'folk'.

Digital culture has brought about an explosion of genre, to the point where almost all digital music can be heard in relation to a known genre or be seen to have created a new genre. In electronic dance music, for example, new genres come and go so rapidly as to constitute the whims of fashion. At the technological level, this genre multiplication has come about because of the possibility of adding digital 'tags' to sound files, giving basic information that will enable future classification or 'sorting'. At a more cultural level, it may be seen as an example of postmodernism, of which more will be said in the next chapter.

The approach to specific genres requires a warning bell. One of the fundamental requirements of the digital musician is to develop an original sound. Genre work is potentially limiting in that respect because genres generally involve conventions and traditions, even constraints. These can be very useful for initiating creative work, but if they dominate the musician too much, then there is a danger of becoming merely a reproducer of other people's ideas. It is important for the digital musician to retain a creative originality, even if working within the confines of an established musical genre.

An extreme example will illustrate the point: *plunderphonics*. The name of the genre originated in 1985 from an essay and CD by John Oswald and refers to music stolen from existing, usually well-known, recordings and subjected to various modifications. There is a political dimension to this music, which attacks the hypocrisy surrounding copyright. The original *Plunderphonic* album fell foul of various laws and its cover, depicting Michael Jackson as a naked white woman, landed Oswald in court. In his various essays and articles,[22] he makes it clear that his work is by no means unique, citing examples from classical and contemporary popular music where composers and artists have openly 'lifted' other composers' music. The influence and practice of plunderphonics can be traced in the work of bands such as Negativland, turntablists like Christian Marclay, 'mashed-up' pop music, and even some works by contemporary classical composers. Plunderphonics could,

Table 7.1 Electronic dance music genres.

Ambient	Breakbeat	Downtempo/IDM	Hardcore	Industrial
Dark ambient	Electro	Balearic Beat	4-beat	EBM
Illbient	Big Beat	Bleep	Bouncy techno	Noise music
New Age	Breaks	Electroclash	Breakbeat hardcore	Old-school EBM
Psybient	Miami Bass	Electropop		Futurepop
Ambient Dub	Brokenbeat	Laptronica	Breakcore	Powernoise
Ambient Goa	Cut and paste	Bitpop	Digital hardcore	
Ambient house	Florida breaks	Chiptune	Gabba	
Lowercase (music)	nu skool breaks	Minimal Electronica/ Glitch	Happy Hardcore	
	Progressive breaks		Hardcore trance	
		Acid jazz	Hardstyle	
	Turntablism	Nu jazz	New beat	
	Grime	Trip hop (aka The Bristol sound)	Nu style gabber	
			Speedcore	
			Terrorcore	

therefore, be seen as a genre that accurately reflects the cut-and-paste culture of sampling and the Internet, and the technique itself offers many creative possibilities, as well as a considerable danger.

The question facing the digital musician is, therefore, to what extent to adopt plunderphonics as a technique, given that others have already developed identifiable voices within that genre? This is a question that will be relevant in any genre. There is no fixed answer, but for the digital musician to retain integrity and to move from the known to the unknown will not allow for simple aping of the mannerisms of others. A technique will not, in itself, guarantee distinctive results; it is all a question of how it is used, what is done with it.

Consider this recent list of (just) electronic dance music genres (Table 7.1).[23] Given that almost all these genres have arisen in the past decade, this will readily illustrate the complexity of the subject. This takes us well beyond the various dance-types in traditional dance halls, and beyond the various types of rock music too. The digital musician could become a kind of alchemist, combining elements from several of these, perhaps even to formulate a new genre. It is likely that none of these genres will remain particularly stable.

All the above-listed genres have something in common: they have arisen as a result of a collective agreement by the community they serve. It may be that there are certain key individuals that are responsible for the distinctive musical characteristics of these genres (beats per minute, effects, activity level, etc.), but the genre has to be validated by a community who is willing to recognise

Table 7.1 (continued).

House		Jungle/Drum n bass	Techno	Trance
Chicago house	Minimal house/ Microhouse	Darkcore	Acid techno	Psychedelic trance/ Goa trance
2Step		Ragga	Detroit Techno/ US Techno	
Acid house	Garage	Drill n bass		Acid trance
Deep house	Hard house	Jump-Up	Electroclash	Vocal trance
Eurodance	French house	Liquid funk	Freetekno	Minimalist trance
Ghetto house	Progressive House/Tribal house	Neurofunk	Ghettotech	NU-NRG
Freestyle house		Techstep	Minimal Techno/ Glitch Techno	Progressive trance
Hi-NRG	Tech house	Clownstep	Nortec	
Funky house	Disco		Rave music	
Hip house	Italo disco		Schranz	
Pumpin' house	Spacesynth		UK Techno/Euro Techno	
Italo house				

it as distinct. There is then a platform for virtuosity within the genre. This is clear enough in dance music but is also present in other forms of music too. The makers are the consumers and the consumers are the makers. This is true for 'art' music just as much as 'popular' music.

This ongoing exchange between the makers and the consumers, the musicians and their audience, the artists and the non-artists, is the sign of an active musical community. Christopher Small need not have worried: process has not been replaced by product. The forming of ideas remains an integral aspect of music creation, and the commodification of music will continue both to provide a useful entry point for the interested listener and to lag behind the changes and developments that make music such a vibrant and life-enhancing activity. In that respect, at least, digital music is no different than the best music from the past.

● Random play

Selected listenings in digital music

This selected listening list introduces some leading digital works that are hard to classify. Each seems to be located in a genre and yet push beyond the limits of that genre. The main questions to ask are not so much 'What genre is this?' as 'What are the defining characteristics of this music?' and 'What is its context?'

▲ Autechre, *Chiastic Slide*. Warp 49.

▲ David Behrman (1983–1986) *Leapday Night*. Lovely Music LCD 1042.

▲ Kim Cascone (2000) *Parasites*. anechoic media a001.

▲ Richard Chartier (2007) *Of Surfaces*. LINE 008.

▲ Farmer's Manual (1998) *Explorers We*. Or SQUISH04.

▲ Bernhard Günther (1998) *Un Peu de Neige Salie*. Trente Oiseaux TOCSE01.

▲ Ryoji Ikeda (1998) *0°C*. Touch TO:30.

▲ Phil Jeck (2003) *Vinyl Coda I–III*. Intermedium INTER 002.

▲ Christian Marclay (1988) *More Encores*. Recommended RER CM1.

▲ Kaffe Matthews (2003) *ebb + flow*. Annetteworks AWCD0005-6.

▲ Merzbow (2001) *Merzbox Sampler*. Extreme XLTD 003.

▲ Negativland (2001) *These Guys Are from England and Who Gives a Shit*. Seeland 0021.

▲ John Oswald (1996) *69 Plunderphonics 96*. Seeland 515.

▲ Steve Roden (2000) *Four Possible Landscapes*. Trente Oiseaux TOC 00.

▲ Scanner (1999) *Lauwarm Instrumentals*. Sulphur SULCD002.

▲ Squarepusher (1998) *Feed Me Weird Things*. Rephlex CAT037CD.

Chapter 8

Critical engagement

In this chapter lies the answer to the difficult question posed in the Preface, 'How do we know what is good?'. Critical engagement arises from a study of the cultural context for music and from a personal desire to engage with it in an informed and intelligent way. In order to achieve successful critical engagement, the digital musician, therefore, needs to be culturally aware and keen to develop. He or she will need to deploy some of the analytical techniques and ideas that emerge from the fields of musicology, critical theory and cultural studies.

The phrase 'cultural studies' describes a broad mixture of investigations into the meaning and practices of everyday life. It is a hybrid discipline that has come to underpin much theorising in universities and colleges, combining aspects of social sciences, anthropology, philosophy, art history, media studies and other areas. It has a background in radical thought and often focuses on issues of race, gender, ideology and class. 'Critical theory' similarly emerges from social science but also overlaps with literary criticism. Some of the early figures of critical theory, such as Walter Benjamin (1892–1940), Theodor Adorno (1903–1969) and Roland Barthes (1915–1980), addressed both music and technology in their writings.

This chapter considers certain key ideas that are directly useful to the digital musician, without in any way attempting a complete survey of cultural studies in music. Traditional musicology has experienced the same changes that have influenced the musicians described in this book. Analysis historically tended to restrict itself to a parametric, or note-by-note, study of music alone. In recent years, however, there has been an increasing interest in exploring the meaning and significance of the music in social and cultural terms. One of the leaders of this 'new musicology', Susan McClary, has described music as:

> a medium that participates in social formation by influencing the ways we perceive our feelings, our bodies, our desires, our very subjectivities – even if it does so surreptitiously, without most of us knowing how. It is too important a cultural force to be shrouded by mystified notions of Romantic transcendence.[1]

- Hooper, G. (2006) *The Discourse of Musicology*. Aldershot: Ashgate.
- McClary, S. (1991) *Feminine Endings: Music, Gender, and Sexuality*. Minneapolis, MN: University of Minnesota Press.
- McClary, S. (1994) 'Constructions of Subjectivity in Schubert's Music' in *Queering the Pitch*, P. Brett, E. Wood and G. C. Thomas (eds), New York: Routledge.

Popular music-art music

It is almost a cliché of cultural studies that a division exists between 'popular' music and 'art' music. It is a central argument of this book that (at last!) this distinction is being eroded in digital culture. Whereas, in the past, a 'highbrow' musician was usually 'classically trained' and a 'lowbrow' musician was not, the new technologies are enabling the emergence of a new kind of musician, whose work resists easy classification in either sector and who may move comfortably into a range of situations. These new musicians have greatly increased access to techniques and equipment that were previously only available to a few. Excellent results can be achieved with readily available hardware and software, and many of the obstacles to making good music are effectively being removed. To be sure, the need to practice, to develop, to evolve as a musician, is as important now as it has ever been, but the easy classification of musicians into those with a 'proper' technique and those without is being exposed as too simplistic.

There are historical reasons for this. At one time, it was commonplace to assume that art music blazed an experimental trail which popular music then exploited. In many instances that was true, but the reverse also occurred. Today, there is simultaneity of discovery, such that it is really impossible to claim the lead for either side of the supposed divide. In fact, digital musicians will be able to exploit their work commercially as well as making ground-breaking musical discoveries. The distinctions that prevailed in the analogue world at this point are no longer so relevant. A digital soundfile is fundamentally data and might just as well be a recorded sound as an electronically generated sound.

This is not a history book, nor is there enough space to recount the whole of the history of electronic and digital musical evolutions in the past century.[2] On the other hand, critical engagement is greatly improved by an understanding of at least some key points of those evolutions. Given their importance, it is surprising that they have not been documented more thoroughly, and in many cases they seem to have been seen more as marginal notes in the history of notated instrumental music. This is partly due to the nature of the medium. The removal of notation makes them less well suited to academic study and, furthermore, the music itself tends to resist classification. Also, it has proved surprisingly difficult to preserve some of this music. The physical medium (usually tape) deteriorates quite rapidly, and even digital formats become unreadable quite quickly.

Another problem is that the history of the musical evolutions is so closely linked to the history of developments in technology. This means that historical accounts often read like a catalogue of technological innovation, with the artists apparently running along behind, forever trying to keep up with what the engineers have developed. It is certainly true that the present culture would not exist were it not for developments in technology, but musical innovations are more important for the musician. It is more significant that The Beach Boys used a slide theremin[3] in *Good Vibrations* than that Leon Theremin invented the original theremin in 1919/1920.

The emergence of the new technologies has, nevertheless, filled a gap between 'art' and 'popular' musics. By placing the full range of audio-processing techniques in the hands of a mass market for a relatively low price, the digital revolution has rendered all kinds of musical activities equivalent. Now the only thing that determines whether a particular technique is used is the limits of the musician's imagination or technical abilities. This began to emerge when The Beatles enthusiastically embraced *musique concrète* techniques in the recording studio or when minimalism swept all before it in the art houses of the 1970s and 1980s, with its motoric beats and harmonic simplicity.

In Indonesia now, a new genre called 'brutal ethnic' combines traditional Javanese melodies and rhythms with Indian film musics and death metal. In Nepal, studio artists deliberately juxtapose music from different traditions and cultures in complex mixes that might include various types of Asian folk and film music alongside reggae and rap, classical and disco. Australian studio engineers use 'secret' techniques to enhance *dijeridu* recordings, the technical challenge being to conceal the 'artificial' element to the point at which the listeners believe they are hearing a purely 'natural' *dijeridu* sound.[4] In their different ways, each of these represents an example of the way in which 'popular' and 'art' practices have become blurred through the creative use of digital technology.

■ Middleton, R. (1990) *Studying Popular Music*. Philadelphia, PA: Open University Press.
■ Jones, A. (1995) *Plunderphonics, 'Pataphysics and Pop Mechanics: An Introduction to Musique Actuelle*. Wembley, Alberta: SAF Publishing.

Listening across the divide

This listening list comprises some examples of music that seem to have their roots either on the 'popular' or the 'art' side of the fence. Yet, there is clear evidence of a convergence and cross-fertilisation, to the point that in some cases the distinction itself starts to break down. Nor is it the case that record sales are a ready indicator of which is 'popular' and which not. The list contains many contradictory examples of that idea.[5]

▲ Laurie Anderson (1982) *Big Science*. Warner 2KNM.
   Includes the hit single 'O Superman'.
▲ Aphex Twin (1994) *Selected Ambient Works Vol. 2*. Warp 21.
   Richard James, aka Aphex Twin, is a DJ and electronica artist, although this album is at times difficult to connect with that world.

▲ The Beatles (1968) 'Revolution #9' from the *White Album*. Apple PCS 7067-8.
According to John Lennon: 'It has the basic rhythm of the original "Revolution" going on, with some twenty loops we put on, things from the archives of EMI. [. . .] There were about ten machines with people holding pencils on the loops [. . .] I fed them all in and mixed them live.'

▲ Glenn Branca (1981, reissued 2003) *The Ascension Acute*. 9EIPG.
Trademark layered electric guitars and a cacophony of riffs, beats and rhythms.

▲ Wendy Carlos (1968, reissued 1999) 'Brandenburg Concerto No. 3'. East Side Digital 81422.
From the celebrated *Switched-On Bach* album.

▲ The Chemical Brothers (1999) *Surrender*. Virgin Records XDUSTCD4.
Clearly club music, but the attention to detail and intricate handling of digital sound seems to root this music elsewhere.

▲ Einsturzende Neubaten (1980–1983) *Strategies against Architecture*. Mute STUMM14.
Classic and shocking work from the pioneers of German 'industrial' music.

▲ Faust (1973, reissued 1993) *The Faust Tapes*. Recommended RER F2CD.
Faust used the studio as a creative tool in the 1970s and spliced together improvised music, electronics, folk music, musique concrete, punk, psychedelia, and jazz.

▲ Lou Reed (1975) *Metal Machine Music*. BMG ND 90670.
A celebrated album comprising layered guitar feedback, and nothing else.

▲ Raymond Scott (1969) *The Pygmy Taxi*. Corporation Basta Records.
This is one of Scott's noncommercial compositions, written as a musical experiment with his Electronium.

▲ Sonic Youth (1999) *Goodbye 20th Century*. SYR 4.
A rock and roll band perform experimental music by John Cage, Cornelius Cardew, Pauline Oliveros, Yoko Ono, Christian Wolff and others.

▲ DJ Spooky (1996) *Songs of a Dead Dreamer*. Asphodel ASP0961.
A New York DJ producing music that sounds quite unlike dance music, connecting with dub reggae and ambient music.

▲ Frank Zappa (1986) *Jazz from Hell*. Rykodisc RCD 10549.
Almost entirely created on the synclavier, and the only all-instrumental album ever to have a 'parental advisory' warning attached!

Critical theory

This began in the 1930s as an activity that aimed to change society through critique. Many of the early critical theorists were dissident Marxists, and the Frankfurt School, in particular, set out to establish a theoretical basis for potential revolutionary action. Later on, critical theory became more linked to aesthetics, and literary criticism in particular. In the 1960s, the critical theorist Jürgen Habermas (b. 1929) redefined the social theoretical approach to include self-reflection and psychoanalysis as emancipatory forces for the individual. He described an idealised 'communicative action' through which people freely exchange intentions and beliefs.

Meanwhile, literary criticism was also expanding to incorporate some of the radical social aspects of critical theory. In particular, there was an ever-increasing focus upon language. Issues of text and meaning became fundamental to the humanities and, once again, psychoanalysis was admitted, to the point that the literary side also became predominantly concerned with communication. Both sides of critical theory were interested in processes, and in particular, the way in which culture emerges or happens. This extended to a study of cultural artefacts (objects) and phenomena. The latter study is called *phenomenology*, which is a branch of philosophy that examines the appearances of things and the way we experience them.

Many recent advances in critical theory have come from a critique of, or reaction against, earlier critical theories. These reactions have taken various forms, ranging from accusations of elitism (after all, who are these people to assume that they can make a better world with their 'critical theories'?) to a reassertion of the thing the critical theorists themselves reacted against: logical positivism. This philosophy asserts that only mathematical, scientific or logical statements can contain truths, so the dependence of critical theory upon language and interpretation makes it meaningless.

Given the complexity and heat of the arguments, it can sometimes be difficult to see the point of engaging at all with these ideas. There are two main reasons why it is worth the effort: first, the theories (whether or not we agree with them) do succeed in identifying certain cultural tendencies and phenomena and, second, in doing so they help us come to an understanding about our own activities and productions. There are several key themes and a number of important texts in critical theory that are directly relevant to music. The key themes include broad cultural ideas such as modernism and postmodernism, structuralism and deconstruction, and, ultimately, the business of forming critical judgements and analysing music itself.

- Barthes, R. (1977) *Image, Music, Text.* London: Fontana.
- Finlayson, J. G. (2005) *Habermas: A Very Short Introduction.* Oxford: Oxford University Press.
- Heidegger, M. (1953) 'The Question Concerning Technology' in *Martin Heidegger: Basic Writings* (1978). London and New York: Routledge.
- Lechte, J. (1994) *Fifty Key Contemporary Thinkers.* London and New York: Routledge.
- McLuhan, M. (1964) *Understanding Media: The Extensions of Man.* New York: Mentor.
- Monaco, J. (2000) *How to Read a Film.* Third edition. Oxford: Oxford University Press.

Modernism and postmodernism

It is much easier to draw lines through history than it is to make sense of the cultural scene today. It is always hard to see what is immediately significant, to 'see the wood for the trees'. History conveniently sifts out what it deems to be relatively unimportant. Critical theorists have created the labels 'modernism' and 'postmodernism' to describe certain broad trends in Western culture of the past

100 years or so. These can be very helpful towards reaching an understanding of today's digital culture but – a word of warning – it is also possible to become seriously lost when applying them.

Modernism, as the name implies, describes a culture that believes in progress, in newness. Although it is mostly a historical term, there are many who argue that modernism is still a part of contemporary culture. The modernist impulse seems to have arisen first towards the end of the nineteenth century, but the event that gave it such a strong impetus was the First World War. The war exposed the cultural values of the nineteenth century as a failure, with a variety of consequences. For some, the only solution was political. The most striking example of this was the Russian revolution. For others, particularly those in the arts, it meant the development of radical, forward-looking movements, such as futurism, which aggressively rejected the past. This tendency was given further impetus by the Second World War, after which some artists even sought to remove evidence of their own hand in their work, seeking instead to create music using less subjective laws, such as those of mathematics or chance.

It is hard to encapsulate the modernist vision in a few sentences, but at its most intense it seems to seek a core emotional truth, uncorrupted by irrelevant cultural information. An essay called 'Purism', written in 1924 by the modernist architect Le Corbusier and the painter Amédée Ozenfant, sums up this quite extreme idea as follows: if you show a billiard ball to a native of Papua New Guinea who has never encountered any other human beings beyond his own village, he will not understand that it is a *billiard* ball. He will, on the other hand, understand the form of a *sphere* (even if he has another name for it). The writers called the sphere a *primary form*, and its function as a billiard ball a *secondary cultural association*. Modernism, broadly speaking, emphasises primary forms at the expense of secondary cultural associations.

One of the most influential writers and thinkers about modernist music was Theodor Adorno (1903–1969). In his book, *The Philosophy of Modern Music* (1949), he made a critique of mass or popular culture, arguing that it manipulates people by offering them an illusion of choice in a process he called *pseudo-individualisation*. He described 'cultural industries' that feed the needs created and satisfied by capitalism, and contrasted these with the 'true needs' of freedom, creativity or genuine happiness. In musical terms, this led to a comparison between the composers Igor Stravinsky and Arnold Schoenberg, with the latter emerging clearly as a standard-bearer for modernism. Interestingly, both composers ended up in Hollywood: Stravinsky through choice, Schoenberg as a fugitive from Nazi Germany. While neither composer achieved commercial success in the film industry (both tried),[6] Stravinsky was generally happy and successful in Tinsel-Town, whereas Schoenberg loathed the place.

Post-modernism, or postmodernism (as it is generally written), is a reaction to and development from modernism. In many ways, it represents a rehabilitation of, and glorying in, the 'secondary cultural associations' of Le Corbusier and Ozenfant's essay. The characteristics of postmodernism are eclecticism, digression, collage, pastiche, irony – in short, a move away from a simple line of historical progression that modernists often called the grand narrative. Postmodernism is highly diverse and suggests that individuals first *construct* their knowledge of the world and, then, in order to make a critique, *deconstruct* it again. Postmodernism asserts that no single global explanation of human behaviour is credible and that technology leads to *reproduction*, rather than the modernist *production*. The leading postmodern theorist Jean-François Lyotard describes the social consequences of postmodernism in *The Postmodern Condition* (1979), declaring that all previous, unified conceptions of society as an organic whole, or a system, or even (as in Marx) as opposing classes, have lost credibility. In postmodernist thinking, there is no possibility of an ultimate truth, and the digital age has brought about a state of ever-increasing complexity.

In music, postmodernism does not take on any one particular style or technique; rather it is just the condition of things *after* modernism. Postmodern music may include more or less any type of music and resists hierarchies, especially those based on notions of 'high' and 'low' art. The music may contain traits of *bricolage* (do-it-yourself), and *polystylism* (multiple styles in a single work), and involve *recontextualisation* (presenting familiar material in a different context), but it need not *necessarily* do any of these. The main quality is a cultural *knowingness*, a cultural awareness, in short: cultural knowledge. It is hard to resist the idea that we live in a postmodern age.

One useful text in the study of postmodernism in music is *Image, Music, Text* (1977) by Roland Barthes. This includes the seminal essay 'The Death of the Author', in which he states:

> The text is a tissue of quotations drawn from the innumerable centres of culture. [. . .] [It] is made of multiple writings, drawn from many cultures and entering into mutual relations of dialogue, parody, contestation, but there is one place where this multiplicity is focused and that place is the reader, not, as was hitherto said, the author. The reader is the space on which all the quotations that make up a writing are inscribed without any of them being lost; a text's unity lies not in its origin but in its destination.

The 'listener' may be substituted for the 'reader' here. The word 'text' is used by Barthes to refer to any kind of cultural artefact, not just literature. The phrase 'innumerable centres of culture' suggests a highly fragmented picture, one in which there is no single culture but instead many different cultures or sub-cultures.

A sub-culture is a set of people with a distinct set of behaviours or beliefs that recognisably sets them apart from the larger culture. Where this is in opposition to the dominant culture, it would be called a counterculture. There are many aspects of the digital music scene, which suggest that people place themselves within particular sub-cultures. Musically speaking, these would be defined by styles and techniques, but this is only part of the story, because lifestyle concerns are also a defining characteristic of sub-cultures.

- Adorno, T. (2003) *The Philosophy of Modern Music*. London: Athlone.
- Gablik, S. (1984) *Has Modernism Failed?* London: Thames & Hudson.
- Gablik, S. (1991) *The Reenchantment of Art*. London: Thames & Hudson.
- Kittler, F. A. (1999) *Gramophone, Film, Typewriter*. Stanford, CA: Stanford University Press.
- Lyotard, J.-F. (1979) *The Postmodern Condition*. Minneapolis, MN: Minnesota University Press.
- Lyotard, J.-F. (1984) *Driftworks*. New York: Semiotext(e).

Structuralism and deconstruction

Structuralism, like most critical theory, has a history that goes back to the nineteenth century. However, the aspect that has significantly influenced today's music arose during the 1960s and afterwards. Structuralism focuses on the way in which structures influence human behaviour. The structures themselves may be social, cultural, linguistic or mental. They are layered upon the deeper elements that make up language, literature and so on. In other words, structures are conventions of meaning or patterns of relationships. Structuralism 'reads' these structures just as one would read a text, literally deciphering them for evidence of the underlying elements. An important part of this process is called *semiology*, or the study of 'signs'. A sign is anything that is used to stand for something else. Codes, such as literary or cultural codes, give a context to these signs. According to Gérard Genette (b. 1930), structuralism is 'a study of the cultural construction or identification of meaning according to the relations of signs that constitute the meaning-spectrum of the culture'.[7]

Structuralism successfully opened up whole areas, such as anthropology, which were previously unavailable to cultural studies. However, debate continues to rage about the merits of structuralism in relation to literary criticism. The application of the linguistic theories of Ferdinand de Saussure (1857–1913) and the anthropological discoveries of Claude Lévi-Strauss (b. 1908) to narrative, in particular, has led to the argument that a text can only be said to be truly new if it creates a new structure, as opposed to new characters or new style. Since most stories are structurally derived from a handful of archetypal narratives or myths, it follows that the text is to be seen merely as the function of a system. The structures may be universal and timeless, and it is they, rather than the individual, that produce the meaning.

An important tool of structuralism is *deconstruction*. This is a very difficult term to define succinctly, but according to the leading writer Jacques Derrida (1930–2004), it is not a destruction, but rather a kind of analytical reading. It employs a questioning of the apparent essences of a text, by finding elements *within the text itself* that seem to differ from its own intentions, thus laying bare a different meaning. As such, it has become a popular way of describing the process of dismantling someone or something by exposing their inherent weaknesses, or just what makes them up. A great deal of artistic product of the past fifty years or so purports to 'deconstruct' meaning, convention, the artist, society or the work of art itself.

Derrida himself moved structuralism into a new phase, usually called post-structuralism, which reappraised some of its key assumptions. Post-structural thought says that the underlying structures are *themselves* the products of culture. In particular, it asserts that the author's intentions are secondary to the meanings perceived by the reader. Barthes described a 'metalanguage', or high-order language that is used to explain language. One result of these developments is that post-structural theories themselves are very hard to read and to understand.

One philosopher whose work fits into this school and who has had a considerable influence on developments in music (and other performance arts) was Gilles Deleuze (1925–1995). His book A *Thousand Plateaus* (1980), written with the economist Félix Guattari, describes a vision of the world that is modelled on a *rhizome*. This is a term from botany, which describes a network of interconnected tubers (such as a lawn). Deleuze suggests that in the rhizome theories and research are connected in such a way as to allow for multiple, non-hierarchical entry and exit points. Knowledge is transferred in a manner similar to horizontal gene transfer, in which an organism transmits genetic information to another cell that is not its offspring. Although Deleuze does not mention the Internet, the description of the rhizome seems uncannily similar to the way in which cyberspace operates today.

Many of the ideas of structuralism and deconstruction have found their way into the writings of artists, critics and media theorists. A good example was Marshall McLuhan (1911–1980), whose famous statement 'the medium is the message', discussed in his book *Understanding Media: The Extensions of Man* (1964), became the basis for much subsequent media theory. Fundamental to his thinking at this point was the idea that percept is more important than concept, in other words that the experience itself takes preference over its subsequent rationalisation. Another key concept was the 'global village', a vision of a future in which society would be organised through 'electronic interdependence', when new media would replace the visual with the aural or the oral. As McLuhan reputedly put it: 'The future masters of technology will have to be light-hearted and intelligent. The machine easily masters the grim and the dumb'.[8]

Jacques Attali (b. 1943) is even more direct about the social role of music. In *Noise: The Political Economy of Music* (1977) he theorises that the only thing common to all music is that it gives structure to noise and that the musical process of structuring noise is also the political process for structuring community. He suggests that music parallels human society, is structured like it, and changes when it does.[9]

For Attali, the way in which music is made in today's society is fundamentally self-deceiving, because modern distribution techniques 'contribute to the establishment of a system of eavesdropping and social surveillance'.[10] Attali was writing before the download culture began and uses Muzak as an example to illustrate his point, but his words still have considerable relevance today:

What is called music today is too often only a disguise for the monologue of power. However, and this is the supreme irony of it all, never before have musicians tried so hard to communicate with their audience, and never before has that communication been so deceiving. Music now seems hardly more than a somewhat clumsy excuse for the self-glorification of musicians and the growth of a new industrial sector. Still, it is an activity that is essential for knowledge and social relations.[11]

● Digital minimalism

■ Attali, J. (1985) *Noise: The Political Economy of Music*. Minneapolis,MN: University of Minnesota Press.
■ Barthes, R. (1991) *The Responsibility of Forms*. Berkeley, CA: University of California Press.
■ Buchanan, I. and Swiboda, M. (eds) (2004) *Deleuze and Music*. Edinburgh: Edinburgh University Press.
■ Deleuze, G. and Guattari, F. (1980) *Mille Plateaux*. Paris: Éditions de Minuit.
■ Derrida, J. (2001 new edition) *Writing and Difference*. New York: Routledge.
■ Deutscher, P. (2005) *How to Read Derrida*. London: Granta.
■ Genette, G. (1983) *Narrative Discourse: An Essay in Method*. Ithaca, NY: Cornell University Press.
■ Saussure, F. de (1991) *Signs, Systems and Arbitrariness*. Cambridge: Cambridge University Press.

Critical judgement

The sheer diversity of postmodern and contemporary culture can be bewildering. It is difficult for an individual to locate himself or herself when things change so rapidly, and newness is always present, where names have to be invented in order to describe things. The digital world is so messy and vague, teeming with information and data, to the point where even 'secondary cultural associations' are hard to pinpoint. One thing, however, is certain: sooner or later, a digital musician is going to have to exercise critical judgement, even if only to decide what *not* to absorb. In fact, making music itself is a decision-making process, and it could be argued that the critical judgements one makes on the way define the quality of both process and product. In many senses, a musician is the sum of all the critical judgements he or she has ever made. An understanding of how to reach good and effective critical judgements is therefore essential.

Contemporary thinking on this subject has developed much more slowly than the art it contemplates. The field of aesthetics is still underpinned by thoughts and writings from the eighteenth century and even before. Although these ideas about critical judgement are very old, a summary of their key points will be illuminating. They are epitomised by two important philosophers, whose approaches to critical judgement will be recognised as still having considerable relevance. It would not be an overstatement to say that these two represent the opposite poles of opinion on the subject.

In 1757, the philosopher David Hume (1711–1756) published an essay entitled 'On the Standard of Taste'. Hume began by outlining a sceptical position that will be very familiar to the reader: the beauty of something is equal to the sensation of pleasure it gives. On this basis, all judgements of artistic products seem to be worth exactly the same, because anybody's opinion of anything is equal. Nobody is ever wrong about anything in art or music.

This view has the merit of being quite simple and very radical. It also gives total power to everybody in the business of making critical judgements. Hume, however, while stating that evaluative responses are neither true nor false, accepted that common sense dictates that some judgements are better than others; otherwise there would not be general agreement about good and bad works of art. He went on to outline five factors that enable people to improve their critical judgement-making: 'strong sense, united to delicate sentiment, improved by practice, perfected by comparison, and cleared of all prejudice'.[12] He did point out, however, that the ability to make critical judgements is not simply a matter of training or education, but there are natural differences between people and their tastes, and there are certain unavoidable preferences due to a person's age (generational differences) and culture (cultural preferences).

On the face of it, there seems to be little to dispute in Hume's argument, and, indeed, the Humean view of critical judgement is the one that generally prevails in culture today. However, there is one significant omission in his theory, which boils down to the clichéd question: is beauty only in the eye of the beholder or (in music) the ear of the listener? By making an individual's critical judgements and taste the decisive factor, standards or no standards, Hume seemed to refute the idea that something can be beautiful *in itself*. This was entirely in keeping with his general philosophical position, so it took another philosopher, Immanuel Kant (1724–1804), to explore the opposing idea.

In his book *Critique of Judgment* (1790), Kant put forward a series of complex arguments that defend a notion of *inherent beauty*. Kant's view was that something may be beautiful in itself, and human perception must develop to unlock that beauty. The sensation of aesthetic taste, or pleasure, is ideally the result of a free play of imagination and understanding that judges an object based on its form rather than its purpose. These judgements must be both *universal* and *necessary* if we are to care about the beauty of, say, a sunset. 'Common sense', therefore, was interpreted literally by Kant as a universal sensing (rather than understanding) of things. Critical judgements may relate to human cognition, but the object being critically judged can be beautiful *a priori* (before everything else, including human perception). For Kant, a work of art becomes universally pleasing when it allows room for reflective judgement or, as he famously said, when it shows 'purposiveness without a purpose'.[13]

Kant's position is much more complicated than Hume's, but one of its key points is that it allows for *transcendence*. The beauty of something is not necessarily dependent upon our appreciation, and is not subject to something as arbitrary as taste. Kant discusses 'the sublime', which he says is something that seems to overwhelm us, that we cannot get our heads around, such as a violent storm or a very large building. In Kant's view, it is not really the storm or the building that is sublime, but rather the sense of scale we get from the ideas of absolute totality or absolute freedom that they seem to embody. However big the building may be, we know it is small compared to absolute totality; however powerful the storm, it is weak compared to absolute freedom. Thus, in Kant's view, we should aim to base our judgements literally *in* the common sense. This is a skill which needs cultivation, and which may also be moral. Beauty may also be a sign of moral goodness. In Kant's philosophy (unlike Hume's), there is room for a faith in God.

Although both these philosophical positions are somewhat old-fashioned, it is surprising to what extent they still represent the poles of critical judgement. For most people, judgements will be formed in some way between the two. There are some situations where a *relativism* in forming judgements is useful, especially when ignorance, or a lack of cultural knowledge, might lead to sudden or rash verdicts; on the other hand, there are times when a sense of the beauty of something may come through *in spite of oneself*, where it is not possible to be sure of one's own taste. One thing is for sure: simple 'I like it/I don't like it' judgements, while not wrong in themselves, are almost never enough. Mere 'instinctive' reactions have to be gone beyond in order to improve critical judgements. One way of doing this is to use analysis.

● Balloon debate

■ Gràham, G. (2005) *Philosophy of the Arts: An Introduction to Aesthetics.* London: Routledge.
■ Meyer, L. (1994) *Music, the Arts and Ideas.* Chicago, IL: University of Chicago Press.
■ Wenzel, C. (2005) *An Introduction to Kant's Aesthetics: Core Concepts and Problems.* New York: Blackwell.

Analysis

The purpose of music analysis is to reveal how music works. In traditional notated music, the elements of harmony, melody, rhythm and so on could be analysed with reference to a score. This led to an assumption that the methodologies of music analysis are abstract. In other words, it was considered acceptable to analyse the music divorced either from its social and political context, or from its effects on the listener. In fact, even traditional musical analysis usually made some effort to account for such apparently extra-musical aspects, but the way they were described was sometimes so impressionistic as to be useless as analysis.

This is one of the great challenges for analysis: how to go beyond the merely descriptive towards something that has some 'scientific' foundation. Both ethnomusicologists and analysts have consequently adopted many of the approaches outlined by critical theory. Various methods of music analysis have emerged, ranging from the structuralist (such as Lerdahl and Jackendoff's 'generative' attempts[14] to specify the linguistic structures that an informed listener hears in a piece of music), through to the anthropological (such as the work of John Blacking[15] and many others that attempt to analyse music in terms of its social function in world cultures).

When analysing electronic and electro-acoustic music, however, some of these methods and approaches can become rather problematic. The tools that work for, say, tonal music or folk music are less satisfactory for analysing a music based on sounds or samples. Harmony, melody and rhythm are not necessarily the main constituents of this music. An analysis of a timbre presents specific difficulties that soon challenge the capabilities of the written word. A piece constructed from digitally processed water sounds lacks the note-to-note procedures that lend themselves well to a database-driven, structuralist approach. The social function of a musical language that is not obviously vernacular can be hard to articulate. The difficulties that are faced by analysts of this music therefore include establishing typologies of sound and standardised analytical terminologies and procedures, through to identifying common musical languages or sets of shared practices.

Some notes about semiotics

The 'semiotics' of a piece of music refers to the distinctive and recognisable *signs* that contribute to its behaviours and stylistic attributes, within a given musical culture or sub-culture. Semiotics has been applied successfully to the analysis of both classical and popular music. In his *Introductory Notes to the Semiotics of Music*, Philip Tagg comments:

> [We need to discover] which sounds mean what to whom and in which context. And this, obviously, is a semiotic matter. That is why [this text] is devoted to (a) basic semiotic terminology, (b) a definition of 'music' and 'musical structures', (c) a sign typology of music, (d) how music can be studied semiotically without knowing what a diminished seventh is.[16]

Tagg's exhaustive analysis of the theme tune for the television series *Kojak*[17] demonstrates a thorough application of these ideas.

Despite its potential, semiotics has so far been relatively under-used in the analysis of digital, electronic or electro-acoustic music. Some useful introductions include:

- Chandler, D. (2001) *Semiotics for Beginners*. New York: Routledge.
- Nattiez, J-J. (1990) *Music and Discourse: Towards a Semiology of Music*. Princeton, NJ: Princeton University Press.
- Monelle, R. (1992) 'Linguistics and Semiotics in Music' in *Contemporary Music Studies, V*. Chur, Switzerland: Harwood Academic.

■ Monelle, R. (2000) *The Sense of Music: Semiotic Essays.* Princeton, NJ: Princeton University Press.

Jean-Jacques Nattiez defines analysis as a 'metalanguage' applied to a musical fact. This metalanguage adopts different types of discourse in its examination of the object, in this case a piece of music with all its many variables. Analysis adopts a methodology to make a 'semiological interrogation' of the music. Nattiez devotes an entire chapter of *Music and Discourse: Towards a Semiology of Music* to a discussion of the 'sound-object' (after Schaeffer), in which he identifies its *neutral, poietic* and *aesthesic* levels. 'Poietic' refers to that which underpins the making of a work: the deliberations or intentions that lie behind it, the operations on its materials, its production. The 'aesthesic' is the enjoyment, contemplation or, indeed, analysis of the experience of a work. He concludes:

> On the neutral level, it would be easy enough to identify and describe the sound-objects that make up these works, to describe the laws governing their succession and their integration into various syntactic arrangements, on various levels. We would then, from this *arrested* description of the material, *proceed to extract* those constituent traits that account for a sense of continuity within the succession of isolated moments that make up the work. But this essentially esthesic explanation (we perceive a 'sense of continuity') will never be possible unless one first has access to a material description of the work; that is to an analysis of its neutral level.[18]

The 'neutral level' presumably equates to a 'scientific' analysis of the sounds themselves, which raises a problem of distinction between the understanding and organisation of sound explored in earlier chapters of the current book. This breaking down of the process of analysis into two distinct levels is reminiscent of structuralism, which leads us back to another layer of theory. What is needed here are some practical approaches to the analysis of digital music.

Analytical approaches

A *parametric* analysis is somewhat similar to Nattiez's 'neutral level', in that it tells the reader what happens when and, perhaps, how. The conventional musical mileposts of bars or measures, key changes and themes, are absent, so the best method is to give timings to indicate the locations of significant sonic events. However, it is important not to ignore the musical features of the work, so any sign of repetition or variation, modality or tonality, rhythmic structures or regular patterns, even phrases and melodies, should be indicated as an overlay on the timing graph. As this comment suggests, graph paper may be a useful way of laying out such an analysis, with verbal comments or descriptions of significant events.

Whereas a parametric analysis is *perceptive*, in other words it objectively describes what we perceive, a more subjective approach is an *affective* analysis. This focuses upon the way in which the music affects the listener, but also to some extent on the way in which it achieves that effect. This can be linked to the perceived intentions of the artist, or to the cultural context for the work, but mostly this is a highly subjective account. This subjectivity, however, does not inevitably produce vague, unscientific, information. A group affective analysis, in particular, can be revealing, as common reactions and threads are drawn out by a neutral figure (usually an educator). In some situations, this kind of analysis may be best deployed *before* the parametric analysis, in order to ensure the listeners' full attention is engaged by the work. The degree of interpretation will often depend upon the method used, whether a graphic score or a language-based description.

A different approach is implied by a socio-cultural or anthroplogical analysis. Here, the interest is not so much in the music itself but rather in the social and cultural position it occupies. Once again, semiotics may be a useful tool, but also some of the methods of social science. A *quantitative* method uses empirical observation and mathematical or statistical information to support its hypotheses. This is probably a less practical (although not impossible) method for music analysis than the *qualitative* methods, which investigate the 'why' and the 'how' of decision-making. A qualitative analysis relies on case studies supported by interviews and other data-gathering, so it is important for any socio-cultural analysis to have access to this kind of information. A typical socio-cultural or anthropological analysis might explore, for example, why and how a particular musical genre arose from a particular group at a particular time.

Comparative analyses, which treat musical examples as cultural 'texts', can be helpful. The aim is to compare and contrast two or more pieces of music. The first step is to identify the frame of reference for the comparison, which might be an idea or theme, a specific question or even a theory. Next, establish the grounds for the comparison by giving reasons for the choices. Now, develop the argument by exploring the relationships between the two chosen pieces, indicating where they appear to complement or contradict one another. This can be presented as a separate discussion of the two works, or as a point-by-point comparison. Finally, some appropriate conclusions should be drawn. This method is a staple of literary criticism and forms the basis of many examination questions and student essays in the humanities. However, the phrase also crops up in computer science, economics and social science with a somewhat different meaning and often used for predicting the behaviour of a system.

All these analytical approaches presume that the 'work' being analysed is a fixed entity that already exists in a completed state. This is by no means the only way to approach analysis, and the creative or making process itself contains an analytical element. *Practical* analysis therefore links directly to the notions of reflective practice, critical engagement and cultural content discussed earlier. Even the understanding, representation and processing of digital sound itself has a considerable analytical relevance, and the computer can be cautiously introduced as an analytical tool at any stage of the process. A spectrogram may be an 'analytical' representation of a sound, but it also needs to be decoded and the sound placed in a context if the analysis is to reveal anything very much about how the music works. Nevertheless, there is a perpetual loop between creation and analysis which is part of the musical process itself and may be captured in some form for analytical purposes.

One excellent way to begin the process of analysis, which can incorporate all of the above approaches to some extent, is the 'Evocative Transcription' project given below. By creating a system of graphic symbols to represent the parameters of the music, analysts can both notate an 'aural score' and develop their listening skills and perceptions. Extending this into a Flash movie can further create a useful 'real-time' map of the work. The evocative transcription can also be useful evidence of analytical listening.

● Evocative transcription

Analytical listening

Faced with a purely aural music (i.e., no score), analysis finds itself severely challenged. The scientist David Bohm once wrote: 'The expression of the new quantum concepts is beset with severe difficulties, because much of our customary language and thinking is predicated on the tacit assumption that classical concepts are substantially correct.'[19]

This is also true in digital music, where the use of a traditional analytical method is inappropriate to the subject and yet often there is no clear substitute. To avoid making the mistake Bohm identifies, it is necessary to start first with the sounds themselves. Digital music is very often built from the smallest element upwards, rather than from the larger structure down. In other words, artists will, more often than not, work directly with sonic materials when building a musical work, rather than sitting down to create, say, a symphony.

So, listening, and especially repeated listening, must become the starting point of analysis (it is surprising how often music analysis has traditionally been undertaken without much listening). Once again, primacy is given to the ear. Listening analytically is a skill which takes time and practice to develop but will greatly help the analyst to become aware of the processes and manipulations applied to sounds and then understand the creative reasoning and cultural significance of those processes and manipulations. Critical judgement is likely to form part of an analysis, so it may be observed that the purpose of analytical listening is twofold: to increase one's understanding of the technical and creative aspects of the music but also to improve one's own musical skills.

The following long (but nowhere near long enough to cover everything) listening list not only illustrates some of the key ideas about modernism and postmodernism, structuralism and deconstruction, discussed in the previous sections but also adds up to a mini-history of the evolution of electronic and electroacoustic music in the twentieth century. It is unlikely that the reader will listen to *all* these works, but any one of them will repay close critical study. Some brief descriptive notes are included to indicate the salient features, but there is no substitute for careful and repeated listening with, perhaps, some attempt to analyse what is heard.

It should be remembered that modernism and postmodernism are not musical styles, nor words that artists and composers use to describe their work, but rather terms from critical and cultural theory that seem to sum up broad tendencies in art. In fact, all the pieces below will probably be heard to exhibit characteristics of both 'isms'. Some useful questions to ask when listening are: What is the artist's intention? How well is it realised? What is the cultural context for the work? What are its compositional techniques? What is the musical language?

▲ Pierre Schaeffer (1948) 'Étude aux chemins de fer' from *Cinq études de bruits* on *OHM: The Early Gurus of Electronic Music: 1948–1980*. Ellipsis Arts M1473 O46 2000.
This was the first time recorded sound was assembled into a musical composition. The sounds included steam engines, whistles and railway noises.

▲ Pierre Schaeffer and Pierre Henry (1950) *Symphonie pour un homme seul* on Pierre Schaeffer: *L'Oeuvre musicale*. EMF EM114.
A 12-movement musical account of a man's day using recorded sounds. This was performed live, and originally required real-time manipulation of many turntables and mixing desks.

▲ John Cage (1951) *Imaginary Landscape No. 4 for 12 radios*. Hat Hut Records hatArt CD 6179.
Two performers are stationed at each radio, one for dialling the radio-stations, the second performer controlling amplitude and 'timbre'. Durations are written in conventional notation, using notes, placed on a five-line staff. The score gives notations for tuning (controlled by player 1) as well as volume and tone colour (controlled by player 2).

▲ Otto Luening (1952) *Low Speed*. CRI CD 611.
Luening and Ussachevsky worked in the Columbia-Princeton Electronic Music Center on tape composition. This piece explores slowed down flute sounds.

▲ Vladimir Ussachevsky (1952) *Sonic Contours*. CRI CD 611.
Ussachevsky worked with tape feedback, looping, and echo effects in this piece that combines piano and varispeed vocals.

▲ John Cage (1953) 'Williams Mix' on *OHM: The Early Gurus of Electronic Music: 1948–1980*. Ellipsis Arts M1473 O46 2000.
Tape fragments of various sounds are recombined in a random order (determined by coin tosses).

▲ Earle Brown (1953) *Octet I for Tape*. New World Records 80650.
An early tape piece for eight loudspeakers surrounding an audience.

▲ Karlheinz Stockhausen (1954) *Studie II*. Stockhausen Verlag CD3.
An early example of *Elektronische Musik* (electronic music) which used sine tones superimposed in groups of five.

▲ Hugh Le Caine, *Dripsody* (1955) EMF EM115.
Created from the sound of a single water drop, and using splicing and speed control to make various rhythms and melodies.

▲ Karlheinz Stockhausen (1955–1956) 'Gesang der Jünglinge' on *Stockhausen: Elektronische Musik 1952–1960*. Stockhausen-Verlag CD3.
This combines electronic sounds and a recording of a boy's voice. It is a serial 2 composition, but with strong connections drawn between the sound of the sine wave oscillators and the timbre of the boy's voice. It not only serialises durations, loudness, and thickness of texture, but also the spatialisation.

▲ Louis and Bébé Barron, *Forbidden Planet* (1956) Planet Records.
This film was the first motion picture to feature an electronic music score.

▲ Edgard Varèse (1958) *Poéme Electronique*. Decca 460208.
Composed for the Philips Pavilion of the 1958 World's Fair, a massive multi-media environment featuring projected images, film, and multi-channel sound. As the listeners walk through the space, the sound moves around them.

▲ Luciano Berio (1958) *Thema – Omaggio a Joyce*. RCA Victor Red Seal 09026-68302-2.
All the sounds are derived from a recording of Cathy Berberian reciting a passage from James Joyce's *Ulysses*. This is a compendium of tape splicing techniques.

▲ Iannis Xenakis (1958) 'Concrète PH' on *Xenakis: Electronic Music*. Electronic Music Foundation, EMF CD 003.
A musique concrète piece made from the sound of burning charcoal.

▲ György Ligeti (1958) *Artikulation*. Schotts Music Ltd. WER 60161-50.
A very short, but highly virtuosic tape composition, made from small electronic sounds that are combined to resemble utterances.

▲ Karlheinz Stockhausen (1959–1960) *Kontakte* (for piano, percussion and tape). Wergo 6009.
The 'contact' in the title is between the taped sounds and the acoustic sounds of piano and percussion. By adding the two together, a richer palette of sounds is discovered.

▲ Pierre Henry, *Variations pour une Porte et un Soupir* (*Variations for a Door and a Sigh*) (1963) Harmonia Mundi.
This is a tour-de-force of tape splicing and editing techniques.

▲ Ornette Coleman (1961) *Free Jazz: A Collective Improvisation* Atlantic 81227 3609-2.
Two independent jazz quartets play opposite each other (one on each stereo channel), improvising on a limited selection of directions, without harmonic structure, driven by melodic and rhythmic concerns, and each musician contributing according to own style. Highly influential in subsequent jazz improvisational technique. Left channel: Ornette Coleman (alto saxophone), Don Cherry (pocket trumpet), Scott LaFaro (bass), Billy Higgins (drums); right channel: Freddie Hubbard (trumpet), Eric Dolphy (bass clarinet), Charlie Haden (bass), Ed Blackwell (drums).

▲ Steve Reich (1965) 'Come Out' on *Steve Reich: Early Works, 1987*. Elektra/Nonesuch 9 79169-2.
An early piece using phasing: looped tape recordings of speech (the phrase 'Come Out to show them') gradually move out of synchronisation. This process is then

repeated and repeated until the multiple layerings remove the meaning of the words.

▲ The Righteous Brothers (1965) *You've Lost That Lovin' Feeling.* Polydor 847 248.

An example of the celebrated 'wall of sound' studio treatment (rich vocals and orchestral accompaniment) characteristic of Phil Spector.

▲ The Beach Boys (1966) *Good Vibrations.* EMI CDEMTVD 51.

Brian Wilson's production was highly advanced for its time, reflected in the fact that it took six months to record this single. It involves unusual instrumentation for a pop song, including an electro-theremin. The mix is mono, but all 5 parts are still clearly audible.

▲ The Beatles (1966) 'Tomorrow Never Knows' on *Revolver.* Capitol/EMI ST 2576.

Early psychedelia, heavily influenced by Indian music and Eastern philosophy. The Beatles' first experiments with tape loops.

▲ Frank Zappa (1968) *Frank Zappa and the Mothers of Invention: We're Only in It for the Money.* Ryco RCD 40024.

This album features radical audio editing and production techniques. The album was highly virtuosic and satirical of contemporary cultural fashions (flower-power and hippie-dom). There also seem to be some tongue-in-cheek references to 'serious' electronic music.

▲ Can (1969) 'Father Cannot Yell' on *Cannibalism* (released in 1980). Spoon CD 004.

Can was a German rock group who had considerable influence on electronic and experimental music.

▲ Alvin Lucier (1970) *I Am Sitting in a Room.* Lovely Music CD 1013.

'Several sentences of recorded speech are simultaneously played back into a room and re-recorded there many times. As the repetitive process continues, those sounds common to the original spoken statement and those implied by the structural dimensions of the room are reinforced. The others are gradually eliminated. The space acts as a filter; the speech is transformed into pure sound. All the recorded segments are spliced together in the order in which they were made and constitute the work.'[20]

▲ Miles Davis (1970) *Bitches Brew.* Columbia C2K 65774.

The Bitches Brew album was not only a landmark in the establishment of 'fusion' jazz, but also important in its pioneering use of studio technology, led by Teo Macero.

▲ Luc Ferrari (1970) 'Presque rien No. 1' (Almost Nothing) on *OHM – The Early Gurus of Electronic Music: 1948–1980.* Ellipsis Arts M1473 O46 2000.

This documents a day on a beach. Ferrari's sound diary includes the sounds of insects and other animals, traffic, and human voices. He referred to this genre of his work, characterised by the use of sounds to tell a story, as 'anecdotal music'. In his words, 'The problem is to try to express ideas, feelings, passing intuitions by different means to observe everyday life in all its realities, whether they are social, psychological or sentimental.'

▲ Wendy Carlos (1972) *Timesteps.* East Side Digital ESD81362.

This was composed for Stanley Kubrick's film *A Clockwork Orange* and used a vocoder to create 'synthesized speech'.

▲ Pink Floyd (1973) *Dark Side of the Moon*. Harvest/Capitol 3609.
Classic concept album that sits between electronic music and blues rock. Employs many musique concrète techniques alongside double-tracking, flanging, panning and reverb effects. 'To this day, audiophiles use The Dark Side of the Moon as a reference standard to test the fidelity of audio equipment despite the fact that it was originally mixed from third-generation tape with Dolby noise reduction.'[21]

▲ Kraftwerk (1974) *Autobahn*. EMI CDP 7 46153 2.
Influential German electronic music group, particularly known for their 1970s work which has had a broad impact on popular music.

▲ The Residents (1976) *The Third Reich and Roll*. Torso CD 405.
Long-standing American underground avant garde group, who consistently maintain their anonymity. Many of their works are cultural commentaries utilising samples and media hi-jinks.

▲ John Chowning (1977) *Stria*. Wergo 2012-50.
This is a classic of FM synthesis and localisation, using the Golden Mean (the ratio 1: 1.618. . .) to determine pitch and duration.

▲ Brian Eno (1978) *Ambient 1/Music for Airports*. Virgin Records EEGCD 17. 1.
Influential English composer, producer, engineer, writer, and visual artist. He is known as the father of 'ambient' music. His production credits include U2 and The Talking Heads.

▲ Gavin Bryars (1978) *The Sinking of the Titanic*. EG Records – CDVE938.
Uses a collection of 'found materials' on tape along with a live ensemble, plus sounds recorded underwater. The music consists of immensely slowed-down hymn tunes and other sonic materials.

▲ Iannis Xenakis (1978) *Mycenae-Alpha*. mode 98/99.
This was the first piece ever to be made with the UPIC computer system. Instead of a keyboard to perform the music, the UPIC's performance device is a mouse and/or a digital drawing board, which trace the composer's graphic score into the program. This then interprets the drawings as real time instructions for sound synthesis.

▲ David Behrman (1978) 'On the Other Ocean' on *OHM: The Early Gurus of Electronic Music: 1948–1980*. Ellipsis Arts M1473 O46 2000.
An improvisation on acoustic instruments with pitch-detection controlling a computer, which in turn controls two handmade synthesisers. This is an early example of an interactive work with live computer response to human performers.

▲ Iannis Xenakis (1977/8) *La Legende d'Eer*. Mode 148.
A 7-channel electro-acoustic composition designed to be played as a multimedia piece with lasers in a specially constructed building called 'Le Diatope'. There are three sound sources: instrumental sounds, noises, and electronically generated sounds.

▲ Robert Ashley (1978/80) *Perfect Lives*. Lovely Music DVD4917.
A highly innovative crossmedia 'television opera' in seven 30-minute episodes.

▲ Jonathan Harvey (1979) *Mortuos Plango, Vivos Voco*. Wergo CD WER2025-2.
'In this work Harvey manipulated recordings of the great bell of Winchester Cathedral – on which is inscribed HORA AVOLANTES NUMERO, MORTUOS

PLANGO, VIVOS AD PRECES VOCO ("I count the fleeting hours, I lament the dead, I call the living to prayer") – and the singing of his son Dominic, at that time a chorister at Winchester. By creating "synthetic simulations" of the bell sounds and of Dominic's singing, Harvey could make spectra or partials from the bell's sound appear to "morph" into his son's singing, or vice versa.'[22]

▲ Charles Dodge (1979) *Any Resemblance is Purely Coincidental.* New Albion 043.
Scored for piano and tape, the latter consisting of electronic sounds and a computer-transformed rendering of Enrico Caruso's 1907 recording of the aria 'Vesti la giubba' from Leoncavallo's *I Pagliacci.*

▲ King Tubby/Roots Radics (1981) *Dangerous Dub.* Greensleeves GREWCD229.
King Tubby is a Jamaican sound engineer who has been highly influential in the development of Jamaican dub. This has heavy reverb and other effects overlaying a remixed reggae/ska track from which vocals and lead instruments are omitted.

▲ Pierre Boulez (1981) *Répons.* Deutsche Grammophon 457605.
A huge work for nine percussionists, orchestra and digital sound system.

▲ Grandmaster Flash (1981) *The Adventures of Grandmaster Flash on the Wheels of Steel.* Sugar Hill Records 310917.
Grandmaster Flash is a New York DJ artist who was instrumental in the development of turntable technique during the 1970s–80s. This track uses samples from Queen, CHIC and Blondie, among others.

▲ Laurie Anderson (1982) *Big Science.* Warner 2KNM.
An important figure in the establishment of performance art, Anderson's stripped-down, ironic tone and technologically quirky delivery helped define the idea of the postmodern in the 1980s.

▲ The Art of Noise (1984) 'Beat Box (Diversion One)' on *The Best of The Art of Noise.* China/Polydor 837 367-2.
An influential electronic music group formed by producer Trevor Horn, helping to define the potential of new digital sampling technology in dance and popular forms in the 1980s. The name of the group is, obviously, a reference to Luigi Russolo's essay of the same name.

▲ Trevor Wishart (1986) 'Vox 5' on *Computer Music Currents, vol. 4, 1989.* Wergo 2024-50.
An English composer who has contributed significantly to the development of computer music.

▲ New Order (1987) *Substance.* Factory Records FAC 200.
English band known for its melding of electronic-dance and post-punk styles.

▲ George Lewis (1993) *Voyager.* Disk Union R-3800029.
'Voyager (the [computer] program) analyzes aspects of an improviser's performance in real time, using that analysis to guide an automatic composing program that generates complex responses to the musician's playing. This implies a certain independence of action, and indeed, the program exhibits generative behaviour independent of the human performer. The system is not an instrument, and therefore cannot be controlled by a performer' (from the liner notes).

▲ Jean-Claude Risset (1984) *Sud*. Ina-GRM INA C1003.

Risset uses synthesis techniques applied to natural sounds. Sud has been a set work in the French baccalauréat

▲ Paul Lansky (1985) *Idle Chatter*. Bridge 9103.

This is one of a whole family of pieces which explore vocal sounds, overdubbed, edited, and processed. The music comprises an inflected babble of barely recognisable sounds.

▲ Denis Smalley (1987) *Wind Chimes*. Empreintes Digitales IMED-9209-CD.

The sound of wind chimes is processed and developed in astonishing detail.

▲ John Zorn (1988) *Forbidden Fruit*. Nonesuch D 100675.

With Christian Marclay (turntables), Ohta Hiromi (voice) and the Kronos String Quartet.

▲ Diamanda Galás (1988)*You Must Be Certain of the Devil*. Mute CD STUMM 46.

'Galás emerged within the post-modern performance art scene in the seventies [. . .] protesting [. . .] the treatment of victims of the Greek junta, attitudes towards victims of AIDS. Her pieces are constructed from the ululation of traditional Mediterranean keening . . . whispers, shrieks, and moans' (Susan McClary, 1991). Galás uses an unusual microphone array and time-varying reverberation to enhance her extraordinary vocal range and the brooding intensity of the music.[23]

▲ Pauline Oliveros (1990) *Crone Music*. Lovely Music LCD 1903.

'As a musician I am interested in the sensual nature of sound, its power of release and change. In my performances throughout the world I try to transmit to the audience the way I am experiencing sound as I hear it and play in a style that I call deep listening. Deep listening is listening in every possible way to everything possible to hear no matter what you are doing. Such intense listening includes the sounds of daily life, of nature, of one's own thoughts as well as musical sounds. Deep listening is my life practice' – Oliveros (from the liner notes).

▲ Michael McNabb (1993) *Dreamsong*. Wergo RWER20202.

Dreamsong was created with the MUS10 computer music language on a DEC KL-10 computer. McNabb programmed the computer to create smooth transformations between different sounds. For McNabb, these shifts were poetically like the shifting experiences of a dream.

▲ Francis Dhomont (1994/6) *Forêt Profonde*. Empreintes Digitales IMED 9634.

Dhomont is one of the leading exponents of 'acousmatic' music, or 'cinema for the ears'.

▲ Goldie (1995) *Timeless*. FFRR CD 697-124 073-2.

The debut album by Goldie, and still one of the finest examples of drum 'n' bass.

▲ Autechre (1995) *Tri Repetae*. Warp Records 38.

Autechre (Rob Brown and Sean Booth) have been influential on the development of IDM (Intelligent Dance Music), but their work does not fit easily into a single genre. They explore a variety of techno instruments and techniques and sometimes use modular software environments.

▲ Tupac Shakur (1996) *All Eyez on Me*. Death Row/Koch 63008.

Probably the most influential rap album of the 1990s.

▲ John Oswald (1996) *69 Plunderphonics 96*. Seeland 515.
'If creativity is a field, copyright is the fence' (John Oswald).

▲ Tortoise (1996) *Millions Now Living Will Never Die*. Thrill Jockey THRILL025.
An eclectic fusion of jazz, electronica and experimental rock (among other influences) from an American 'postrock' band.

▲ Hildegard Westerkamp (1996) *Transformations*. Empreintes Digitales IMED 9631.
'Hildegard Westerkamp is a composer, radio artist and sound ecologist' (from the liner notes).

▲ The Prodigy (1997) *The Fat of the Land*. XL Recordings.
Controversial British 'Big Beat' band.

▲ Aphex Twin (1997) 'Bucephalus Bouncing Ball' on *Come to Daddy*. Warp Records 31001.
Richard James, aka Aphex Twin, is an innovator in contemporary electronic ambient, drum and bass, and related genres.

▲ Steve Reich (1998) *Different Trains*. Signum Records SIGCD066.
Combines recorded speech with string quartet.

▲ Coldcut (1998) 'Timber' on *Hexstatic*. ZencdS65A.
'In Timber all sound components are linked to their video sources. Whole rhythms have been painstakingly edited out of individual beats and video frames.'[24]

▲ Pan Sonic (1999) 'Maa' on *Album A*. Blast First BFFP132.
Pan Sonic is a Finnish electronic music duo: Mika Vainio and Ilpo Väisänen.

▲ Various Artists (2000) *OH: The Early Gurus of Electronic Music: 1948–1980*. Ellipsis Arts M1473 O46 2000.
A very useful compilation album of the history of electronic music.

▲ Bernard Parmegiani (2000) *De Natura Sonorum* Ina-GRM. INA C3001 CD.
A huge, 12-movement composition that explores the nature of sound materials in comprehensive depth.

▲ Kim Cascone (2000) *lparasitefordeleuze*. anechoic media a001.
The title explicitly references *Milles Plateaux* by Giles Deleuze and Félix Guattari.

▲ AMM (2001) *Fine*. Matchless Recordings MRCD46.
A highly influential free-improvisation group. They are said to never discuss the content of a performance ahead of time.

▲ Squarepusher (2001) *Go Plastic*. WARPCD85.
'The modern musician is subject to a barrage of persuasion from manufacturers of music technology. The general implication is that buying new tools leads to being able to make new and exciting music. While it is true that certain degrees of freedom are added by new equipment, it is not the case that this entails wholesale musical innovation. What seems more likely is that new clichés are generated by users unanalytically being forced into certain actions by the architecture of the machine. For me it is parallel, if not synonymous with a dogmatic consumer mentality that seems to hold that our lives are always improved by possessions' (Tom Jenkinson, aka Squarepusher).[25]

▲ Matthew Adkins (2002) *Fragmented Visions*. MPS Music and Video MPSCD015.
'Walk into the games arcade of the future and you walk into a world of liquid neon: a world of high stakes, high energy and high risk' (from the liner notes).

▲ Missy Elliot (2002) 'Work It' on *Under Construction*. Goldmind/Elektra 7559-62875-2.
Highly successful American singer, songwriter, and hip-hop artist, who also uses
some sophisticated digital techniques.

▲ DJ Spooky (2002) *Optometry*. Thirsty Ear THI57121.2.
A virtuoso and seamless mix of live and sampled materials in this landmark hybrid of
free jazz and dub.

▲ Tetsu Inoue and Carl Stone (2002) *pict.soul*. Cycling '74 c74-005.
'pict.soul documents the first meeting between these two giants in the experimental,
ambient, and post-ambient world. [. . .] As is always the case with Inoue and Stone,
their source materials remain mysterious, identifiable for fleeting instants. The precise nature of the collaborations for each of the ten pieces on *pict.soul* is equally mysterious' (from the Cycling '74 website http://www.cycling74.com).

▲ Björk (2004) *Medúlla*. Atlantic Records, One Little Indian 6294.
An album made entirely from digitally manipulated vocal sounds, including the
throat-singer Tagaq, hip-hop beatboxer Rahzel, Japanese beatboxer Dokaka, avant-
rocker Mike Patton, Soft Machine drummer/singer Robert Wyatt, and various
choirs.

Chapter 9

The digital musician

> What I like about the Futurists is that they didn't just make groundbreaking art and music: they published recipe books and had Futurist dinners too![1]

This chapter addresses some very practical aspects of *being* a digital musician, including employment and career prospects, skill sets and education, and a range of 'real world' situations and practices. To illustrate some of the key ideas that emerge, a collection of 'case studies' of leading digital musicians is provided. These consist of brief biographies and interviews, from which a picture of the diversity of the lives of such musicians will emerge.

A digital musician is an amalgamation of performer, composer, engineer and informed listener, all to a certain extent. It is highly likely that each individual will have more skills in one of these areas than the others. The 'sound designer', the 'sonic artist' and the 'digital musician' have overlapping skill sets and, for the purposes of this book, are practically the same. As Ronald Herrema points out, what all these people share is 'an understanding of the manipulation of sound in time, how that relates to gesture and how it relates to drama, or the dramaturgy of the work'.[2]

A digital musician is conscious of the questions posed in the Preface to this book. The time has come to attempt some succinct answers to those questions. This is not easy, because there is no single answer that is good for everyone. The following are the author's own personal responses, based on what is written here. The readers will, it is hoped, make their own replies.

All this potential to make music, but what music?
The music that has your voice, which has been found with integrity, out of curiosity, and through awareness.

What is there to 'say'?
John Cage said 'there is nothing to say, and I am saying it'.[3] This neat paradox illustrates the central purpose of music, or of any art: to reveal the human condition. There's no need to get too hung up about this – what needs to be said will be said.

Why create music?
The reasons are many. However, the most successful musician will not be somebody who wants to make music, but somebody who has to make music.

And what about existing music? How to approach that?
With cultural awareness and critical engagement.

And which music to approach?
The music that is unknown.

And how do we know what is good?
By forming our own judgements, informed by the judgements of our peers.

The changing workplace

Over the past few decades, the workplace for any musician involved with technology has changed, from a large fixed recording studio, through a miniaturised version of the fixed studio called the digital audio workstation (DAW), to a laptop studio that is 'on the move'. The fixed studios and the DAWs still exist, of course, and the laptop equivalent is often modelled to a greater or lesser extent on them. In the recording studio situation, the digital musician is normally confronted with the paradox of a glass barrier that separates the 'musicians' from the 'engineers'. There is often an assumption that the former neither understand the work of the latter, nor are allowed to get involved. However, the most creative and productive musical developments often start when this demarcation breaks down.

To explore this point a little further, consider the works of Glenn Gould (1932–1982), Frank Zappa (1940–1993) and Sir George Martin (b. 1926): three quite different artists who all saw the potential of the recording studio and devoted much, even nearly all, their careers to the use of the studio as a creative device.

Glenn Gould was a virtuoso concert pianist who gave up performing in 1964 because he preferred to work in the studio. He saw tape-editing as part of the creative process, and positively embraced the use of dubbing to produce effects that are not possible in live performance. The second of his two recordings of Bach's *Goldberg Variations*, made in 1981, was the first digital recording issued by CBS. There is much documentation by and about Gould, including several documentaries and a film: *Thirty Two Short Films about Glenn Gould* (1993, dir. Don McKellar). The Glenn Gould archive is also available online.[4]

Frank Zappa managed to fuse many different musical styles and idioms during his prolific career, including rock, jazz, R&B, doo-wop, disco, reggae, new wave, serial and electronic music. The methods he used, even in live performance, were based on an almost obsessive use of the recording studio, where he developed unique techniques with many pieces of equipment. These included 'xenochrony' or, literally, 'strange time', which used a collection of material (usually guitar solos) as a kind of database to be accessed and included anywhere on an album. Many writers have discussed Zappa's 'intertextuality' and his critical stance towards the 'culture industry',[5] and Zappa himself gives an entertaining account of his career in *The Real Frank Zappa Book* (co-written with Peter Occhiogrosso).

George Martin is often called 'the fifth Beatle', because his mastery of the recording studio was so crucial to the sound produced by the 'Fab Four' as they moved increasingly towards studio albums. He worked with a vast array of other artists too and may justly claim to be the most influential record producer of all time. There is so much documentation about his work that further discussion is largely unnecessary. However, at the time of writing, he (with his son Giles) has just issued 'Love', an experimental digital remix from original Beatles tapes.

The DAW represents a logical development from such studio creativity, by placing both the recording and editing tools in the hands of the digital musician and, in effect, making everyone a potential Glenn Gould, Frank Zappa or George Martin. This does not entirely remove the need for high-quality recording studios, however, because most DAWs do not have the kind of sound-isolated environments, monitoring set-ups and recording equipment needed to produce the best results. The laptop workstation embraces those very limitations, reinforced by ever-greater processing power, data-storage capability and accuracy, along with mobile connectivity. Audio quality and monitoring have improved, but also the limitations of the portable system have become a conditioning factor for the music itself.

There has been one very significant consequence for music-making from these changes to the workplace. The typical computer workstation is designed for the single user, often further isolated under a pair of headphones. The act of music-making becomes an act of production, with perhaps a CD or DVD, film or website as the outcome. This object may be passed on, once again, with only minimal social contact. If the musician in question does not engage in live performance, then he or she becomes an almost completely isolated figure. It should be stated and restated that *music is a social activity*. Isolation can be musically unhealthy, and the pervasive culture of individualism has a downside.

Another consequence has been for the notion of *repertoire*. Whereas in the past there were generally agreed bodies of repertoire which all musicians could share, the tendency of digital culture towards individualism is creating a situation where each musician invents their own. One of the major challenges facing the digital musician, then, is how to engage musically with others, including the public. Such engagements can take place live or across a network, but social and acoustic communication are crucial to their success. The new generation of social-networking tools on the Web have made it easier for digital musicians to connect with others, but these will never entirely substitute for face-to-face interaction.

Digital musicians will find themselves in a range of situations beyond the studio or workstation. Real-time music-making and studio production have expanded to include a range of new media and multimedia situations. The phrase 'real time' means that there is no significant time gap between the production of a sound and the listener's perception of it. So, a conventional live concert is real time, but so are many types of network performance and life-linked performance activities. The live concert situation covers a vast array of different activities ranging from laptop gigs to electro-acoustic music concerts, from working with traditional orchestras and ensembles to playing with bands or solo. The role of the digital musician may be different in these situations: here, as a performer originating sound; there, as a diffuser projecting sound into a space; here, as a DJ or turntablist; there, computer programming.

Musical performance does not have to be delivered in a traditional situation. In fact, many digital musicians prefer to avoid the conventions of a concert. Life-linked performance, where there is a seamless transition between daily life and the performance activity, has increased steadily since its early days in the 1960s. The use of mobile and flash technologies, real-time sampling and soundscape composition, as well as the activities of bootleggers and plunderphonicists, hackers and net-artists, can create a situation where the distinction between the 'concert' and 'life' breaks down. Here, the digital musicians develop a reciprocal relationship with their cultural context. They become their own audience but, at the same time, the wider audience (the 'non-musicians') are drawn into the musical process to the extent that they can share in becoming musicians.

An interesting special case is *telepresence*, in which a live musician may interact with a virtual entity or in a remote environment. This gives the experience of being fully present at a live real world location but remote from the actual physical location. Someone experiencing telepresence would therefore be able to behave, and receive stimuli, as though at the remote site. This is an unusual (and currently fairly rare) musical situation that presents particular challenges and properties. To achieve good results through performance requires first what might be called 'action and agency' (audible and visual cues) and then 'choice and intention', in other words, the psychological aspects of musical activity. There needs to be a human presence in the social area that is the auditorium. Real-time networked interactions have a way to go before they can emulate these.

What is intriguing about the role of the digital musician in the above situations is the extent to which it changes day by day and hour by hour, moving from a performative mode here to a compositional mode there, from originating creator to critical listener. This is especially evident in the context of *interart* such as music for theatre, dance, performance, interactive installations, video art and so on. The extent to which new media and new technologies appear in these contexts will determine to what extent the musician draws upon the knowledge and skills discussed in this book, but it is clear that there is an increasingly subtle use of digital technologies in everything from virtual environments to sound environments, from *son et lumière* to *cirques de soleil*.[6]

- Kac, E. (2000) *Telepresence, Biotelematics, Transgenic Art.* Maribor: KIBLA.
- Nisbett, A. (2004) *The Sound Studio: Audio Techniques for Radio, Television, Film and Recording.* Oxford: Focal Press.
- Rumsey, F. (1996) *The Audio Workstation Handbook.* Oxford: Focal Press.

Careers

Given the enormous range and diversity of these overlapping situations, it might be objected that we are in fact talking about several different types of musician, who work in one or other of these areas. It is certainly true that it is unlikely that a single individual will undertake work in *all* these situations in a lifetime. To develop a career, it is probably necessary to specialise to a certain degree. However, the digital musician who has acquired the skills outlined in this book *could* work in any of these situations, because the technology allows it and because there are certain musical abilities that are useful in all of them. In other words, the skills of a digital musician are transferable. The application of these skills in the development of a career is a skill in itself. The challenge facing digital musicians is to find a situation for their work, to exchange, to disseminate.

The hardest thing for a digital musician to decide is not what skills should be acquired but what *not* to learn. Given that the skill set draws upon so many different and well-established disciplines, it is always possible to go further into any one of them in order to specialise in a particular area. A theme that emerges, therefore, is the sheer number and variety of employment situations or careers. Here is a quick list of just *some* of them: programmer, music and effects for games, music and effects for cinema (location sound, ADR, Foley, sound effects, re-recording engineer, composer, session engineer, etc.), music and effects for industrial video, audio-loops designer, audio-effects designer, mobilephone ringtone designer, radio producer, studio engineer, record producer, mastering engineer, music-related retail sales, music software support, jingle writing, music-events producer, live-sound engineer, band member, session musician, arts administrator, self-promoted musician, Internet-based microsales, record-label manager, talent scout, A&R (artist and repertoire) representative, acoustic designer, arts/sound museum/events coordinator, events/festivals technical support, PA system consulting and installation, DSP inventor, instrument inventor, writer for electronic music magazines, sound for web (commercial record sales samples, sound design for sites, interactive sound), bulk media reproduction, teaching, music therapy, new-age market (relaxation tapes, mind manipulation, etc.), Muzak, corporate sonic environments, multimedia development, busking, lawyer, music librarian, artist.

Most of these (and the list is by no means complete) have the capacity to offer either full-time or, more likely, part-time or temporary employment. The digital musicians, ready to respond to a variety of situations and demands, can transfer knowledge and skills from one arena to another. They are multi-faceted, and their skills can always be applied. But, as everybody knows, the job market changes as constantly as the rest of culture. To enter this market, therefore, requires a willingness to change and engage in different activities.

Many of the jobs are in emerging areas relating to new media. It is hard to predict exactly how these emerging areas will develop, so the skills and abilities outlined in this book may be regarded as basic prerequisites for most situations, but the need to *specialise* will also be important as the career develops and the culture changes. To give a simple example: thrity-five years ago the Internet did not exist, but now it is a fact of life. Those musicians who have adapted to the Internet are achieving a greater success than those who have not.

Once again, the challenge is to identify the fixed elements in a changing world. Industrial models are often invoked to describe the digital-music culture, such as: 'the music industry', 'the entertainments industry', 'the cultural industries' or 'the creative industries'. Where the work undertaken is purely commercial, these models can be useful, and the 'product' (whether music or musician) can be successful within that context. However, a more fluid approach is often needed, particularly where the work is either non-commercial or unclear in its industrial aim. There are porous boundaries between contexts, between sub-cultures, between industries. Music flows, and music's contexts change. The digital arts and technologies tend to blur into one another, and the people who work in those areas often have ill-defined roles. In fact, many successful digital musicians may never have set out to be musicians in the first place. They may have found themselves making sound or music by accident or default.

■ Kusek, D. and Leonhard, G. (2005) *The Future of Music: Manifesto for the Digital Revolution.* Boston, MA: Berklee Press.

Social networking

The best approach the digital musician can take, therefore, is to be prepared for a variety of real-world situations. Much of this preparation is identical to that undertaken by any other musician, but some is peculiar to the digital musician. There are many good sources of information about this in books and periodicals, which will also take into account regional and national variations. The following is a brief summary of general advice that will be useful in a range of situations.

Whatever the field of work, social networking and self-promotion is always essential if people are to be aware of the musician's name and abilities. This can be done in person or through third parties, through marketing or by reputation. The aim is to convince people of the value of the work, whether that is financial or artistic value. The digital musician, therefore, has a vested interest in avoiding contributing to activities that generally cheapen music, whether commercially or artistically. At the time of writing, the proliferation of cheap music (in both senses) is doing exactly that, and the service industries are becoming a major employer. If musicians are to avoid becoming only servants, then the digital musician needs to value both his or her skills and the work that he or she produces. This is not an argument against novel methods of dissemination but rather in favour of self-promotion. This sense of value *will* come across to a prospective client or employer.

One much-overused term is 'professionalism', which seems to have become synonymous with a certain slickness in marketing. There are certain situations where slick marketing techniques will produce results, but a far more important aspect of 'professionalism' is the ability to be easy to work with and reliable. This is as much a question of interpersonal skills as musical abilities, is worth a thousand marketing campaigns and may be summarised by a common-sense statement: if other people find you a pleasure to work with, then they will call on you again. This skill is not easy to acquire, however. There will be many situations in which artistic goals contradict one another, or ideas and approaches fail to cohere. In a commercial situation, the client has bought the right to define and change the brief. In a non-commercial situation, individuals are free to define their own path but, even so, remember that everything a musician does will contribute towards their reputation. Word of mouth and contacts will get much further in any aspect of the music business than a slick image and an over-confident manner. Negotiating skills will also be essential, particularly when making artistic as well as the more obvious financial, contractual or professional decisions.

One unique aspect of all this for the digital musician is the need not only to know the market but also, to some extent, to *create* the market. Many of the skills they will bring to bear are unfamiliar to musicians, let alone to the non-musicians who often end up being clients or employers. This means that the musicians themselves will sometimes need to do some consciousness-raising about what it is that they do or bring. Many people in business will already have a notion that 'creativity' is valuable, but this will be quite unfocused. The musician will need to be ready to explain how digital creativity works and what makes it special. The level of detail in the explanation will be a judgement-call, because people vary in their ability to absorb either artistic or technical ideas, but at the same time it is important that the newness and uniqueness of the musician's activities comes across clearly. Doing so will be infectious, and the very presence of a digital musician will start to alter the surrounding culture. When people are meekly accepting clichés and well-worn formulae, it is the digital musician's job to show them the benefit of going beyond that and investing time, money and attention in interesting new areas.

The single most important aspect of networking and self-promotion for the digital musician is Internet presence. This generally means building a website, but it can also mean rather more than that, so it needs to be considered separately. The web is now the first port of call for anyone seeking information about anything. It is also the location for a great deal of cultural activity. The digital musician *must* have a website that is representative and accessible. It will also pay dividends to develop other forms of Internet presence such as a blog or a personal web space where people can download the music, interact, make contact and so on. E-mail lists and online forums or discussion groups are also a good starting point, and the digital musician should join those which cover areas of interest. Online communities form and dissolve rapidly, but what they all have in common is a shared and mutual interest on the part of their inhabitants.

The best way to become involved in an online community is to begin by 'lurking', in other words, to become a member but say nothing for a while until the 'feel' of the group sinks in. However anonymous the characters may seem to be, there is always a real person behind the avatar or virtual character. People will often behave online in ways in which they would never behave in '3D'. This can make Internet interaction quite different from real-world interaction. Speech, in particular, lacks a 'tone of voice', hence the pepperings of 'emoticons' (smiley faces, etc.) in online interaction. Remarks that are intended to be ironic or humorous can often be taken literally and give offence. Similar comments apply to online game playing and interaction in virtual worlds. Although the audio capability of these worlds is limited at the time of writing, it seems likely that it will improve. In some of the worlds, people build and sell or exchange virtual objects including musical instruments, give performances and concerts and design virtual environments. This can be a fertile situation for a digital musician, a different kind of 'real world'.

■ Kimpel, D. (2005) *Networking Strategies for the New Music Business*. Boston, MA: Artistpro.
■ Spellman, P. (2002) *The Musician's Internet*. Boston, MA: Berklee Press.
■ Yeung, R. (2006) *The Rules of Networking*. London: Cyan.

Business

In matters of business, there is little difference between being a 'digital' and a 'non-digital' musician. Good organisation and time management are as crucial to the digital musician as to any other creative or performing person and form a significant aspect of any attempt at self-promotion. Musicians of all types live by their calendars and contacts. It is vital to have these in good order.

Two professional types who will prove themselves invaluable are *accountants* and *lawyers*. It is very difficult to do without the former, and it is a brave soul who takes on their own tax returns and royalty collection, although it is not impossible to do so. Lawyers are essential if moving into contractual negotiations with large companies but not necessary for small-scale work. There are enough horror stories about musicians being exploited to make anyone think twice before entering a significant contractual negotiation without the support of a lawyer.

Professional arts managers and agents exist and may, under certain circumstances, be useful, depending upon the kind of career that is being developed. Music publishers, too, where appropriate, will provide a degree of management and guidance. But, on the whole, the digital musician is a self-managing entity and would be well advised to retain as much artistic control as possible. It is generally not a good idea to grab at a deal at any price. If there is sufficient interest in the work for one deal to be on offer, then often another, perhaps more favourable, deal may be found.

● Pecha kucha

■ Spellman, P. (2000) *The Self-Promoting Musician.* Boston, MA: Berklee Press.

Production

Music production relies on software. To specify precisely *which* music software packages might be useful to the musician is futile, because the software market changes so rapidly. However, it is possible to identify generic types of music software, as follows:

- sound recording, editing and sequencing software
- processing applications (including plug-ins)
- software samplers
- virtual instruments
- synthesis software
- live-performance software
- notation software
- composition software
- analysis or representation software
- modular or build-it-yourself software.

Additions could be made to this list, in relation to new media, aural training and other less obviously musical applications, but the digital musician should know more than one example of each of the above. It is also highly advantageous to be able to work across platforms and, specifically, to have abilities in both the Windows and Mac operating systems. Knowledge of Linux and open-source systems and software may also be regarded as desirable.

Of course, software is always designed by somebody, and the nature of that design will often (although not always) be linked to a perceived commercial market. The digital musician will need to be aware that such software can try to steer musical content in a particular direction, even towards a specific genre or style. Sometimes music production is a matter of finding ways to achieve something original *in spite of* the software design. Everybody has favourite applications (usually the ones first learned), but in order to unlock the potential offered by a general understanding of computer music, the tendency to be driven by the design and interface of a particular piece of software must be overcome.

Unless the artist is very lucky indeed, the creative process will produce large quantities of discarded material along the way. This is by no means irrelevant to the final production, even if it is never heard. There can be confusion between process and product, even to the extent of regarding 'music production' as having a set of 'production values' which have nothing to do with creativity. This might derive from film, where the post-production phase is a separate part of the creative process. To take one well-known example to illustrate the point: the contribution of George Martin's studio techniques and creativity to the *Sergeant Pepper's Lonely Hearts Club Band* album was as integral to the compositional process as Paul's melodies, John's lyrics, George's guitar-playing and even Ringo's drumming. Any musical 'product' is the result of a process, in which all the various elements have played a part.

Some composers produce a lot, some produce very little. This is unimportant unless it is *too* much or *too* little. But if musical integrity is to be the goal then, whatever the quantity of product, the creative process must be subject to some rigor, some set of value judgements. If fulfilling a commercial brief, then the client must be satisfied and the brief fulfilled to the highest standard. If working more freely, then the artistic imperatives of that particular project, of the musician's own beliefs, must be met. A compromise in these areas will result in a very short career. People are generally good at sniffing out a fraud.

In multimedia and new media, the music exists alongside other disciplines, such as text, graphics, animation and video. Multimedia is a pervasive aspect of digital culture. The digital musician might take a particular interest in the following types:

- *text-sound work* which came out of poetry (text-sound or phonetic poetry) and is designed to be heard, rather than read
- *'audiovision'*, in which the sound and image combine holistically, with neither taking precedence over the other[7]
- *sound design* in which the sounding element is one constituent part of an interdisciplinary art work and is never intended to be heard alone.

Music for film and television is a separate study in its own right but is plainly a fertile ground for the digital musician too. However, many films still tend to divide their soundtracks into 'music' and 'sound effects'. The great Hollywood film composers, such as John Williams, are musicians in the traditional sense, writing scores that mimic classical techniques. Not all film music is like this, and there are numerous examples of sound designers, such as Walter Murch and various Foley[8] artists, who have achieved extraordinary results, but, even so, it is a relatively rare thing to find a director who treats sound as music. The various new media described earlier are probably a more appropriate location for this kind of work.

The term 'new media' is generally taken to refer to various interactive and multimedia technologies that have arisen during the 1990s and since. This includes the Internet, computer games, portable technologies and interactive media in general. It is likely that the digital musician will be active in some or all of these. Certain new media such as computer games, interactive DVDs and online environments are rooted in concepts of virtual reality (VR). This may be defined as a computer simulation of an environment and is generally focused mainly on the visual domain. Sound is often used purely to reinforce the illusion of reality and so normally simulates the behaviour of sound in the physical world, often with only limited means. The processing and memory demands of the video stream frequently require a degraded sound quality (generally stereo, but often with low sampling rates and bit depths). However, a creative musician will always accept limitations when they occur and find ways to work within them. There are many examples of good music produced for new media, and this looks set to be the most expanding market in the immediate future.

● Sonic branding

■ Cunningham, M. (1999) *Good Vibrations*. New York: Sanctuary.
■ Nardantonio, Dennis N. (1990) *Sound Studio Production Techniques*. Blue Ridge Summit, PA: Tab Books.

Education

One major consequence of the emergence of the digital musician is a change in music education. There is almost a 'chicken-and-egg' relationship between the education system and the musicians it produces, because of the sudden rapid proliferation of 'music technology' as a subject at all levels. Of course, it is not necessary to have studied music academically *at all* in order to be a good and successful musician of whatever type. However, in the case of music technology, it can help enormously to have pursued some kind of course or training programme. Whereas, at one time, formal musical training was essential for a classical musician (and sometimes a handicap for a band musician), a digital musician will benefit from education in a wide range of areas, and not just 'music'.

The differences between 'music' and 'music technology' curriculums do summarise the somewhat confused picture of education in this field. As Dr Matthew Adkins observed in a recent paper, there is a strong contrast between the two:

> On the one hand we have those from a traditional music background, who have had little use of technology (perhaps notation software) but are highly musically literate. On the other hand we see those from an unorthodox music background, with high technological literacy, but no notational skills.[9]

In addition to these observable tendencies are the financial constraints upon schools and colleges which have reduced instrumental tuition to a fraction of its former level and failed to equip classrooms or train teachers adequately in technology. This situation is changing, but it is quite common at present to find school pupils who have greater access to, and better understanding of, the technology than their teachers.

There is a general agreement among young people, at least, that a good knowledge of music technology is an essential part of contemporary musical life. The curriculum, on the other hand, struggles to keep pace with the rate of change. In universities, meanwhile, a large number of music-technology programmes have sprung up based largely upon the ideas and skill sets outlined in this book. These degree and sub-degree level courses may include the words 'creative' or 'sonic art' or even 'commercial' in their titles but, whatever their particular flavour, they are all fundamentally based on the same observable developments. The first-year programmes on these courses are frequently devised specifically to fill in the gaps in either musical or technological education that have appeared at school level.

For the digital musician, all this offers a great opportunity both to receive a varied and stimulating education but also to some extent to set the agenda for the future. The education system is becoming increasingly flexible where music is concerned. This does not mean an outright and wholesale rejection of traditional skills and knowledge but rather an *opening up* of these to a wider, less restrictive, understanding than previously. Music technology as a subject area is in the process of maturing and will eventually find its own roots and produce its own flowers.

The very real and exciting prospect is that the digital musician can readily develop a unique voice. The new technologies have enabled people to create, to share and to develop together in ways that would have been unforeseeable thirty years ago. Education and practice are at last beginning to correspond more directly, and this trend will continue, to the point that a higher qualification will represent an enlivening and growth of the available set of possibilities. The final product of this process will be not 'digital musicians' as such, but musicians for whom the digital technologies are just as familiar as conventional acoustic music technologies. These remarkable individuals will be responsible for the growth of new forms and new musical experiences that will prove every bit as satisfying and rich as anything heard to date.

Case studies

This section contains case studies comprising interviews with a number of leading digital musicians, chosen from a range of backgrounds and each representing a different approach or way of working. There are representatives from the USA and Latin America, Europe and Scandinavia, Canada and Japan, from academia and the commercial world, from pure digital to mixed-media backgrounds. Many areas of music are represented, including popular and electro-acoustic, film and television, multimedia and installation work, networked music and new media, music for theatre and dance, laptop work and instrumental performance.

Each musician was asked to supply a short biography, describe their creative use of technology, particularly digital technology. and answer a fairly general set of questions, as follows:

- What music do you make?
- Why do you make music?
- Is any of your sound-based work not 'music', as such?
- Do you consider yourself a performer, a composer, a technologist, an engineer, some combination of these or, indeed, something else?
- What is the cultural context for your work? Are you influenced by music in other cultures? And the other arts?
- What skills and attributes do you consider to be essential for you as a digital musician?
- Do you have any other useful or relevant things to say about being a digital musician today?

The answers echo a number of the key themes that have been explored in this book, sometimes from some unusual or particularly interesting angles.

Oswald Berthold

Please supply a biography, giving an account of your career and current activities.

enter world. awakening of the internal program. learned to play an instrument. formed a band. acquaintance with more instruments including electronic devices. left home. meet computer. short studies in music technology. meet internet. establishment of a studio and founding of a collective that lives until today. embeddance in an electronic music scene. playing concerts. start learn programming. playing more concerts. doing regular work in website construction. shifting interest to installations. picking up studies in computer science. still going. vacillate between art and science.

Please describe your creative use of technology, particularly digital technology.

i am interested very generally in wave phenomena as they are evident in, or rather, constituent of all of nature's processes. sound then seems well suited for conveying information about the trajectories of these processes' variables, particularly as they unfold along time, be they external and tapped or simulations. this suggests a toolbox equipped with devices such as supercollider, octave, R, and a good text editor, a lot of glue, utilities and scripts of diverse provenience and a box filled with I/O apparatus, sensors, soldering iron and such.

What music do you make?

barely any. or put extremely, it's not making music but rather transforming music. consider music as the continual evaluation of a vector valued function of multiple variables. whew.

phenomenologically it's again a progression, one of parameterised sounding entities, elements that vary mostly microscopically, that recur among diversely different timescales, maybe slowly evolve. hums, hisses, buzzes, tonal drones, optionally and quasiperiodically pulsed, also blips, squeaks, tweets, squirts, grunts and other more short lived creatures.

Why do you make music?

i slipped into this, not noticing myself and now i can't find a way out.

Is any of your sound-based work not 'music', as such?

referencing above preemptive statements, most of it, yes. it appears to me i have arrived at this definition (the one with the function, above) by searching for a local optimum in personal manoeuvring space. i enjoy a lot of music 'as such' but i enjoy in a very similar manner many more temporal structures occurring in my immediately perceptible surrounding and wonder about the imperceptible.

Do you consider yourself a performer, a composer, a technologist, an engineer, some combination of these or, indeed, something else?

clearly, all of the above and then some. maybe not quite a generalist but at least a student in many disciplines.

What is the cultural context for your work? Are you influenced by music in other cultures? And the other arts?

sorry to be unsubtle in unwrapping subquestions.

1   white elitist western art music, sound art, sound hacking, slow code, media art + theory.
2   in no way directly. only through the filter of being published on recording media.
3   i draw inspiration from all over movies, literature, people, visual, sculptural, electronic and/or performing arts, physics, biology, mathematics, electronic and hacker culture, (in ad-hoc order) and other unworldly terrain. generally i go with the notion of arts and sciences overlapping, a tendency to syn rather than sci.

What skills and attributes do you consider to be essential for you as a digital musician?

verbalised positively in the order of descending generality: humor, curiosity, persistence, luck, classical literacy, having readily access to electronic calculating machinery of recent make including libraries of open software for their operation, literacy in mathematics, the internals and black magic of aforementioned machinery.

Do you have any other useful or relevant things to say about being a digital musician today?

no, not today.

Nick Collins

Please supply a biography, giving an account of your career and current activities.

Nicholas (Nick) Collins has indulged in both mathematics and instrumental composition in the past. His interests run the gamut of topics in electronic music, but particular specialisms include algorithmic composition, live electronica, machine listening and interactive music systems. He occasionally tours the world as the non-Swedish half of the Swedish audiovisual laptop duo klipp av.

He was born near Oxford, grew up in Burntwood, Staffordshire, received a first degree in mathematics, a masters in music technology, worked for Sony for a year on film SFX software, then became a programmer and part-time lecturer in London. Nick escaped to Cambridge to sort out a PhD, where he also learnt the dark art of writing in the third person about himself. He is now a lecturer in computer music at the University of Sussex.

In a recent interview, he said: 'I am trying to build an artificial musician, some kind of autonomous unit that can sit on a concert stage and interact with human musicians. It would have to analyze acoustic music in real time, and then play back something that fits in with that music or compliments it.'[10]

Please describe your creative use of technology, particularly digital technology.

I am active in: machine listening and interactive music systems; generative music/ algorithmic composition (especially for large-scale 'infinite length pieces' exploring non-standard tuning systems and other mathematical musical systems, and in tool development for algorithmic electronic dance music and more abstract compositional modes); live coding (this grew out of earlier experiments in laptop music); live audiovisuals (this is probably where I've had the most concerts with klipp av, novel non-standard sound synthesis algorithms (see the SLUGens plug-ins for SC).

What music do you make?

I used to create fixed products including 'impossible tape music illusions' but the past three years especially have seen me focus full time on live performance. The various facets of this described above include an audiovisual experimental electronica duo (live improvisation of mappings), designing systems for real-time interactive situations and competitive live coding battles.

Why do you make music?

The answer to this would itself vary based on the work and the time of day. But here is a selection of responses:

- to make social contact with people I'd be too shy to talk to, to assist communal forgetting of the everyday, for particular functions (a club event, promoting dancing) to undermine particular functions (deliberately awkward music disrupting dancing)

- to create artefacts as a challenge to my own and other's intellectual and emotional states
- to become lost (or transcendent, meditative?) in the flow of composition and performance. I can both achieve such direct flow in more intellectual pursuits (though I also play piano in traditional musicianship and can become lost there in a motor memory assisted kind).

I'll stop before your patience wears thin . . .

Is any of your sound-based work not 'music', as such?

I made one installation in my life, a failure, a bit of a joke – a large banner proclaimed an 'Anti-Copyright Installation, copyright Nick Collins' and below was a red button (and this was in the foyer of the Royal Festival Hall!). Granulated shards of sound of sufficient shortness to have unidentifiable origin were played, but the envelopes would be extended if you touched the button. To reveal copyrighted sources. I have nothing against sonic art – it's still organised by humans, and it's healthy to not always be sat 'consuming' in the dark but to wander a space and reach out to an artefact.

Do you consider yourself a performer, a composer, a technologist, an engineer, some combination of these or, indeed, something else?

I've made the comparison before of nineteenth-century composer/pianists and twenty-first-century composer/programmers. People are an implicit and untangleable blend of characters and change as the context suits; so I can be any of the above, but certainly, happy to be labelled a digital musician where this might simply mean someone working at the cross-disciplinary juncture of these types.

What is the cultural context for your work? Are you influenced by music in other cultures? And the other arts?

I am interested by all musics, but am especially drawn to those of counter-cultures and experiments. Of course, from a Western perspective, sometimes the mainstreams of other cultures can seem like subversive voices! All arts and sciences are good sources of human richness. In particular, I'm actively involved in multimodal art (audiovisuals).

What skills and attributes do you consider to be essential for you as a digital musician?

Some are in common with and critical to an acoustic musician: dedication/enthusiasm, networking, effort/practice, but some are exclusive, these are possibly more what you're asking for: computer programming ability in a number of languages (i.e., SuperCollider, C, MATLAB); instrument builder's/system designer's spirit – desire to tinker and explore potential (and the necessary patience to defer outcomes here, plus the necessary impatience not to spend the entire time designing); grasp of electronic musician's music theory: psychoacoustics, DSP, discrete math, representations/formalisms and some I'm developing and currently weak in but might like to improve; ability to be operating system and platform/software free; essentially to reach to ideas independent of particular implementations (helping with future proofing in this over anxious environment of upgrades – we should have a moratorium on progress for some years and take advantage of what we have right now!) live electronics/interfacing.

Do you have any other useful or relevant things to say about being a digital musician today?

The avenues for truly experimental new music are highly centred on digital technology. However, a few of the debates and themes seem to me chimerical or unnecessary: there's nothing special about laptop music, cognitive skills have a lot in common with physical skills, and we shouldn't be too biased against either. Sometimes we want to listen to acousmatic music; sometimes we want to be dancing; sometimes we want to talk during a concert. A mixture of functions is great!

Julio d'Escriván

Please supply a biography, giving an account of your career and current activities.

Julio d'Escriván (b. 1960) is a composer who uses music technology, both for concert music, and in its applications to film, video and new media. From 2002 onwards he was in-house composer at A&E Mundo, a Latin-American cable network which is part of the HBO group. He also directed bitBongo, a highly successful recording and production studio running out of Caracas. His clients included Kraft, Pepsi, Gatorade, P&G and the local Venezuelan banking industry. In the UK he has worked as a consultant for Yamaha Research and Development in London, on sampling and synthesiser voicing projects. He is now a lecturer in creative music technology at Anglia Ruskin University.

D'Escriván's musical work includes CDs of purely acousmatic music, and his electro-acoustic music has been performed at numerous music festivals in countries such as The Netherlands (Gaudeamus), Spain (Centro Reina Sofía), The Basque Country, France, England, Scotland, Ireland, Argentina, Sweden, Norway, USA and Venezuela. It continues to be broadcast in America and Europe and has been heard on BBC Radio 3, VPRO Amsterdam, Radio Nacional de España, and RAI (Italy) among others. He is interested in the 'traditional' literacy of non-traditional laptop musicians.

Please describe your creative use of technology, particularly digital technology.

I use digital technology for the transformation, archival and sequencing of sound and visuals. I also make use of programming languages such as SuperCollider and MaxMSP in order to design algorithmic music structures that may aid the composition and performance process as well as use live synthesis for sound-design tasks.

In my orchestral piece which features USB game controller as a soloist, *Con cierto Demente* (2005), I created a system that would not only let me cue in prepared sound files at various points but also the facility to trigger random processes of live synthesis and sample playback.

In my piece for laptop, harpsichord and baroque flute, *Tonada Recursiva* (2006), I used the SuperCollider language to record and transform the live sounds to provide a backdrop and dialogue between the laptop processing and the performers.

Finally, I have used and hope to deepen my understanding of sensor technology to extend the instrumental capabilities of music performers as exemplified in my recent piece *Sueño con Ranitas* (2006), where, with the use of accelerometers on the wrists of the marimba performer, she can control the spatialisation of the electronics in performance.

What music do you make?

I am a composer of electronic music. I straddle all the styles currently practised in this field. My main output has been in the electro-acoustic field with, as well as those recent works mentioned above, pieces such as *Salto Mortal* for tape solo (1989) and *Sin Ti Por El Alma Adentro* (1987) for flute and tape and *Hocketus Creole* (2001) for chamber orchestra and Venezuelan 'carrizo' panpipes. In the electronica genre I have produced two CDs, *Vox* (1998) and *Inventos Barbaros* (1999), which had a successful run in Venezuela where they were released. (A piece from Vox was broadcast on BBC Radio 3 on the excellent Friday night *Mixing It* programme in autumn 2003.) In the film and commercials music areas, I have worked extensively for advertising as well as scoring four feature films and one short in Venezuela, I also scored *Balloon* (1991, dir. Ken Lidster) in London which won the BAFTA for animation. I have played and arranged Venezuelan folk music and Latin salsa.

Why do you make music?

This will sound silly, but I am like the Blues Brothers, on a mission to make music! It is, with the exception of my family, the most important thing in my life. I feel a strong calling to recombine, transform and place sounds in a musical way, even if I don't think the results are destined to fame and fortune; I view it as beautiful inevitability.

Is any of your sound-based work not 'music', as such?

No. Even my commercial work as sound designer, whenever I am called upon to do that, I view as a musical task. Sounds cannot (should not!) be organised except according to musical criteria.

Do you consider yourself a performer, a composer, a technologist, an engineer, some combination of these or indeed, something else?

I am a composer in the twenty-first century. I am no more a technologist for using computers and electronics than Bach was a carpenter for playing the harpsichord. A twenty-first-century composer can easily be a performer through the use of 'macro musical' devices such as sound cueing and live diffusion, in a manner not too different from that of a conductor who also happens to have created the music he is directing.

What is the cultural context for your work? Are you influenced by music in other cultures? And the other arts?

My context is a mixed baggage of urban world popular idioms, South American and Latin folklore, world folk/ethnic musics and delightfully highbrow pretentious European concerns which I can afford to never take very seriously because I am a foreigner everywhere I go, including Venezuela. Like a lot of my contemporaries, I am sensitive to visuals and visual art forms such as cinema and video. Internet communication through art media is also an important influence and concern.

What skills and attributes do you consider to be essential for you as a digital musician?

An open mind is the principal attribute. Technological shamelessness is the second most important. The latter allowing me to plunder code (a useful skill) and recorded sound whenever necessary to produce my music. A digital musician must be more concerned with the final sonic output than with beautiful programming. Being an elegant coder/programmer is an irrelevant bonus. The main thing is to get the sound you are looking for. Digital musicians need to start thinking of themselves more as simply musicians in possession of new musical literacy paradigms. Otherwise, why not talk about 'pianist musicians' or 'woodwind musicians'? How different does our choice of instrument really make us?

Having said all that, it is politically useful to be ghettoised, as it has created an identifiable niche market for electronic music and it fosters a spirit of experimentation and innovation all but absent from much present day 'acoustic' music.

Do you have any other useful or relevant things to say about being a digital musician today?

I may have used all my gunpowder in the above response!

Chris Joseph

Please supply a biography, giving an account of your career and current activities.

I am a writer, artist and musician who works primarily with digital text, sound and image. My past projects include 'Inanimate Alice' (www.inanimatealice.com), a series of interactive multimedia stories, and 'The Breathing Wall' (www.thebreathingwall.com), a digital novel that responds to the reader's breathing rate. I am editor of the post-Dada magazine and network 391.org (www.391.org), and a founding member of The 404 (www.the404.org), a group of digital and traditional artists exploring early modernism within new media.

Please describe your creative use of technology, particularly digital technology.

My creative process is completely suffused with digital technologies. I use them for inspiration; to create text, images and sounds; to edit, program or otherwise manipulate those elements; to allow the reader/audience to respond to and influence the works ('interactivity'); to collaborate with other artists around the world; to publish, distribute and promote my work; and many other related uses between and besides.

What music do you make?

Electronic music in a wide range of styles, often with collaborating singers or musicians who are part of the 391.org network.

Why do you make music?

This is a question I often ask myself, and a difficult one to answer. The best answer I can give for now is that it is a kind of compulsion – a need that must be satisfied to remain happy and sane. I think part of the reason may be that when I make music I often feel completely absorbed in the process/moment, to an extent that comes more rarely when creating with other forms. I almost want to say that it is a more 'pure' form of creation, but maybe better would be to say that it is more immediate, and there is something in that immediacy that makes it a hugely enjoyable activity.

Is any of your sound-based work not music, as such?

Aside from the creation and manipulation of sounds as part of my multimedia works, many of my longer sound pieces would probably be better described as something other than music. What that something is, I wouldn't like to say . . .

Do you consider yourself a performer, a composer, a technologist, an engineer, some combination of these or, indeed, something else?

Any of these terms would fit some part of my practice, which is why I always have difficulty answering the question 'What do you do?'. I tend now to describe myself as a writer and artist, which is sufficiently vague to cover and leave open all possibilities.

What is the cultural context for your work? Are you influenced by music in other cultures? And the other arts?

My major musical influences would probably be post-war popular musics, principally rock, pop and electronic music; the classical music I played in orchestras when I was younger; and Dada. But there are a huge number of other influences that wax and wane. I am certainly influenced by the other arts and digital arts in particular.

What skills and attributes do you consider to be essential for you as a digital musician?

As with any musician, a basic love of music, an ability to be happy sitting alone for (sometimes long) periods of time, and an awareness of copyright; for the specifically digital musician, an interest in learning new musical softwares and other related digital skills. Beyond that, there are lots of useful skills, but probably none essential.

Do you have any other useful or relevant things to say about being a digital musician today?

The relative ease with which anyone can create electronic music today is a great thing; however, it sometimes obscures two important issues. First, that the majority of people in the world do not have the resources (financial or other) to become digital musicians (or digital artists of any description). Second, traditional music theory and skills can greatly help electronic musicians with their art.

Thor Magnusson

Please supply a biography, giving an account of your career and current activities.

I studied music from a young age and was involved in various bands in Iceland until I moved out of the country in my early twenties. My academic background is philosophy, focusing on the philosophy of mind, language and aesthetics, but also on Indian philosophy. This got me interested in computing and AI. When I learned programming, it became obvious that a meta-machine like the computer is a fantastic tool for creating musical instruments and compositions, so I've spent a decade now researching and creating digital instruments and algorithmic/generative music. I am the co-founder (with Enrike Hurtado Mendieta) of the ixi software project (www.ixi-software.net) which concentrates on experimenting with graphical user interfaces in musical software. We also have a label and regularly run workshops all over Europe where we teach audiovisual software development for artists and designers. At the moment I am a PhD student at the University of Sussex – in the Creative Systems Lab, which is part of the Informatics department, concentrating on human–machine interaction and intelligent tools for musical production and playing.

Please describe your creative use of technology, particularly digital technology.

I use all technology that I can get hold of. I consider my guitar a sophisticated technology; guitar pedals and amplifiers, all kinds of flutes and a clarinet that I'm practising. On the computer, I work most of the time in a programming language called SuperCollider, which is specifically designed for audio *programming*. My work with SuperCollider can be roughly divided into two areas: (a) building instruments that are designed for live improvisation and are, therefore, quite flexible and allow for spontaneousness; (b) algorithmic compositions where I create software that generates music that is never the same when you listen to it.

I always try to make software that supports working with acoustic instruments, hopefully creating a symbiotic relationship between the acoustic and the digital.

What music do you make?

I mostly play with improvisation bands, using a mixture of acoustic instruments and electronics, but I also enjoy improvising with other electronic musicians which happens frequently in various club or festival settings. I also make generative music in the form of software, the latest piece in a collaboration with Runar Magnusson where we used field recordings from Iceland to create 'schizotopic' soundscapes where the pieces/ locations are never the same. We intend to release the software so the user can generate an endless amount of music and share with others.

Why do you make music?

For me, music is an outlet of ideas and states of mind that I am dealing with. I get inspiration from everything I hear, see or read, and working with music in an environment like SuperCollider, which allows you to deal with musical elements from the level of samples to the score level, is a highly engaging activity where you feel you can get your hands (and mind) really dirty with direct connection to the musical material, i.e., the sound waves themselves. Sound is an important part of my world, and researching and experimenting with sound and its physics is for me a meditative process of understanding the environment. For example, recording sound in nature gives me a richer and deeper 'presence' and 'experience' of the nature itself. It is as if the ears become hypersensitive. I imagine this is analogous to a painter painting nature or even a hunter that has to pick up signs from the natural environment in order to find the prey.

Is any of your sound-based work not 'music', as such?

Yes, some of my research is on the effects of sound on the mind or direct explorations of sound physics. I don't consider that necessarily 'music', and it changes according to contexts, so it's quite hard to answer this question really. Some of the installations I have made emphasise the notion of space and ruptured temporality, often without formal or narrative structure. For myself, music tends to be more about the temporal in the 'here-and-now' sense where formal structures are important.

Do you consider yourself a performer, a composer, a technologist, an engineer, some combination of these or, indeed, something else?

All of these in addition to being an inventor. As with the term 'music', I don't find it productive to define myself (neither for myself nor others), so it depends on context what mask one might have to wear. In fact I prefer the term 'musician' as it is vague and meaningless enough. I consider everybody a musician, just of varied skills, practice and maturity.

What is the cultural context for your work? Are you influenced by music in other cultures? And the other arts?

The cultural context of my work is a mixture of the cultures of experimental music and academia. I play regularly in various concerts and music festivals, but over the past years I have been working on my project – ixi software – in an academic setting, and that has taken me to various academic conferences and festivals. I enjoy both worlds, although I think the most interesting stuff musically is happening outside the academic settings.

As for music from other cultures, I have to admit being obsessed with Indian music (and philosophy), and this has had strong influence on my own musical practice. I studied music in India for a while, which was an amazing experience. I'm also interested in various African musical cultures, such as those of western Africa – Mali and Morocco in particular. All music inspires me, and often the most obscure location of the world contains some amazing musical performers.

What skills and attributes do you consider to be essential for you as a digital musician?

Personally, I think knowledge of a programming language and sound physics is the most important. Learning those things takes time and practice, but not any more than learning to play an acoustic instrument well. In order to escape the limitations that commercial software imposes on the musician, I think it is important to be able to work in an environment where you are free to compose your own instruments or tools. But, at the same time, working with sound on the computer also requires that you understand sound physics and digital signal processing. For specific things like algorithmic composition, machine learning, signal analysis or other generative approaches I think a textual programming language suits better than graphical environments, but that's just my opinion/experience, and I acknowledge that people's minds work in different ways.

Do you have any other useful or relevant things to say about being a digital musician today?

I don't consider myself a digital musician, but simply a musician that makes use of digital technology as part of what I do. I think all instruments afford certain ideas and work processes, and it would be limiting to constrain oneself to one tool or technology.

Regarding useful things to say, I don't know what those would be. It is almost a cliché, now in 2007, to talk about the change in the music industry with the advent of the Internet and the social networking that is happening through this wonderful, but at the same time dangerous, technology.

Kaffe Matthews

Please supply a biography, giving an account of your career and current activities.

See www.annetteworks.com for all details on Kaffe works; also see current developments in www.musicforbodies.net. Kaffe Matthews has been making and performing new electro-acoustic music since 1990. She is acknowledged as a leading figure and pioneer in the field of electronic improvisation and live composition, making, on average fifty performances a year worldwide. In 1997, she established the label Annette Works, releasing the best of these events on the six CDs, 'cd Ann', 'cd Bea', 'cd cecile', 'cd dd', 'cd eb and flo' presenting an annual document of ever developing sound worlds. Currently she is rarely performing, instead directing the collaborative research project Music for Bodies with multidisciplinary professionals and the community, bringing new music and some ideas about listening to everyone.

Kaffe became known for making live site-specific sound works, playing in the dark in the middle of the space, the audience surrounding her, the sounds moving around them. She uses self-designed software matrices through which she pulls, pushes and reprocesses sounds live, using microphones, a theremin and feedback within the space; the site becoming her instrument. It is this practice that she has shifted to sonic furniture building, with Sonic Bed London (Distinction, Prix Ars Electronica, 2006) and the Worldwide Bed Project being a central pin in this ongoing collaboration.

Kaffe has worked and performed with many artists worldwide including AGF, Ryoko Kuwajima, Eliane Radigue (The Lappetites), David Muth, Shri, Mandy McIntosh, Zeena Parkins, Sachiko M., Brian Duffy, Leafcutter John, Janek Schaeffer, Ikue Mori, Marina Rosenfeld, Pan-Sonic, Alan Lamb, Christian Fennesz and ongoing democratic struggles with pan-European electronics orchestra MIMEO. Her most recent collaborative release, *Before the Libretto*, with the Lappetites, was voted in the *WIRE*'s best Top 10 new releases for 2005.

She has also been making a growing body of composed works through collaborations with a variety of people, things and processes. From working with NASA astronauts researching the sonic experience of space travel, making BAFTA-awarded *Weightless Animals*, kites and the weather on an uninhabited Scottish island, Sanda, *Weather Made*; *Taut Wires* in the Australian outback with Alan Lamb; *Touching Concrete Lightly* for MIMEO and the Oscar Niemeyeer Pavilion 2003, Serpentine Gallery; and the innovative Radio Cycle, a concept and works for maps, bikes and radios.

She played classical violin from the age of seven, singing badly in one band but getting further with bass and drums in another which recorded and toured for four years; in 1985 she discovered electricity and sound and with that, her current trajectory. Since then: acid house engineering, electrically reconstructing the violin, Distinction for a Masters in Music Technology, introducing and running a performance technology course at one of the leading live arts colleges in the UK and establishing the label Annette Works. She also set up a shop and did a zoology degree along the way.

What music do you make?

I make experimental electronic music, but I use the word 'electronic' music only because to most people, the word 'electro-acoustic' means nothing. In fact, I make both electronic and electro-acoustic music.

Why do you make music?

I don't know. I just know that that is what I have to do. But, if you want a story: in the mid-1980s, when I was in a band playing bass and drums, I went to West Africa for a couple of months. I lived with some drummers, and they taught me traditional rhythms on tam-tams, and, within that, I learnt very simple things about how the texture of the skin on your hand, and the shape of the hand, and the tightness of the drum skin and the shape of the drum, these tiny, tiny details, would change the sound of the drum when your hand hit the skin. The changing of that sound would alter the pattern and so completely alter the music and its meaning. Also, how the simple patterns, simple cells, interlocking with each other, would produce music of great complexity.

I came back to Nottingham, where I was living at the time and had this epiphany – I just had to make music. Sound essentially is my medium. It's not emotional expression, or personal experience. I'm more of a channel. Overall, making music and using it is a continuously questioning journey that never stops which makes some sense of living.

Is any of your sound-based work not 'music', as such?

No. I consider everything I make with sound to be music.

Do you consider yourself a performer, a composer, a technologist, an engineer, some combination of these or, indeed, something else?

I am a person who makes music through constant questing. I'm always looking and listening and thinking and challenging and proposing and moving. I very much work with now-time: what's happening now and now and now: now where I am, what's happening politically, socially, emotionally, geographically, historically. I live in the middle of London. It's a very noisy, fast, complex, fascinating place that is full of cultures, of people from all over the world, all of us struggling to survive in our different ways. We mash with each other and we don't. It's the antithesis of Quebec city, which I've just visited, where there are clear blue skies and lots of space, absolute clarity to think.

I am a performer. I can get into showing off too, one of the reasons I no longer go on stage – I don't want audiences to get distracted by my prancing about rather than just listening.

I am a composer in different ways. I compose on the fly in live performances, improvising and working with software to create chance events to which I respond then and there. I also slowly make carefully constructed, thought-out pieces for dance and film. Right now, I am also designing multichannelled interfaces for which I compose pieces to feel through and moving around your body in never repeating combinations of sounds.

Part of the skill which I have been trying to acquire through practice with the live work is to ask: is this decision I am making now the best one? Is it right? (Whatever that means.) Is that interesting? Is this a decision that's worth making? Or should I actually not do what I think I should do? Of course, I begin with an idea, launch off, I'm playing and I have no idea what will come next, like life really. So sometimes it's great, and then slam, a disaster, and I have to deal with that. And all witnessed with an audience.

I'm not a technologist. I use digital technology as my instrument, my tool. I'm not an engineer either. But I got into what I do now because I went to work in a recording studio in the early days of acid house and discovered that you could use technology to make sound accessible as a material. At that point, I stopped making conventional tunes and began to play with what the machines might do, crashing and coming up with things I would never think of. That's where the collaboration began, and I began to feel that music-making was really possible. I also made the decision then not to be an engineer but to use the studio and its gadgets creatively. I wouldn't be doing all this if computers didn't exist.

What is the cultural context for your work? Are you influenced by music in other cultures? And the other arts?

About two years ago, I started to realise that I no longer wanted my work to be available just to those who already know about the kind of music I make; the largely young, male, white audiences who come to galleries, warehouses, basements, cellars and so on to enjoy shows.

I think that experimental electronic music, if you can find a way into it, can be profoundly rewarding, even life-enhancing. It gives you a way of tuning in to what life is like through your ears, through listening. If you listen, rather than look all the time, it can transform your life.

I realised back in about 1997, when I made my first sonic armchair, that old women and kids would queue to be able to have a ride in this chair. All that they were actually listening to was a piece made from a recording of a jumbo jet, which I had processed, looped and filtered so that it moved up and down your body as you sat in the chair. It gave you an audio massage and was great to sit in. However, if you had played that piece to any of those people through speakers, they'd have said, 'Give me a break love, where's the tune?'

So, having realised that sonic furniture had potential, I went on to make a sonic bed. So the sonic bed is for lying down, can be a social space (there's room for three to six people) as well as a social experiment around listening and unbeknownst intimacy with strangers in public spaces. It has a high quality twelve-channel sound system so the music really spins and wraps and massages visitors. No more stereo. The response has been stunning.

So, my music is no longer just about me performing solo with a space but is now working with collaboration. I have set up and direct this collaborative research project, Music for Bodies (www.musicforbodies.net) exploring sound, architecture, furniture and the vibrations of the human body to make new music and ways of enjoying it. It works with professionals from other disciplines such as an architect, a social psychologist, a biofeedback practitioner, an acoustician, a software programmer pooling ideas. A lot of musicians end up working with image, but not me. I'm interested in sound and the future of sound, and now it seriously is involving looking for wider audiences.

What skills and attributes do you consider to be essential for you as a digital musician?

All kinds of skills, but the main one has been collaborating with other people, such as programmers and other musicians. As a result of meeting the programmer David Muth, for example, I am able to think about sonic shapes and sonic movements as different entities, so I can link them separately to other things. I am no longer the digital musician in my studio practising for hours every day.

My intention when performing was always focused on the live event. I started with an empty hard drive and a sense of the occasion and a responsibility to the audience. I don't want to work like that anymore. People used to love the spectacle of me as a person performing, but it was a distraction. Another important skill is to jettison stereo and to work with the acoustic properties of the space you are in at the time. I'm no longer a soloist. Now I work with other people and aim for a wider audience.

Do you have any other useful or relevant things to say about being a digital musician today?

Quebec was a delight because it was the antithesis of what I just said! I was a complete recluse, making my bed. One other thing I wanted to say is that I've got very bored of watching people playing with laptops. People even still mime to what they produce from their laptops or mixers. I want to be in a social space and experience music with other people.

I also really want to make music that is not restricted by time, that doesn't have a middle and an end but is about the sonic experience that is happening right now. What's happening around me right now could be music. And I want to make music that is always different, every time you come back to it.

So I'm asking more from technology. I set up the rules and the ingredients, and something different must happen. That's why I'm making installations. Let's replace a few of these new gyms with huge multichannelled sound systems for people to come and spin around their favourite disco, opera or swing CDs.

Randall Packer

Please supply a biography, giving an account of your career and current activities.

Randall Packer is internationally recognised as a pioneering artist, composer, educator and scholar in the field of multimedia. His book and accompanying website, *Multimedia: From Wagner to Virtual Reality* has been widely adopted as one of the leading educational texts in the field. He is concerned with the aesthetic, philosophical and socio-cultural impact of new media in an increasingly technological society.

In 1988, he founded Zakros InterArts and has since produced, directed and created critically acclaimed new-media performance, installation and net-specific works. Since moving to Washington, DC in 2000, his work has explored the critique of the role of the artist in society and politics. He founded the virtual government agency US Department of Art and Technology (www.usdat.us) in 2001, which proposes and supports the idealised definition of the artist as one whose reflections, ideas, aesthetics, sensibilities and abilities can have significant and transformative impact on the world stage.

Please describe your creative use of technology, particularly digital technology.

My work is based in performance and has incorporated nearly every form and genre of new media. Currently I am working with HD video and surround sound for an upcoming music theatre production.

What music do you make?

Music that supports a variety of media and interdisciplinary projects.

Why do you make music?

Because I can.

Is any of your sound-based work not 'music', as such?

No.

Do you consider yourself a performer, a composer, a technologist, an engineer, some combination of these or, indeed, something else?

I am a composer of media.

What is the cultural context for your work? Are you influenced by music in other cultures? And the other arts?

My work is influenced by social and political issues. Currently, I am at work on a political music theatre work entitled *A Season in Hell*, a project of the virtual government agency I created shortly after 9/11, the US Department of Art and Technology.

What skills and attributes do you consider to be essential for you as a digital musician?

The ability to integrate ideas with technical skills.

Do you have any other useful or relevant things to say about being a digital musician today?

It is no longer possible to be concerned only with music; we live in a global world where interdisciplinary approaches are critical to artistic expression.

Quantazelle

Please supply a biography, giving an account of your career and current activities.

A self-proclaimed 'multi-hyphenate', Liz McLean Knight – the sole woman behind Quantazelle – is thoroughly immersed in technology, fashion, music and the often-surprising overlaps between. When attempting to circuit bend battery-powered music toys for an upcoming music performance, she discovered that electronic components can be turned into elegant jewelry and started an entire tech-fashion line called Zelle (www.zellestyle.com).

While devising a content-management system for her online experimental electronic music magazine, *Modsquare* (www.modsquare.com) she learned various web-based programming languages and related technologies, having a head start from her one-time computer-science college major. With that knowledge she then started an online store, Fractalspin (www.fractalspin.com), to sell not only her jewelry but also accessories and gear for the technologically-sophisticated yet fashionably-minded crowd.

Desiring to assist similar artists reach a greater audience as well as provide gear for electronic musicians, she started Subvariant (www.subvariant.com) – a record label and accessories company behind the well-received Electronic Musician's Emergency Adapter kit (www.emergencyadapters.com).

As laptop-DJ Liz Revision (www.lizrevision.com), she selects both experimental ambient and glitchy techno in response to the aura of each night (including a recent co-promotion and residency at Ramp Chicago's (www.rampchicago.com) Sonotheque nights). As Quantazelle (www.quantazelle.com) she combines complex percussive programming, sonic innovation and engaging sound design together with an approachable melodic sensibility and often booty-shaking result.

Quantazelle has contributed a track to the upcoming compilation by Black Dog's self-tagged Future Sound of Sheffield label, Dust Science (www.dustscience.com), called *Faith is Fear.*

Liz lives and works in the Wicker Park neighborhood of Chicago, IL, sharing a cable-strewn apartment with her boyfriend, their two dogs and stacks of music gear and computers.

Please describe your creative use of technology, particularly digital technology.

What's great about computers is that they are amazing tools that allow you to completely stretch, distort, invent and reinvent sound like no other instrument. And, there's usually an 'undo' command. :-)

What music do you make?

Perhaps 'edgy experimental-yet-melodic electronic' or 'glitchy-yet-catchy instrumental electronic'. It continues to evolve as I do.

Why do you make music?

I feel that I have a particularly unique audio perspective on creating music that's not dependent on any particular instrument, machine, plug-in or genre to make it sound like it came from me. I've participated in this Iron Chef of Music competition put on by the kracfive label (www.kracfive.com/ironchef), but which has worldwide participation via the Internet and various 'nodes' (physical meet-ups) throughout the world. The idea is that they give you one audio sample, and two hours, and you can use any program or effect to create a track from that one sample, but you can't use any other instrument. I thought it was absolutely fascinating how everyone who participated took the same source material but used it in completely different ways. And I was able to recognise the ones that were produced by my friends, because it just 'sounded like them'. Even though all of us who participated started from the same place with the same materials, we each produced something uniquely different. I sort of feel that way about what I do – I have a particular approach that sounds like me that you'll never hear anywhere else, even though there are people using the same software and plug-ins as I do. I feel as if I'm contributing something unique to all the available recorded electronic music. If I ever stumble across anyone who sounds like I want to sound, but doing it better, I'll just retire and subscribe to all their future albums. :-) Also, I wrote about my experience at Iron Chef on my blog: lizrevision.com/general/iron-chef-of-music-kracfives-sample-chopping-beat-dicing-producer-battle.

Is any of your sound-based work not 'music', as such?

Well I suppose my mother might say yes, but I don't think so. :-)

Do you consider yourself a performer, a composer, a technologist, an engineer, some combination of these or, indeed, something else?

I'd say all of those on some level. These days, I've toned down the actual 'performance' of my shows a bit (haven't worn a costume in for ever, haven't done any costume changes or participated in any laptop cage matches in quite a while) and have just been focusing on the sonic experience that I create as a sound technologist in a live setting. Plus, just creating all the musical intricacies in one track requires a few days of such focused nerdery in front of my laptop that I kind of run out of time and energy to think about how I could make it more 'performative' in a live setting.

What is the cultural context for your work?

Here in Chicago, the only stations that play instrumental music are the classical-music station and two low-signal-power college stations, one that plays dance music and one that plays absolutely anything from field recordings to noise punk. There really isn't a mainstream cultural channel that my work would fit into, although I can think of about twelve Internet-based podcasts or websites that are a near-perfect fit. And that's why the Internet is just so wonderful – you can discover all kinds of new music and network and interact with people with the same connoisseur-level taste in this kind of music that you wouldn't find in mainstream cultural channels.

And I do think that people who love IDM/experimental/abstract electronic music are connoisseurs along the same level as classical-music buffs. Both sorts of fans generally have a technical knowledge of how their music is created (although classical has a 'canon' of pieces by established composers that can be played by different groups of musicians and compared side by side with each other to highlight technical differences), and both rely on emotions created only through the interaction of all the sounds and not through a sung narrative. That's likely what's behind the perception of IDM as being pretentious and over-intellectual instead of fun, but it definitely can be both.

What's interesting to me though is the response I get when I play my music or my favorite tracks by other musicians for people who've never heard this kind of music – and they really are into it. I think this sort of music can be appreciated by more people, and I'd like to see it have a higher profile than just background music for car commercials.

Are you influenced by music in other cultures? And the other arts?

I think *gamelan* is really interesting. It's heavily and sometimes complexly layered, with different parts coming in and out with variations or in another time signature. Some of it reminds me of earlier Autechre.

What skills and attributes do you consider to be essential for you as a digital musician?

Technically: keeping up on current technologies, upgrades, plug-ins, processor speeds, available VSTs. Knowing how to optimise the performance of one's computer for digital audio, keeping an eye on the sort of peripherals and MIDI interfaces and whatnot that become available, and looking at tech news to think about the future of one's set-up as technology progresses (i.e., I use a PC, but with the advent of imminent-failure Vista, I'm going to have to start thinking about either switching everything over to a Mac, or pray that the software and hardware I use now can either be emulated in WINE under Linux or that those manufacturers will port everything to Linux).

Professionally: networking and sharing ideas with fellow digital musicians, having a local peer base, having an Internet peer base, being committed to the larger digital musician community and helping out others with talent (either by sharing knowledge or helping to connect musicians with labels or musicians with venues to perform in), not letting one's ego get in the way, keeping in touch with people in the press who've been supportive in the past, as well as labels or promotions crews that have booked me.

Mentally: commitment, goal orientation, foresight and planning ahead, just doing things that are musically fun (like DJing privately or in a low key setting and not being constrained by a genre, or participating in the Iron Chef of Music competition), having another income stream so I don't have to care if my music is commercially viable, going to music events that aren't electronic just for a change of pace.

Do you have any other useful or relevant things to say about being a digital musician today?

It's a very exciting time to work with computers, software and new interfaces – I can't wait to see what people will invent next. For a new musician, I would recommend learning Max/MSP, PD, or Reaktor, since those modular software interfaces allow for all sorts of innovation, both sonic and in the sort of things that you can begin to program through it (like, the ability to use external sensors, and being able to control free-standing lighting or even robotics in Max). I'd recommend against learning a program like Reason since it's built as a sort of program with 'training wheels' to help analogue musicians make the transition to digital. If you're just learning, you should go as digital as possible in a platform that allows as much flexibility as possible in regards to how you're going to be composing your music.

John Richards

Please supply a biography, giving an account of your career and current activities.

John Richards' work explores performing with self-made instruments and the creation of interactive environments. He performs regularly with electro-noise improvisers kREEPA and the post-punk group Sand (Soul Jazz Records), and he is actively involved in the performance of improvised music and community music projects. In 2002, his work with kREEPA helped initiate the OIK project at STEIM, Amsterdam that involved the hacking of commercially available hardware to create economic musical interfaces.

He has worked with many leading improvisers and musicians in the field of live electronics and has performed extensively across the globe, predominantly in Europe, as well as Japan, Australia and the USA. He completed a doctorate in electro-acoustic composition at the University of York, UK, in 2002, and he is currently part of the Music, Technology and Innovation Research Centre at De Montfort University, Leicester, UK. Since 1990, he has also taught improvisation at Dartington International Summer School.

Please describe your creative use of technology, particularly digital technology.

My use of digital technology, particularly in my performance work, is not obvious. This is the case with the Kreepback instrument: a modular environment of analogue DIY electronic devices, audio hardware and digital bits and pieces patched together to create a feedback labyrinth. The instrument's name is derived from my work with the group kREEPA and the idea that sound creeps back on itself. Since 2000, I have been developing the instrument and approaches towards performing with it. Some of the modified 'physical' objects (see answers to questions below) tend to catch the 'eye'. However, as far as the ear is concerned, digital technology plays a big part. I have been hugely influenced on different levels by object-orientated programming languages. I initially conceived the feedback network of the Kreepback instrument using Max/MSP and the inputs and outputs of an audio interface. Despite being quite a different instrument to the one I currently use, the genesis of the instrument is here.

Max/MSP has also offered me a way of prototyping environments for performance and installations. The Kreepback instrument is really a hybrid technological system designed for solo and group improvisation. It combines both analogue and digital technology as well as the acoustic and physical properties of objects. For me, although digital technology has been formative in my creative work, it is not simply just about being a 'digital' musician. In regards to specifically digital technology I currently use in performance, the Nord Micro Modular is used as a 'module' in the Kreepback instrument. The programming language of the Nord offers great flexibility, and its small size, robustness and control features make it a really powerful device to help coerce and steer the feedback produced by the other modules that make up the Kreepback instrument. For example, using a mixing desk as a matrix, I can use a low frequency oscillator (LFO) from the Nord to modulate some of the analogue signals. Within the digital domain of the Nord I also have created feedback labyrinths and networks that I control with MIDI: there are feedback loops within feedback loops within the overall instrument. Having worked with Max/MSP, programming the Nord was an extension of the same modular approach.

What music do you make?

I make predominantly electronic and improvised musics, as well as having written 'composed' electronic pieces. Such terms as 'industrial jazz' have been applied to some of this music, where free improvisation meets the broad genre of 'noise'. Although a lot of the music I have created has dense textures, complex rhythms and could be considered as 'loud', I am also interested in extreme contrasts, the use of silence and sparse musical landscapes. Similarly, the idea of contrast in my music is also explored through the relationship between the performer's involvement and non-involvement (total process) in performance.

Why do you make music?

I do not really have a rational answer to this question. Making music is part of my fabric as a human being and is something that has always been there. I have sometimes thought about how I might stop making music, but these thoughts have been fleeting.

Is any of your sound-based work not 'music', as such?

With some of the instruments I have created there would seem a clear link to sculpture and found art. For example, the Mincer – a modified meat mincer (grinder) where turning the handle outputs different resistances that in turn controls other sound-generating devices – is very much like a piece of commodity sculpture. With the Mincer there is a striking resemblance to the ready-mades of Marcel Duchamp. I have also used other found objects to create sound generating devices/instruments. These include two Victorian teapots (*Loud Tea*), a wooden plank with drill-hole patterns (*Resonating Wooden Sculpture No. 1*) and brass candlesticks. In some of my instruments, the appropriation of found objects is purely cosmetic, such as whiskey-bottle corks for knobs and old tins to house the electronics. Then there is the *Automaticiser*, a brass etching produced automatically that acts as a random touch control. Often there is as much interest in the way my devices look as sound. With an audience, I like to set up a visual dynamic. Devices, cables, objects are arranged, normally on a table, very much like an artist's still life. The tabletops of Keith Rowe and David Tudor have been influential in this respect. These objects also act as a score to the performance. Before and after concerts, my still life or 'installation' is meant to be viewed. The audience more frequently than not want to more closely explore the devices used in performance. There is intrigue with regards to how such objects are used to create sound or how they work. I find that the digital elements in my hybrid system are often overlooked by the audience or overshadowed by the more visual curios.

Do you consider yourself a performer, a composer, a technologist, an engineer, some combination of these or, indeed, something else?

I have found it increasingly difficult to call myself a 'composer', although I am, at times, clearly composing. There is a lot of baggage with the term 'composer', some of which, I do not like. For example, the composer as someone that sits at the top of a musical hierarchy, the limited reference of the term in regard to Western culture, and the composer as something distinct from a musician. I have previously remarked in other interviews I have given on a comment made by Harrison Birtwistle in an interview with Paul Griffiths. In this interview, Birtwistle states that for him, playing the clarinet and composing were incompatible. This seemed anathema to me. Never at any point whilst composing did I ever feel the need to give up playing or performing. If this meant my compositional output was smaller or compromised in some way, then so be it. I like to think of myself as a musician, the term 'musician' also embracing the composer.

I am also a technologist, engineer, designer, programmer and artist. However, for cultural reasons I do not call myself any of these. To be, for example, a sculptor, you have to earn the right to be called this: have a studio and exhibitions, a commitment to sculpting. Some of my instruments are arguably sculptures, but their *raison d'etre* is to create sound. I recently remarked in a seminar entitled 'Inscribing Instabilities' that I gave with Simon Atkinson at the Institute of Electroacoustic Music, Sweden, on the *Resonating Wooden Sculpture No. 1*. This is a piece of wood from my workshop that I have used for years on my drill press. Random patterns have been made on the wood from the drill holes. The piece of wood is aged and worn. It has a history, and there is something visually appealing about it. Justifying it as a work of art, however, is another matter. Yes, I would like to hang it in an art gallery, but as a sculpture, I have no artist authority to do this. But, as a 'musical' object, I can justify it. Working with these types of objects has been very important to me and has enabled me to express different artistic sides of my personality.

Furthermore, I feel very strongly that the distinctions associated traditionally between science and the arts are perfunctory. In the UK, for example, people study to become a Bachelor of Science or Arts. It is clear that many students do not fit into either of these categories. This is also true of the majority of digital musicians.

What is the cultural context for your work? Are you influenced by music in other cultures? And the other arts?

'The Twenty-First Century is a Better Place for Me.' This is the title of a paper I have had an idea for, although I am struggling to start the paper due to the enormity of the issues it keeps throwing up. In brief, the idea for the paper was to attempt to place my and other people's work within a cultural context. Being born in the 1960s, I have been fortunate to experience making music in more traditional ways with acoustic instruments such as the piano and double bass, as well as witnessing the incredible rise of the PC and being part of the digital era. Also, through teaching, I have seen the emergence of the first generation of purely digital musicians. Consequently, I am a polyglot musician: I speak many musical languages. I remember at university where I was studying music, there were those who could improvise and those who could not. Never the twain met. I suppose one of my attributes as a musician was that I could move across different musical terrains. It seemed completely natural. I had learnt some of the canon of Western classical music; I played in a jazz band and spent a good many years of my youth playing 'axe murdering' bass in a punk band. I also have experienced the dissemination boom of music. By this, I mean the opportunity to have on CD, for example, a vast range of music from around the globe. Some of my tutors would see my eclecticism as a problem, arguing that it was artistically incoherent to be involved in and have such an interest in such a broad range of music, to have more than one musical personality. For them, it was all about artistic integrity, creating a coherent body of work and 'purity' of an idea. I never really saw it this way. My broad interests were a result of my cultural background. My artistic integrity, therefore, should be informed by this plurality. So, for the past twenty years, in certain circumstances, I have kept supposed different musical personas under my hat. The idea behind the paper 'The Twenty-First Century is a Better Place for Me' simply recognises the cultural phenomena that I have been part of and that has arisen.

The high-versus-low-art debate really does seem to have run its course. Likewise, the stranglehold of high modernism, which seemed to dominate a lot of my music education, has loosened. I often joke with myself about being a musician representing the true 'middlebrow'. Now, this may sound abhorrent, but this is something I am beginning to think more positively about. There really is a cultural revolution going on, and a lot of very exciting new music being made as a result.

My work is very much influenced by the other arts. This is particularly evident in, for example, the Kreepback instrument. These influences include the futuristic imagery in Fritz Lang films, the architecture of Richard Rodgers, the ready-mades of Marcel Duchamp, constructivist sculpture, the Young British Artists and pop art, the writings of William Gibson and automatic art.

What skills and attributes do you consider to be essential for you as a digital musician?

File management and archiving is something I should be better at and really is a skill the digital musician needs. Over the years, I have created thousands of files that are now sprawled across many hard disks. I sometimes feel it is easier to create a new sound rather than try to retrieve a file I made, for example, five years ago. Also, understanding ins and outs and patching skills is essential. The binary world has no in between with regard to this. Being a digital musician is not any different for me from being a musician in general, where, for example, I would want to experiment, explore and find the 'edges' of the medium.

Do you have any other useful or relevant things to say about being a digital musician today?

Being a digital musician is not just about the practical application of technology but also a way of being or thinking. I have recently presented a paper at Stanford University entitled 'The Short-Circuited Digital Mind'. This paper discusses how 'virtualness' has had a major impact on how we interface with the physical world and how the digital has reinvigorated our interest in 'old' technology in relation to music. In Nicholas Negroponte's seminal text *Being Digital* there is the sub-heading 'Don't Dissect a Frog Build One'. Negroponte uses this sub-heading to suggest that the digital age is all about 'doing'. In the digital, it is possible to try things out, lots of things and at speed, for there is more often than not the 'undo' key if mistakes are made. Digital technology has enabled me to have a better understanding of acoustics and synthesis through different software programs and to experiment with making performance environments and musical instruments. I have been able to 'do', and this mentality has affected my entire music-making.

Marshall McLuhan has stated how a new technology is often concerned with technology of the past. In regards to music, the digital has helped reinvigorate and excite musicians about pre-digital analogue technology. Take eBay, for example: I can systematically search and find hundreds of digital images of old reel-to-reel machines that are for sale or have been sold. Digital technology, in this case eBay, can constantly bring to life the past. It is not just about buying and selling but what we are 'experiencing', albeit virtual or digital through an image or description. And there are all of the softsynths and computer programs based on analogue models. Eventually after using, for example, virtual patch cables or valve-amp simulators, it seems inevitable that a musician is going to want to use and experience the 'real' thing. Negroponte also considers that we have not even got to base camp in as far as the capabilities and potential of digital technology, yet terms such as 'post-digital' are gaining usage. Perhaps this is due to the fact that digital technology has become so all-pervasive that it is often taken for granted, or even ignored. This is true in the case of the Kreepback instrument I discussed earlier. So, it is in this sense that the digital mind has been short-circuited.

Sophy Smith

Please supply a biography, giving an account of your career and current activities.

I have been involved in music since the age of five. Essentially, I am classically trained with three grade 8s in piano, French horn and singing and a first class BA Hons in music and inter-arts. I played and sang in classical choirs and orchestras until the age of twenty-four, but then stopped orchestral performance when it was no longer necessary for my formal education. Although I enjoyed playing in music ensembles, it became dull playing the same repertoire over and over, especially being a French-horn player where the parts are usually unchallenging.

My undergraduate degree was also in inter-arts and this cross/interdisciplinary approach to my work led me to complete a MA in contemporary performing arts. It was during this course that I began to write music. I had studied and enjoyed composition at GCSE level, but it was not advised as a 'safe' option for A-level music, and so, by the time I began my degree course, I was unconfident in my compositional abilities. However, I did some composition at university and enjoyed the work, where I was able to follow my own path! My undergraduate degree course had no music technology provision, and so my compositions were all for orchestral/vocal ensembles. This had a direct effect on my future compositional development and style, as I am essentially self-taught in all aspects of music technology. This lack of experience (and equipment!) resulted in my early music technology experiments involving any cheap lo-fi equipment I could access, and using it in any way I could find: for example, cheap 1980s sampling keyboards, electronic toys, tape recorders and four-track machines. Early music technology work was essentially sound-based, as I had neither the equipment nor expertise for sequencing! A lack of keyboard or computer-based sound-generating equipment forced me to focus on sample-based music and creating my own sounds by recording and manipulating found sounds. When I began to work as a professional composer being commissioned by other people, this reliance on sound-based and sample-based work was too restricting for the different types and styles of music that I was being asked to write, and so I learned sequencing and editing software and techniques to widen my skills.

My professional work covers a wide range of work. I currently work as a professional composer, writing music mainly for dance and theatre companies as well as running my own live art company Assault Events. The company creates original devised performance events as well as planning and delivering a range of specialist residencies. We also undertake research and consultancy projects for clients including the Creative Partnerships, regional arts organisations and local education authorities. In 2007, I completed my PhD in music technology (the compositional processes of UK hip-hop turntable teams) and am currently working part-time at the Institute of Creative Technologies at De Montfort University, Leicester as a research fellow with responsibility for the Masters programme in creative technologies.

Please describe your creative use of technology, particularly digital technology.

I compose using an Apple Mac running Logic Pro, Pro Tools and Wave Burner. I use soft synths including Absynth and Sculpture. My music also uses a wide range of samples which I manipulate in Logic. I use the technology both as a palette where I can create and mix new sounds and as a canvas where I can compose the work. Digital technology is a tool for creating sounds as well as putting them together, and having both these elements in one place means that I can work quickly and allows me to be much more flexible and effective. Digital technology is ideal as it allows me to quickly re-edit/and alter pieces of music, which is vital in the situation I compose in where I often compose in the rehearsal studio with the dances/actors whilst they are devising. This allows the work to be a much more collaborative experience than it would if I had to keep going back to a large analogue studio or writing for instrumentalists who were not present.

What music do you make?

I mainly write music for dance and theatre companies for touring shows. This involves creating soundtracks of between 40 and 75 minutes in length, comprising of a number of shorter tracks. Usually, all these tracks are 'written through' so that the soundtrack is heard as a complete piece of music without gaps. The type of music I write depends on the movement/action that it works with, but includes orchestral pieces, sound-based work, vocal work and electronic dance music. I think I am more defined by my approach to composition through collaboration with other art forms rather than a particular style. Although my music is commissioned, I have free reign to experiment with different styles and approaches to create the soundtracks.

Why do you make music?

I enjoy creating things from scratch – music is one of my outlets for doing this! I find it challenging and stimulating and hugely enjoyable. I do not write much music for its own sake but rather enjoy writing music for collaborative things (e.g., environments, events) in which music is one of a number of parts that go to make the whole. I can't remember choosing music – I just can't remember doing anything else!

Is any of your sound-based work not music, as such?

Yes, if it is the best medium through which to reflect/support the 'action' on stage.

Do you consider yourself a performer, a composer, a technologist, an engineer, some combination of these or, indeed, something else?

Mostly a performer and composer. I don't really see myself primarily as a technologist, as first and foremost I write music, and the digital technology is my means for doing this. I definitely don't see myself as an engineer, probably as I have no formal training in this area. My music often drives my engineering-orientated collaborators mad as my engineering is 'wrong'! In terms of engineering, I tend to experiment until I find what I like, rather than knowing what to look for. Really, I suppose, I see myself as a facilitator of sorts. On one side of me, I have the whole world of music (or as much of it as I know!) and, on the other, I have the needs of the piece. My role is to pull in relevant forms/styles/sounds/approaches of/to music and create effective sound/music for the piece. I find this approach really exciting as it means I am not restricted to one style or approach and am constantly challenged.

What is the cultural context for your work?

I have probably covered this in answers to the other questions. I primarily compose as part of collaborative projects involving a number of different art forms, some digital, some not. My work is not really of any particular style, though it does lean towards Western traditions, both of 'art' music and popular music. Because of the collaborative nature of my work, I tend to begin with an aim of creating a particular 'feel' or atmosphere rather than with a desire to write a particular style/type of music.

Are you influenced by music in other cultures? And the other arts?

I am influenced in some way or another by all music I hear, but I don't think that I am hugely influenced by any particular music in other cultures. I am influenced by any music that I like and find interesting – usually something that has an instant emotive hit! Some of my music does have different cultural nuances, but this is really because the sound itself reflects what I want to convey in the music for a particular scene or dance sequence. I am very influenced by the other arts as I have a very cross/interdisciplinary approach to my composition. This manifests itself in two ways, either in creating collaborative work with other disciplines or experimenting with different creative processes and concepts used in other art forms. If my music is influenced by anything, then it is a combination of my past experiences as an orchestral instrumentalist and vocalist and a desire to create music that will connect with people and that they will find interesting and enjoyable.

What skills and attributes do you consider to be essential for you as a digital musician?

In no particular order . . .

- creativity to work within 'constraints' of technology
- ability to use the technology creatively and push its boundaries
- flexibility
- patience(!)
- knowledge of music outside the digital domain – trying different compositional approaches, etc.

It does seem *sometimes* that some digital music applications favour a particular approach to music-making and it is important to get the technology to work for you rather than it directing your work.

Do you have any other useful or relevant things to say about being a digital musician today?

I love being a digital musician as digital technology gives me the tools to be an extremely creative and flexible composer. It allows me to experiment in ways that would not be possible with 'real' instruments, e.g., different approaches to creating 'new' sounds and the speed of digital processing means that I can experiment with, and where necessary change, aspects of my music very quickly, which would not be possible without digital technology. This makes me much more likely to take risks and try new things. Also, digital technology has speeded the day-to-day processes of collaboration. I can send music to collaborators virtually instantly and get feedback much quicker than sending tapes through the post. This sounds extremely mundane but means that I am engaged with my work constantly, rather than having to come back to it days later. Also, because of the prevalence of and (relative) cheapness of some digital music packages, many more people I work with across art forms have some experience of creating digital music and so have an understanding of the process and some shared vocabulary. Also, in terms of collaborating across art forms, many of my co-collaborators work with digital technology (e.g., film and photography) and so tasks like swapping and inputting files, time-coding, etc., that used to take a long time and could be quite complex are much easier and at times extremely straightforward. This means that there is more time to be creative as less time is being spent trying to get the technology to work!

Atau Tanaka

Please supply a biography, giving an account of your career and current activities.

Atau Tanaka is a Japanese/American composer and researcher based in Paris. He bridges the fields of media art and experimental music, artistic and scientific research. His work seeks the continuing place of the artist in democratised digital forms. He creates sensor-based musical instruments, searching for the idiomatic voice in the interface. He composes for network systems, considering data transmission delay as the acoustic of the network. His works include solo and ensemble concert works and exhibition instal-lations. His work in the 1990s with the trio Sensorband continues today in gestural sound-image performance with Sensors_Sonics_Sights. He publishes theoretical writ-ings and conducts fundamental research at Sony CSL Paris to develop and document his socio-artistic approach. His work has been presented at Ars Electronica, SFMOMA, Eyebeam, La Villette, ICC, V2 and ZKM. He has received support from the Japan Foun-dation, the Fraunhofer Society, the Daniel Langlois Foundation and is mentor at NESTA.

Please describe your creative use of technology, particularly digital technology.

I have been interested in the use of interactive technology for musical expression. I perform with musical instruments built from sensor systems, create network music infrastructures, sound-image installations and participative mobile locative music expe-riences.

What music do you make?

I make music as a function of the medium or infrastructure for which I am composing. I seek out the sonic voice of the chosen medium.

Why do you make music?

I continue to make music because ideas continue to come, and I have been unsuccessful to stop making music despite efforts.

Is any of your sound-based work not 'music', as such?

I do not make a distinction for myself between sound-art and music. I invite myself into musical situations that put in question the nature of music itself, seeking purely artistic sonic structures. Conversely, I try to impart musical life to sound installations, shaping electronic signals and acoustic patterns into structural forms.

Do you consider yourself a performer, a composer, a technologist, an engineer, some combina-tion of these or, indeed, something else?

I am a composer who performs, an artist who uses digital technology as his canvas.

What is the cultural context for your work? Are you influenced by music in other cultures? And the other arts?

I have lived in several countries in my life so feel no direct identity with one particular culture. I draw upon the different cultures of my background in ways that I could not have if I had not left them. Also, I believe that there is a culture of technology, as well as a culture that questions technology. My works sits at this intersection, ultimately embracing a visceral vision of digital sound.

What skills and attributes do you consider to be essential for you as a digital musician?

A musician is a musician, digital or not. This being said, we need to move beyond the vocational skill set often associated with musical training. Today, knowing the physics of acoustics and the physiology of auditory perception is more important than knowing functional harmony.

Do you have any other useful or relevant things to say about being a digital musician today?

Digital makes us appreciate analogue – not just for the specific sound qualities of certain historical instruments but for the qualities of analogue electronics as a medium of sound transmission. You can keep adding to analog, you can feel analog. Digital is not in the impossibility of acquiring these capabilities, but the digital musician must sensitise himself to this potential.

Martyn Ware

Please supply a biography, giving an account of your career and current activities.

Martyn Ware was a founding member of both The Human League and Heaven 17 and is one of the UK's most successful and in-demand producers. His work includes Terence Trent d'Arby's *Hardline* album and hits for Tina Turner and Marc Almond. Martyn has also worked extensively writing music for film, theatre, television and radio. His most recent venture is The Illustrious Company, formed with long-term collaborator Vince Clarke (of Erasure, Yazoo and Depeche Mode), which makes original music soundscapes often in visual contexts. They recently staged a series of events called 'The Future of Sound'. See www.illustriouscompany.co.uk.

Please describe your creative use of technology, particularly digital technology.

I'm a Mac addict. I had one of the first Macs in the country in the 1980s. The Mac is central to just about everything we do, from composition through to soundscape assembly, through to 3-D surround-sound convolution. We use a proprietary system that has been built with our advice by Paul Gillieron Acoustic Design which enables us to move things around in three dimensions and actually see where things should be in a wireframe diagram. It can move up to sixteen different sound frames simultaneously at 25 frames per second. We also use Logic, an industry standard product, as a front-end. We also use Macs for all our business needs, designing websites, etc. And, although we are famous for using analogue synths, nowadays we use virtual instruments as well, so more or less everything we do is mediated through technology.

What music do you make?

It varies. My collaborator, Vince Clarke from Erasure, and myself compose together, creating soundscapes for exhibitions, events, etc., etc. We also do Hollywood-quality sound design in three dimensions. So, the work we do ranges from 3-D 'narratives' that have nothing to do with traditional music, through to traditional music pieces that are rendered in three dimensions.

The kind of music we create tends to be generally electronic and can be completely abstract or based on, say, folk history or recordings of the human voice. We are currently working on a project for the Royal Observatory at Greenwich which uses seven different sound fields based on sounds, from various observatories around the world, created by celestial events. That's pretty abstract for the listener, but it's all predicated on sounds that are relevant to the particular environment.

We're also designing the reopening of the National Film Theatre, accompanied by giant projections from their newly digitised film library. So, we're doing a lot of stuff that involves reinterpreting in space existing historical or contextual content. From a commercial point of view, we work closely with commissioners to create a sense of immersion. So we did a piece for BP last year based on their six core values, from 'innovation' to 'green'. We extemporised around those ideas to create a sense of immersion in a sound environment.

Why do you make music?

Because it's the only means I have of making a living. And for pleasure. I tolerate no interference with the creative process. I never have done, throughout my career as a musician and writer, composer and producer. One of the conditions of me working is that I can't deal with working by committee, particularly when composing. For that reason, we don't do much work with the advertising world, for instance. The presumption in that kind of world is that if they pay you enough money they have the right to interfere. I'd rather earn less money and provide a clean path towards resolution of a creative idea. And it's my life, and has been before I got signed as a professional musician, since about 1972 when I bought my first synthesiser and started playing with imaginary bands, with my mates in Sheffield. It makes me laugh when people talk about retirement, because I'll be doing this until the day I die, if I can.

Is any of your sound-based work not 'music', as such?

I regard it all as music. Some people would say: 'that's not music'. It all has an artistic element. An example of the closest we would get to something that is not music is a piece we did for the Swansea National Waterfront Museum, with a friend called David Bickertsaff and a company called New Angle. One of the rooms was about how people used to shop in South Wales and the historical attitudes to money. This particular room had a long table with a responsive projection on it where you could touch items and they'd go into your shopping basket as you went along. They needed a sound element to make clear the information they wanted, and we had to do it in two different languages simultaneously. So we took this approach where we had multiple streams of information together with sound effects in three dimensions which, if it was done in stereo would sound confusing, but when they are separated in space sound not confusing at all. It's like having several people in different corners of the room speaking several things in several languages, almost like a Samuel Beckett play, where some of it is abstraction but the majority is about getting information across in an interesting way. Without an artistic sensibility and experience of handling spatialised sound, this could be an absolute mess. So I regard the whole thing as being very creative at every level and very based on a knowledge of musical assembly, both in a compositional sense and a production sense (my career is half-and-half composer/performer and producer).

Do you consider yourself a performer, a composer, a technologist, an engineer, some combination of these or, indeed, something else?

Good question. Nowadays, less of a performer, although during the 'Future of Sound' events I MC the whole thing, because I'm the most famous person involved and it's my baby anyway, so I can do what I want! I like public speaking now, whereas it used to horrify me. I've turned from a performer in the music sense to a performer in the didactic sense. Since I've had children (now aged eleven and nine), I've become much more interested in distributing the experience I've acquired over thirty years.

I think of myself more as a composer now, in the real sense of the word, than a writer. I'm a producer-composer. The skills I acquired as a producer were invaluable in terms of organising the material required to get a message across, especially in the complex world of 3-D sound and how that information is imparted to the observer.

I don't like the word 'technologist', but I have become fascinated by technology. Our 3-D sound needs to be, or rather often is, accompanied by visual imagery. Interesting new forms come out of that collaboration. So I have become, of necessity, much more *au fait* with all the technologies that are out there to do with interaction, with digital manipulation of information, infomatics and new forms of coding that enable you to do things that weren't previously possible in combining digital visual generative work and sound. So, I've expanded my skills base to incorporate a lot more things.

I'm not an expert on all those things, but I know the *implications* of what a certain technology can bring. I don't need to know how an engine works to drive a car is the analogy, I suppose. But it's fascinating, and a prime reason for doing the Future of Sound, in which I encourage artists to collaborate with what we do, but also do works in progress. They're not always finished or polished, they're edgy. Sometimes they don't work properly or do totally unexpected things on the night. That interests me a lot more than creating something that's finished and polished.

The most exciting thing for me has always been the early stages of creativity. The more things converged to the point of being finished, the less interested I became. For instance, mixing never excited me that much because I always knew exactly how I wanted a track to sound, and that was just a boring process of getting there. The creative process of collaboration and bouncing off other people was what excited me down the years, and that's why I've now created the seed conditions like when I started in the late 1970s/early 1980s.

What is the cultural context for your work? Are you influenced by music in other cultures? And the other arts?

I'm definitely influenced by music from all around the world. I've always been very eclectic in my tastes, from way back before even I was involved in making music. I don't think 'ooh, I've just discovered music from Mali, or Tuvan open-throat singing'. Everything is music to me.

I can't alter the context for my work. Everyone knows I'm an electronic musician. We've always tried to do electronics with soul, and that's what interests me, not just in musical terms but also in personal terms. I only work with people who approach what they do with soul, with a sense of humanity, of generosity and openness to new ideas. So the context for me is *innovation*, I think. I'm more interested in new forms than I am in perfecting existing forms.

What skills and attributes do you consider to be essential for you as a digital musician?

I can't think of anything that's particularly special about being a digital musician as opposed to any other kind of musician. You need a degree of talent, a good ear. I'm not a talented musician in the traditional sense: I struggle to play keyboards properly, I can only read music at a snail's pace, I never had any formal training. The important thing is that I can conceptualise how I want something to sound, based on the timbres and melodic aspects – counterpoint, etc. I can hear a multitrack going on in my mind that I just have to get out. If I can't play some things I know people who can, or I can programme it.

Open-mindedness is very important. People who buy a sequencer package have an interest in learning how to use it, but there is a big mistake that digital musicians nowadays often make. They have in their computer a tool of enormous power and diversity that enables them to create very quickly pieces that, on the surface, seem very complex and well rounded. The problem is that the ease with which it is created means that there is a lot of stuff out there that is, frankly, as shallow as a puddle. (I can't really criticise them because I would have done exactly the same thing in the early days, if I had had the tools.) What I would encourage digital musicians in particular to do is: take a step back, do a little thought and research about what you want to achieve before you start. We're in a situation now where you can switch your computer on and, within ten minutes, you can have something that 'does the job'. This is particularly prevalent in advertising, or when people put mp3s on a website. They say 'Isn't this brilliant?' The answer is: 'No, it's not brilliant, it's only OK'.

What digital musicians have to aim for is to escape the normal, pre-set paths that are offered to us at all times. All musicians, myself included, can go for the easy option, the lazy way, and it is always on offer today, particularly in computer composition. The most valuable advice I can offer people starting out on this path is: take a step back, look at what you trying to achieve and do a bit of research. Make it hard for yourself. Limit your palette, even. Deliberately limiting yourself can enable more unique creations.

Do you have any other useful or relevant things to say about being a digital musician today?

The future is very exciting. We are in the early stages of virtual synth abilities. I do quite a bit of lecturing, and one warning flag I'd raise is that the standards in universities and colleges are not generally agreed. I personally think Logic is as good as anything, in terms of its breadth of capabilities and depth of possibilities. But I know a lot of colleges use Reason. I find a lot of these more 'user-friendly' platforms tend to lead you in facile directions. It is more constructive to start from scratch. I'll give you one interesting example.

When I was working with Vince [Clarke] at a studio in America, he used to have, as people know, every synth on earth. He used to control them all using CB and Gate, and his programming controller was a BBC B computer (this was only four years ago) running a program called UI, of which he is the only remaining user. We'd discuss what we wanted to do for a while, then he'd say, 'go away for half an hour'. When I came back, he'd got loads of different synths plugged up together, and programmed it . . . really amazing. If I suggested a change to more than one sound, within ten minutes he'd re-programmed *everything*. To me this is a fantastic example of apparent complexity actually being much simpler than being preguided by software.

We're all under more time and financial pressure than ever before, but I would still urge people to go off-piste from time to time, and even to start with a blank canvas, no presets.

Chapter 10

Projects and performance repertoire

This chapter contains the many projects which are indicated in the main text. They will provide the basis for practical study of the issues and ideas explored in the book. As a general principle, the more technical or abstract the discussion, the more hands-on and creative the project, and vice versa, because the projects provide a counterpoint to the text itself.

Although the projects do relate specifically to the preceding discussions, they (the projects) may also have a more general relevance and so do not need to be undertaken in a specific order. Nor is it easy to ascribe levels of difficulty to them. The first project, which seems very simple to do, can be one of the hardest to do well. Some of the projects will take a long time to complete, others are fairly swift exercises, but the duration does not necessarily reflect their potential significance. Any one of the projects has the capacity to bear musical fruit, and many will benefit from repetition.

There are also two performance repertoire pieces included, by Ambrose Field and Rob Godman, which will be useful where a more formal concert is in preparation.

● Project: *Listen, listen*

Introduction

There have been many versions of this project published over the past fifty years or so. It was a staple of the 'acoustic ecology' movement, founded by R. Murray Schafer, and has appeared in numerous other contexts, but its familiarity should not hide its importance. This is both the simplest and the hardest project in this book, and will repay frequent repetition.

The project

1   For a predetermined period of time (less than five minutes is best), listen intently to the sounds around. Become aware of sounds not normally noticed.
2   Follow the first instruction again, but this time try to write down what is heard

using a system of symbols. A good way to start is to draw out a timeline on graph paper first.

Notes

The project can be done using only the first instruction. It can also be adapted to specific situations, for example, near a major road. In this case, the process of notation becomes particularly challenging.

● Project: *Soundwalk*

Introduction

The *Handbook for Acoustic Ecology* defines a soundwalk as follows:

> A form of active participation in the soundscape. Though the variations are many, the essential purpose of the soundwalk is to encourage the participant to listen discriminatively, and moreover, to make critical judgments about the sounds heard and their contribution to the balance or imbalance of the sonic environment.
>
> Truax (1999)[1]

A soundwalk is, therefore, a walk that is led by the ears rather than the eyes. It may be short or long, highly structured or free, varied or repetitive and take in a range of environments or just stick to a single area.

The project

Make a soundwalk. Think about every aspect of the aural experience. The soundwalk may be prescribed (with a fixed beginning, middle and end) or it may be free.

Notes

One way to approach this project is to identify *soundmarks*, which are the aural equivalent to landmarks. These are prominent sounds which have a high importance to the local area. The soundwalker can navigate the aural landscape using these sounds. A different approach is more freely to explore a given geographical area, with the ears 'wide open', perhaps recording both what is heard and reflections upon what is heard.

● Project: *Soundscape composition* (with thanks to Barry Truax)

Introduction

Soundscape composition was developed by (among others) the World Soundscape Project at Simon Fraser University, with the aim of invoking 'listener's associations, memories and imagination related to the soundscape'.[2] In the early days it often consisted simply of a recording of environmental sounds taken out of context, with little editing beyond selection and, sometimes, cross-fades. In recent years, sound transformation and manipulation have been increasingly used, usually with the aim of revealing aspects of the sound to the listener.

The project

Make a soundscape composition, following the guiding principles outlined by Barry Truax, as follows:

- The listener recognisability of the source material is maintained.
- The listener's knowledge of the environmental and psychological context is invoked.
- The composer's knowledge of the environmental and psychological context influences the shape of the composition at every level.
- The work enhances our understanding of the world and its influence carries over into everyday perceptual habits.

Notes

In his article 'Genres and Techniques of Soundscape Composition as developed at Simon Fraser University',[3] Barry Truax identifies a range of general characteristics of this project, as follows:

found sound ←—————————→ abstracted

Fixed perspective: emphasising the flow of time; or a discrete series of fixed perspectives.
Variants: time compression; narrative; oral history.
Techniques:

- layering in stereo; layering in octophonic
- found sound (with or without time compression)
- narrative; poetry; oral history
- transitions between fixed perspectives.

Moving perspective: smoothly connected space/time flow; a journey.
Variants: simulated motion; real ←—————————→ imaginary/remembered.

Techniques:

- classical cross-fade and reverb
- parallel circuit cross-fade
- layering part and whole
- layering untransformed and transformed.

Variable perspective: discontinuous space/time flow.
Variants: multiple or embedded perspectives; abstracted/symbolic.
Techniques:

- multi-track editing – 'schizophonic' embedding
- abstracted perspective.

● Project: *Hearing fast*

Introduction

Understanding the way hearing works is important, but for the musician wakening up the sense of hearing is even more so. Notice that this is distinct from developing listening skills. This is simply a way to get the sense alive and receptive.

The project

Buy a pair of good quality earplugs and wear them for an hour while going about normal daily business. Be ready for the moment at which they are removed and sound rushes in! This is a simple yet effective way of refreshing the sense of hearing, a bit like fasting for the digestion.

Notes

This is a useful exercise to repeat every so often. It also has the effect of focusing attention upon 'inner' sounds, as the head and body resonate or produce sounds themselves. At first, the dislocation from the outside world will feel strange, but after a few repetitions of this project, it will become natural and easy.

● Project: *Inner world, outer world*

Introduction

This is really a kind of technologically mediated soundwalk. It is also something that many people do every day but probably without the musical intentions suggested by this project. The purpose of the project is to observe how listening to music affects perceptions of the world.

The project

Create a playlist on an mp3 player or other wearable music player. Turn up the volume and walk a fixed route of, say, half an hour's duration. Now do the same again with a completely different playlist. Try it again . . .

Each time, observe how the playlist alters perceptions of the world around, of space and of time. Relationships with the buildings, or other people, seem to change. What are those changes? How to explain them? Why do they happen?

Notes

It can be useful to make written notes on each walk, describing how perceptions change. Is the sense of distance altered by the sense of musical time passing?

● Project: *Speech patterns*

Introduction

Musicians have always been fascinated by the patterns of human speech. The composer Leos Janácek (1854–1928), for example, would jot down 'speech-melodies', which he heard around him, in a process rather similar to the one described in this project. More recently, Steve Reich has used recordings of spoken text to generate short melodic phrases in a number of works, including *Different Trains* (1988) and *The Cave* (1994). The word-phrase-sentence structure of speech is replicated in much music, particularly where the human voice is the basis of the melodic construction. This is even true in some electronic music, where the limitations of the instrument are not normally a factor in determining the lengths of phrases. There is something fundamental to musical communication in the patterns of speech, even if direct comparisons with language are not always helpful.

The project

Sit in a crowded café or restaurant and listen carefully to the patterns of human speech. Try not to understand what people are saying, just the sound they make when they say it. Just the same, ask if you can hear meaning in the sound? Are there recognisable rhythms and shapes? How long do these go on? In what ways does the overall level of activity vary? Document the sessions in writing and do several sessions in different locations on different days.

Notes

The same exercise can be tried using recording. It is interesting to note the difference between what the ear hears and what the microphone 'hears': the two are not necessarily the same.

● Project: *Masking experiment*

Introduction

This experiment will require audio software which is capable of generating two sine tones through separate tracks. There are plug-ins for various commercially available packages which can do this.

The project

Create two mono tracks, each with a signal generator. Pan both tracks to the centre. Mute one of the tracks and set the sine tone signal generator frequency of the other track to 1,200 Hz, at a just comfortable listening level. Then set the other generator to 2,400 Hz, and bring its level down to inaudible. Now, unmute it and slowly bring the level of the 2,400 Hz tone up, noticing when you can hear it. Now, mute both tracks and reset the 2,400 Hz tone to 600 Hz, at an inaudible level and repeat the experiment. At what level does the 600 Hz tone appear?

Repeat this with various tones, and observe what happens. Repeat this with the 1,200 signal generator set to a square wave. Set the other signal generator to a 2,400 Hz sine wave to a level where it can be heard through the square wave (probably just round 6 dB lower than the square wave). Now switch the second tone back and forward between a sine and square wave. What happens?

Notes

This is a fairly simple way of investigating a complex acoustic phenomenon. Acousticians would take such experiments much further, but this is a useful exercise in its own right to demonstrate an aspect of masking.

● Project: *Sound types*

Introduction

There have been many attempts to classify sounds in the same way that one may classify, for example, birds. Pierre Schaeffer's *Traité des objets musicaux* states that a sonic object is not the instrument that was played, nor the medium itself (in his day, magnetic tape), nor a state of mind. This project is surprisingly difficult and will waken up the ears to previously unconsidered aspects of the sounds.

The project

Make or download a collection of up to six sounds. Find sounds that are as different as possible from one another. Listen to them repeatedly under studio conditions or on headphones. Try to hear every last detail of the sound, then classify the sounds according to what they are and classify the sounds according to what they are not.

Notes

Of course, sound is not really divided into 'objects' but is rather a continuum. One question to ask during this project is to what extent the recording or sampling of these sounds removes this sense of continuum. Also, ask whether the concept of a 'sonic object' is useful.

● Project: *Extreme quiet*

Introduction

There is a tradition of 'silent' pieces of music, of which the most famous is John Cage's *4' 33"*. However, that was not the earliest example: the first was probably the humorously titled 'Funeral March for a Large Deaf Man' composed in 1884 by Alphonse Allais. In recent years, new technologies have enabled the creation of all sorts of music that is not exactly silent but extremely quiet, including sounds that sit outside the range of human hearing. It may seem strange, but these sounds are felt by the listener, even if they cannot be obviously heard: their absence is as strong as their presence.

The project

Make a piece that consists only of human breathing. The level should never rise above 10 dBSPL. Try to work towards as much silence as possible, without losing atmosphere. The aim is to keep the listener's attention with the least possible information. At what point does the listener lose contact with organised sound and connect with environmental sound? Can this be controlled?

Notes

The use of human breathing will keep this piece within the (just) audible range. The volume levels during playback need to be carefully controlled.

● Project: *Exploring harmonics*

Introduction

There are many ways to explore harmonics and the harmonic series. If this is being done for the first time, then the project below may well be the occasion on which the acoustic properties of sound first burst into meaning for the musician. Certainly, it is a revelation suddenly to become aware of the 'interior' of a sound in this way.

The project

First, repeatedly sound a low piano note. Move a finger along the string until a bell-like pitch is clearly heard. Mark it off in chalk (and measure the length if you want to check the ratios given above). Keep going until the individual nodes become too small to be distinguishable.

Now, refine this process by playing the open string and attempting to hear the harmonics it contains. Lightly touch the appropriate nodal points and then play the open string again to bring out the effect. The ears will gradually awaken to the pitch contents of the sound. It should be possible to hear the fifth harmonic quite clearly and, with practice, up to the seventh and even beyond.

Notes

This can be tried with other instruments. Then, try using the voice. Sing vowel sounds: a–e–i–o–u (pronounced aah, ay, eeh, oh, uh) in a continuous rotation. The word 'why', sung slowly and extending all the vowel sounds, works well (especially in a bathroom!). Sing through the nose somewhat, and gradually awaken the harmonics present in the voice. A buzzing electric toothbrush can also boost the effect.

● Project: *Spectral study*

Introduction

The use of computers to analyse sounds spectrally has great musical potential, because music is all about repetition and variation. The creative potential of spectral analysis resides in an understanding of how sound behaves through time.

The project

This project begins with finding some objects that have interesting sonic properties. These could be natural objects, or pieces of junk or, indeed, musical instruments.

The first exercise is to try to describe each sound. Is it periodic or aperiodic? What are its timbral characteristics? How does the sound change over time? Try to make a diagram of the envelope of the sound. How does it begin and end?

Now, listen closely and try to deduce spectral information. Are the harmonics true, or partial? Or a combination of these? Is there variation over time in the harmonics, or do they seem stable? Can individual harmonics be identified and do any take precedence during the sound?

Finally, make a recording of the sound. Try cutting off the attack – is it still recognisable? Now, consider the complete sound: look at the wave form and then at a spectrogram. To what extent does this confirm the impression gained by your ears? Are there any obvious differences?

Apply this process to a number of 'sonic objects' and compare the differences and similarities between them. Can you classify the results or divide the sounds into meaningful groupings? Finally, ask whether thinking of these as 'sonic objects' is a useful thing to do.

Notes

This can be a useful substitute for Stage 1 of the . . . *from scratch* project (see p. 255), if that is being undertaken.

● Project: *Singing bowls*

Introduction

This is a sound recording exercise that investigates the properties of various microphones, but it also has considerable potential as the start of a more creative piece. The sound samples obtained this way may be useful for a number of the other projects in this book.

The project

Place a Tibetan temple bowl on a table and surround it with a selection of microphones. Record some strikes or rubs of the bowl simultaneously onto separate tracks per microphone. Compare the results.

Notes

In the absence of a Tibetan temple bowl, any kitchen bowl or pan with a long, clear resonance will do. Adjusting the positions (height, distance) of the microphones can add another interesting dimension to the project.

This project can be extended by positioning microphones all around (above, below, inside, etc.) a piano.

● Project: *Reverse EQ*

Introduction

This creative studio technique can produce some surprisingly useful musical results. It can even be undertaken in real time as part of a performance.

The project

Take a sound with a clear decay and reverse it. Now apply EQ and other filters to modify the reversed sound until it becomes musically interesting. Finally re-reverse the sound to discover a new timbre.

Notes

This technique can be repeated and adapted for both composition and performance. There is even a conceptual aspect: imagining the reversed sound and the re-reversed sound.

● Project: *Analysis-synthesis*

Introduction

This will require some sound analysis/processing software that allows detailed study of a sound's spectrum, wave form, fundamental frequencies and partial contents, preferably through a visualisation.

The project

Record or download a guitar sample (a single note or a chord will do). Using appropriate software, find the frequencies of all the partials in the sound. Then create a synthesised version of the sound by adding sine tones of those frequencies together.

Does the synthesised version sound the same as the original sample? If not, why not?

Observe the spectrogram of the original sample closely. What can be heard 'inside' the sound? What are the relative strengths and weaknesses of the various partials? How are they shaped through time?

Notes

This useful exercise can be performed with a variety of original sounds. With practice, it is possible to become very good at 'hearing' a spectrogram.

● Project: *Visual score*

Introduction

Around the turn of the twentieth century, a number of leading painters began developing an abstract art that drew heavily on music. The Blue Rider group, *Der Blaue Reiter*, included Arnold Schoenberg and Wassily Kandinsky (1866–1944), who began to paint 'improvisations' and 'compositions' during the years immediately preceding the First World War. Kandinsky was inspired by theosophy and other spiritual ideas to create work that aspired to the condition of music. He also experienced synaesthesia, in which the senses become confused, by 'hearing' specific sounds when seeing certain colours or shapes (yellow as the note 'C' played on a trumpet, for example). Many other artists and composers explored these ideas, for example, Alexander Skryabin (1872–1915) whose *Prometheus: The Poem of Fire* (1910) included a part for 'light organ', which was intended to bathe the concert hall in colour from electric lights corresponding to the changing tonality of the music.

The project

Make a musical realisation and performance of a painting or drawing by Wassily Kandinsky. The image can be interpreted in any way.

Notes

This project should be carefully planned and not done as an improvisation. There are various aspects of the painting to consider: line, point, shape, colour, motion. These can be mapped in various ways to musical parameters. The overall aesthetic may also be captured, along with the dynamism of the composition.

The following book may be useful for this project:

■ Maur, K. V. (1999) *The Sound of Painting*. Munich: Prestel-Verlag.

● Project: *File formats*

Introduction

This project is quite easy to achieve but is a very useful way to understand the musical implications of different audio file formats. Musicians can tend to accept what the computer presents to the ear as a standard, but in fact there is considerable variation between file formats, often depending on the type of music that is encoded. Even lossless formats can exhibit certain audible characteristics, depending on the sample rate and bit rate.

The project

Choose some music containing a wide range of contrasting dynamic (loud and soft) levels and sounds. Now, use a software package to save the file in various formats and vary the settings to achieve different quality levels. Listen carefully and comparatively to the results. It might be a good idea to try this with several different examples. The aim is to try to hear what has changed, what has been lost, and what has been emphasised. An extension of this project is to create some music which is designed specifically for a certain file format.

Notes

In an mp3 culture, certain kinds of music adapt better to the file format. This project will quickly establish what those might be and why that is the case. This has implications for music that does not work so well in that format. Formats will change and music will adapt, but one interesting question to explore is whether the arrival of lossy compression formats has changed musical culture, particularly with reference to the kind of music that is made?

● Project: *FFT processing*

Introduction

Digital sound processing might appear to transform a sound in a particular way (altering the pitch, slowing down, etc.), but this is merely the aural consequence of the production of a new collection of data. Any digital process can produce strange or unwanted artefacts, sounds that do not contribute to the aural impression the process is designed to create. In most cases, good software means that this is not a problem. This project, however, positively explores the creative possibilities that endless repetitions of a process can produce.

The project

Take a recorded sound and apply an effect (timestretch, reverb, pitch shift, distortion, anything), repeating the effect over and over again until the sound is nothing like the original sound. Retain a copy of each step in the process. Now listen back to the sounds one at a time in reverse order.

Notes

Notice how the process diverges further and further from how it might be imagined to sound. Rather than going deeper 'inside' the sound, the process is in fact generating a new sound. Ask each time: What is heard? What does it mean? What is its source?

● Project: *Brassage stew*

Introduction

'Cut-up' was a well-known technique in literature in the 1950s. The 'beat' writer William S. Burroughs famously used it many times. Its origins lie in the Dada movement that emerged around the end of the First World War. The Dadaist Tristan Tzara created a Dada Poem by drawing words randomly from a hat. Burroughs and his contemporaries applied the same techniques to phrases and sentences, attempting to break up the linearity of both literary and journalistic texts.

The technique has also been used in music: David Bowie and Thom Yorke of Radiohead have made many of their lyrics that way, and Genesis P-Orridge, of 'Throbbing Gristle', has made it into a whole philosophy of life and art. 'Dub' reggae and other remixing genres deploy it as a key musical technique. It has even become an e-mail 'spam' tactic, using randomly generated cut-up texts to get past certain types of spam filter.

The project

Take a short (under one minute) piece of music or a recorded sound. Use the computer editor to chop it up into small segments. This can be done so it makes musical sense (i.e., by phrase) or randomly. Now, chop up the segments again. Keep chopping until the segments, heard individually, fail to evoke the original music. Now assemble a random playlist and play back the segments one after another in any order, but with no time gap between them. Observe the differences from the original.

Notes

This may be de-composition, or even re-composition. It is hard to resist the anarchistic feel of brassage as an activity. However, once below the level of recognisable musical phrases, this exercise starts to acquire a very different quality. New sounds can be discovered this way with persistence and a good ear.

● Project: *Hearing hearing*

Introduction

John Cage wrote: 'one way to study music: study Duchamp'.[4] In many ways, Marcel Duchamp (1887–1968) set the scene for 'sound-art'. There are numerous references to the sonic properties of objects in his work, such as *With Hidden Noise* (1916), a ball of string compressed between two metal plates and concealing a mysterious object, which rattles when shaken. There are even some musical compositions, including an early experiment with chance entitled *Erratum Musical* (1913). However, the most useful aspects of Duchamp for the digital musician are his ideas and concepts. In his *Green Box* (published in 1934), for example, he observed: 'one can look at seeing; one cannot hear hearing'.[5]

The project

Meditate upon Marcel Duchamp's statement 'one can look at seeing; one cannot hear hearing'. Create a technology-based system that hears itself.

Notes

At its simplest, this project suggests some kind of feedback loop. Think about the flow of acoustical information into and through the system. This could be modelled upon the ear–brain relationship. It might take place entirely within a computer, or it might involve external devices. What is actually heard as a result of the process? Can heard hearing be represented? And what is the relationship between music and hearing?

● Project: *Diffraction experiment*

Introduction

This simple experiment demonstrates diffraction, but it will also act as a stimulus for the creative potential of working in a space.

The project

Set up a sine-tone generator feeding a single easily moveable loudspeaker. Place the loud-speaker in front of an obstacle, such as a piece of furniture. Vary the frequency of the tone, and observe how audible it is. Wavelengths longer than the width of the obstacle should diffract better than shorter ones. Confirm this by using the formula 'wavelength = speed of sound ÷ frequency'. Do the same experiment with a speaker directed at a doorway or other opening, and see what happens to the sound as you move past the doorway.

Notes

Although this is a technical experiment, it might also suggest more creative possibilities. Is it possible to combine two or more tones, and two or more loudspeakers, in a controlled way? Does a human presence affect the sound?

● Project: *Composed space*

Introduction

The aim of this project is to create a spatial 'image'. The project may be realised in (or out of) a room, across loudspeakers, or in 'headphone space'. The objective is to explore the relationship between the sound (or sounds) that is used and its spatial distribution. To give an example: a fly buzzing through a space would follow a typically zigzag route, which can be reproduced in a sound-diffusion spatialisation. Now, consider a sound which does not have such a readily associated trajectory (a reversed piano sound, or a square wave, for example). What would be an effective way to spatialise that sound?

The project

Take either a musical gesture, or the attack and continuant features of a given sound, and use it to 'compose' a space.

Notes

The main objective is to find a way to spatialise the chosen sound so that its environmental or dramatic properties are fully realised. The choice of sound is important, as is the choice of listening situation.

> Spatial imaging is commonly thought of by the composer in a relatively objective way as a means of enhancing the sounding properties inherent in spectro-morphologies and structural relations. Simply stated, a musical gesture can be more vividly dramatised through spatial displacement, just as a texture can be made 'environmental' through spatial distribution.
>
> Smalley (1991)[6]

● Project: *Extended duration*

Introduction

On the face of it, this is quite a simple project. However, it has the potential to develop into an entire extended musical composition. It will require some audio editing software, but this need not be particularly sophisticated. Some of the free downloadable software will do perfectly well.

The project

Find a sound with a natural decay (e.g., a gong, or a piano, etc.) and use digital processes to extend its length to at least twice its original duration, without losing interest in the sound.

Notes

This is more than just a technical exercise. The last part of the instruction contains a hint of how this could develop further. Keeping up interest in the sound implies some amount of transformation or development in what is heard.

● Project: *Sonic morph*

Introduction

Morphing is more usually found in animation, video and photography, where software enables one image to morph with another. In digital audio, a morph is a more sophisticated version of a cross-fade, in which the content of the two sound files is actually intermingled during the intermediate stage. This project, however, concentrates on the perceptual, rather than the technical aspects of a sound morph.

The project

Take two recorded sounds, such as a hi-hat hit and a snare drum. Using any available tools (pitch shifting, time stretching, etc.) operate on one of the sound files only until it sounds as nearly as possible like the other. This may involve repeating the sound numerous times. Then do the same with the other sound file.

Notes

This is a fairly laborious exercise, and morphing software can perform what would be probably a more effective and smoother morph between the two files readily enough without all the effort. So why undertake the task? Because the aural awareness and understanding of the acoustic content of the sound it will produce will be invaluable. There will also be a spin-off benefit in understanding the time-based processes. Ask the following questions: Is there an obvious point in time at which the character of the sound changes? Can this point be moved? Is the point the same for other people?

● Project: *Inspiration box*

Introduction

This is a creative exercise in inspiration and meaning. It is designed for at least two participants and can produce powerful results.

The project

Assemble a box containing several objects that offer inspiration. These may include sounding objects or recordings but also evocative or personal items such as photographs, writings – in fact anything at all that has some meaning.

Pass the box to another person who will create a piece of digital music inspired by what it contains. The personal meanings may be revealed before or after the music is completed by prior agreement.

Notes

It is important that this project is undertaken seriously and with respect and open-mindedness on all sides.

● Project: *Sunset*

Introduction

This project needs no introduction.

The project

Watch a sunset. You will need to set aside a couple of hours or more to do this properly. You should watch from the moment at which the sun hits the horizon, to the point at which all trace of its colour has gone from the sky.

Now try to imagine how a sunset would sound. What are the main features? How do the elements of a sunset translate into sound? And, most importantly, how do the feelings the sunset produced in you translate into sound? How do you convey the impression created? Make written or aural notes to help you if necessary.

Now, create a piece that reproduces as nearly as possible what you have imagined. Observe and note the gaps between what you have imagined and the finished result. Have other people listen to the piece, without telling them what the piece is about. Do they get it? Try again with a title ('Sunset' is the obvious one), or more information. Does that change things?

Finally, get hold of some video footage of a sunset and attempt the same exercise but with the addition of the visual imagery. What has changed? Is the imagination liberated or constrained by the visuals? Can anything be done to improve the imaginative experience?

Notes

The addition of the final phase takes this beyond a traditional composition exercise inspired by nature and into a more mediated, cinematic treatment. However, the first parts of the project are very important. Time passing, a sense of awe and mystery, the power of nature, are good sources of inspiration for an artist of any description.

● Project: *Types of space*

Introduction

Consider the notion of 'space' in music. 'Outer space' is one of several types of space. Inner space, or the space of the imagination, is one. Personal space is a familiar concept from psychology: the area that is felt to be the property of the individual, which can be 'invaded' by others. A private space suggests something intimate, secret. A piece of music itself could also be said to occupy a 'cultural space', in other words, it represents something about the culture from which it has emerged. Finally, there is the sense of 'spaciousness' that you might get from contemplating a natural phenomenon such as the Grand Canyon, or a cloud. Given that music is a time-based art form, these ideas of space are difficult to imagine made in sound. And yet they can, and have, been conveyed. To hear examples from history, listen to the following:

▲ Outer space (1): Richard Strauss (1896) *Also Sprach Zarathustra*. Deutsche Grammophon 447441. This was used in Stanley Kubrick's film *2001: A Space Odyssey* and carries all kinds of associations, including the television broadcasts of the moon-shots.
▲ Outer space (2): Louis and Bebe Barron (1956) *Forbidden Planet* (film soundtrack). Planet Records/GNP PRD-001. This film was the first motion picture to feature an electronic music score. Here 'outer space' is evoked by 'otherworldly' sounds.
▲ Inner space: Erik Satie (1888) *Gymnopédie No. 1*. Philips 028944667226. This manages to convey an inner world by restricting the amount of musical material and adopting a direct simplicity of style.
▲ Personal space: Alvin Lucier *I Am Sitting in a Room*. Lovely Music CD 1013. This is a classic meditation on the relationship between an individual and his surroundings.
▲ Private space: Luciano Berio (1961) *Visage*. BMG Ricordi CRMCD 1017. A disturbing insight into a private imaginary world.
▲ Cultural space: Karlheinz Stockhausen (1966–1967) *Hymnen*. Stockhausen Verlag 10. Stockhausen's attempt to explore the music of the world, which ends up revealing a great deal about his particular time and space.
▲ Spaciousness (1): Gustav Mahler (1888) *Symphony No. 1*. EMI Classics 56972. Listen specifically to the opening of the first movement for an illustration of natural space.
▲ Spaciousness (2): György Ligeti (1961) *Atmosphères*. Teldec 8573882612. A good example of the musical creation of a cloud-like space.

What is impressive about all these works is the way in which they successfully map the evident musical imagination of the composer. Their intention seems to match the outcome (even in the case of the Stockhausen).

The project

Choose one of the types of space (or find another of your own) and make an electro-acoustic piece that creates that space for the listener.

Notes

In 2001, the Cassini–Huygens space probe passed the planet Jupiter. There is no sound in outer space, because it is a vacuum, but, nevertheless, the NASA scientists produced a sonification of the effect of the solar wind in the interstellar dust that surrounds the planet. A quick search on the Internet will locate the relevant sound files. One approach to this project could be to use only this source recording.

● Project: *Narrative*

Introduction

There have been so many films and theatre pieces that use music and sound effects to assist in the telling of the story that it might be assumed that music itself is naturally suited to narrative. However, this is by no means always the case. Once sounds are separated from their sources or visual cues, and the mode of listening changes, the nature of the narrative also changes. In classical composition, thematic material itself might function as a 'character' in a 'drama'. But in a music where the sounds themselves already contain a certain dramaturgy, such as a recorded sound effect, this becomes complex. Somewhere between Foley work and abstract composition lies the reality of sonic narratives.

The project

Devise a short story (or borrow one from somewhere) that lends itself to sonic illustration. Using only sounds attempt to convey the story.

Notes

A common mistake when making musical narratives is to use sound effects (often from a sample bank) in a sequence, which fails to capture either the timing or make a convincing acoustic simulation, of the imaginary model. Here is a cliché as an example: a man is walking through a park and is shot. What is heard might be: footsteps on gravel; bird song; gunshot. These are all standard sound effects on sound modules. Each will have certain duration and have been recorded under different conditions. Sequencing them together will not necessarily tell the story in the way that is intended. This pitfall gets even larger when dealing with more abstract music, where no sound effects are used. A narrative structure can work, but it needs careful handling if the listener is to 'get' the idea.

● Project: *Sonic collage*

Introduction

'Collage' was originally a technique in the visual arts, derived from the French word for 'glue', *coller*. Artists would literally stick 'found objects' (bus tickets, cigarette ends, whatever) to the canvas. A sonic collage, then, will use no 'original' material at all, but only sounds and samples gathered from elsewhere. Important note: extreme care should be taken in this project to avoid breaching copyright law, and copyrighted material should only be used with prior permission.

The project

Make a sonic collage lasting two minutes.

Notes

The compositional decisions in this project are therefore: What material to use and why? How to combine the materials? When to start and stop materials?

Warning: collage can be a perfectly effective way of making music, but in order to achieve its effects, it needs to show an awareness of its own dramaturgy. This means conveying a sense of what it would be like *not* to be a collage. In other words, the formal juxtapositions of collage need to be clearly heard as such, if the listener is to understand that a collage is taking place. To avoid a problem in this area is really up to the composer's own critical faculties. The act of making a *random* collage in itself does not guarantee interesting results.

● Project: *Sudoku*

Introduction

Algorithms are sets of rules that produce a finished state. Using algorithms to make music has a long history. As Jon Appleton observed:

> In both the Middle Ages and the twentieth century, composers have celebrated music's link with the logic of mathematics by introducing parametric systems of organisation (primarily in the pitch domain), which are largely unrelated to aural

5	3			7				
6			1	9	5			
	9	8					6	
8				6				3
4			8		3			1
7				2				6
	6					2	8	
			4	1	9			5
				8			7	9

5	3	4	6	7	8	9	1	2
6	7	2	1	9	5	3	4	8
1	9	8	3	4	2	5	6	7
8	5	9	7	6	1	4	2	3
4	2	6	8	5	3	7	9	1
7	1	3	9	2	4	8	5	6
9	6	1	5	3	7	2	8	4
2	8	7	4	1	9	6	3	5
3	4	5	2	8	6	1	7	9

Figure 10.1 A typical Sudoku puzzle and its solution.

perception. In the Middle Ages these techniques were invariably hidden, existing below a surface that conformed to stylistic norms. In the twentieth century, some composers used a technique that introduced a novel way of ordering pitches, but did so within the context of traditional musical forms.

Appleton (1992)[7]

Algorithmic music has expanded to include stochastic and chaotic, formal and linguistic, generative and quasi-neurological algorithms. AI, in all its various forms, provides a fruitful area for much digital music creation today.

The purpose of this project is not necessarily to create new algorithms or to investigate this field, but rather to understand the relationship between the musician, the computer and the algorithm. The popular puzzle Sudoku provides a useful tool for this purpose. Sudoku may be found in many newspapers, puzzle books or on the web. The rules are simple: fill the 9 × 9 grid so that each column, each row, and each of the nine 3 × 3 boxes contains the digits from 1 to 9 (see Figure 10.1).

The project

Make three digital musical versions of a Sudoku puzzle:

1   computer-controlled
2   'user'-controlled (where the user is someone other than the person making this project)
3   composer/performer-controlled.

The numbers may map to any parameter of the music (sounds, rhythms, intensities, etc.)

Notes

Mapping decisions are significant here. The computer-controlled version is straightforward to execute, but how can the results be made musically interesting? Giving the user control may require some kind of training, if they are to complete the puzzle successfully. Is it the solution, the original, or the processes involved in solving the puzzle, that is being mapped? If this is to be performed by the composer, to what extent (if at all) can the algorithm be used to reflect compositional intentions?

● Project: *Night piece*

Introduction

The night piece, or 'nocturne', is a classical form. This is something which can either be absorbed into the artist's aesthetic for this project, or ignored. Some typical examples include the 'night music' that appears in several works by Béla Bartók or, before that, Frédéric Chopin's collection of Nocturnes for solo piano. What these works have in common is a poetic evocation of night.

The project

Start by making a list of all the things you associate with night. These do not necessarily have to involve sound. Now start to think about creating mood and atmosphere, about resonance and silence, about presence and sound, about imagination and reality. Fix upon a duration for the piece. Finally, create a piece that evokes night . . .

Notes

Night is a particularly good time for listening. It is generally quieter than daytime, and the absence of light means that the ear is heightened. For this project, 'night life' does not mean parties and clubs, but rather the sounds of the night (which might include distant music) that bring it to life.

● Project: *Pastiche*

Introduction

Pastiche composition has a long history as an academic exercise. In fact, most of the famous classical composers used pastiche as a way of teaching and learning. In the post-war years in Western music, it fell out of use to a certain extent, because the goal of modern music was to be original or new. Pastiche was felt to be risky, because it seemed to imply a willingness to accept orthodoxies.

Perhaps, in the digital world of endless reproduction, the time has come to re-evaluate pastiche. The aim will be to understand technique, but also style, aesthetic and process. Short of actually sampling the original, it is highly unlikely that the pastiche will come close to its model in detail, so the chances of discovering something new along the way are quite high. At the very least, the pasticher will learn about the technology and how it could be handled.

The project

Try to reproduce a chosen digital piece. Mimic its sounds and processes.

Notes

This exercise succeeds with pieces that are noise-based and/or with lots of effects and processing. Some pieces that seem to work well are *Meta-abuse* from *Making Orange Things* by Venetian Snares; 'Glitch' from *Amber* by Autechre; and *#15* from *Selected Ambient Works Vol. 2* by Aphex Twin. However, the aesthetic qualities of these tracks may not be to everyone's taste. It is important that the pastiche exercise should be valued and seen as worthwhile, so the choice of music should be individual.

▲ Venetian Snares (2001) 'Meta-abuse' on *Making Orange Things*. Planet Mu ZIQ028.
▲ Autechre (1994) 'Glitch' on *Amber* TVT Records TVT 7230-2.
▲ Aphex Twin (1994) '#15' on *Selected Ambient Works Vol. 2*. Warp 21.

● Project: *ping – hack – rom – seed*

Introduction

There are many ways to create a networked ensemble. A quick search of the web, using a string like 'networked music performance', will bring up many more examples. This project is aimed at getting the musicians to think about the philosophical and aesthetic aspects of networked performance, rather than providing a 'how-to' manual for putting one together.

The project

Create a networked ensemble of at least three members. Give the ensemble a 'digital' name, either: 'ping' or 'hack' or 'rom' or 'seed'. Now try to create music that lives up to or evokes the name of the ensemble.

Notes

These names seem to imply things: a different kind of repertoire, perhaps, or a different approach to music technology. Some immediate thoughts:

- *ping:* communications ('pinging' another machine), signs, insignificance
- *hack:* coding, programming, manipulating the materials of others
- *rom:* processing, memory, data mining
- *seed:* evolution, growth, development.

● Project: *Mobile phone piece*

Introduction

Music is an integral part of mobile phones, and the ringtone-download culture is firmly established. However, the provision of music for ringtones does not necessarily make a musician into a 'digital musician'. This project is designed to explore the creative potential of mobile-phone networks.

The project

Devise a performance in which the audience's mobile phones become the instruments.

Notes

This idea is not new, and there have been several high-profile projects which have attempted to choreograph ringtones. The most successful was probably *Dialtones (A Telesymphony)* (2001) by Golan Levin, Scott Gibbons and Gregory Shakar, which is also available on CD (Staalplaat STCD160). Research into that piece might provide a useful source of inspiration for this project, but the challenge here is to devise some new way in which to realise the idea.

● Project: . . . *from scratch*

Introduction

This project is designed to strip away previous ideas of 'musicianship', in order to re-evaluate the sounding properties of objects, how they may be made into instruments, how playing techniques might be developed and how music may be created as a result. It is not necessarily a 'digital' project as such, but its value to anybody working in a digital context should quickly become apparent, especially through its ability to awaken the ears. It is potentially a long-term project lasting several weeks and can work well with small or very large groups.

The project

Participants find objects with interesting sonic properties to develop into a performance machine. Participants will develop new performance techniques using these objects, avoiding using their existing technical skills – the project is 'from scratch'.

1   Find sonic objects. Analyse the sonic properties of the objects. Can they be modified or tuned? Does an object have obvious musical potential? How can it combine with other objects?

2   Research other people's uses of similar objects. Is there a history of musical use of such an object? Are there any obvious musical or aesthetic associations? How have other people used and developed similar objects?

3   Make an instrument. How can the object be turned into an instrument? What are the best ways to exploit its sonic potential? How can it be made playable? Can it be combined with other objects to form a single instrument?

4   Develop a performance technique. What are the performance issues? Is it possible to become a virtuoso on this new instrument?

5   Create some original music. Will this instrument work best solo or in an ensemble? What kind of music would work best for the instrument? Is there any similar music which can be used as a model? Is the music notated or non-notated?

6   Give a performance. How best to present this music to an audience? How much rehearsal is required? What would be an appropriate performance mode?

Notes

This is a beneficial project for any group of musicians, but the particular importance for the 'digital musician' lies in the experimental approach, the sonic exploration and the removal of anything that resembles familiar technique. Computers may be used at every stage for analysis, research, planning, structuring, recording and even in performance, so there may be some obviously 'digital' component, but this is not essential.

● Project: *Sonic wiki*

Introduction

Collaborative work is, perhaps, one way in which digital music can rediscover a social dimension that is generally lost to classical music. Through the past 300 or 400 years in the West, composing became a solo activity for many social, practical and artistic reasons. One example of this trend was the story of Beethoven's solo piano work *33 Variations on a Waltz by Anton Diabelli*, Op. 120.

Diabelli was a music publisher, who attempted to create a collaborative composition project by sending a short waltz of his own to all the leading composers of the day, asking them to each write a single variation. Beethoven refused, on the grounds that the waltz was too banal. The other composers contributed, and the variations were duly published. Beethoven then rethought his position and published a complete set of his own, which astonished everyone (including Diabelli) and is still thought to be one of his great masterpieces. Although the original project was not fully collabora- tive, because each variation was written separately, Beethoven's towering achievement nevertheless seemed to show that a single vision is superior.

There have been plenty of successful musical partnerships, particularly in popular music, and several bands in which the members have all contributed to the composition of the material. Jazz and improvised music have been at the forefront of what might be reckoned real-time collaborative composition. But it was unusual to find formal group composition projects such as the one described below until the arrival of digital tech- nologies. These have made sharing files easy and enabled the kind of communications and exchange that produce interesting results. Working collaboratively in this way seems to echo the nature of the digital medium itself.

The project

Prepare a 'sonic wiki', a collaborative piece made by a process of collective editing of material. A wiki is a collectively edited document (see wikipedia, for example).

Agree in advance who is contributing to the project. Each participant provides a 'parent' sound. Next, each participant should apply a range of digital processes (time- stretching, brassage, interpolation, pitch-shifting, etc.) to the parents to create a collection of 'children'. These may be posted to a group forum or message board, or shared in some other mutually agreed way.

Decisions can be taken about the fate of each 'child'. They may be saved, dumped (i.e., deleted) or, if especially good, made into a new 'parent'. Decisions can be made by majority vote or by unanimity; it is really up to the group how to do this.

Notes

This is more of a process than a product, but if a finished presentation of the results is desired, the sequencing and combination of the results should also be agreed by the participants.

● Project: *Infra-instrument*

Introduction

In a recent paper, John Bowers and Philip Archer criticised recent developments in instrument making, arguing that all the 'hyper' and 'meta' instruments extend the capabilities of existing instruments with a view to increasing the virtuosity and complexity of the music made. The same is true of virtual instruments, but often replacing the hand gesture with some kind of controller or motion-tracking device. They identify a different kind of instrument, called an 'infra-instrument', which 'engenders relatively simple musics' and is 'restricted in its virtuosity and expressivity', but is 'nonetheless aesthetically engaging and technically intriguing for all that'.[8] They offer a number of examples. This project uses a couple of those.

The project

Make, and perform on, an infra-instrument. Do this by using materials that are 'partway to instrumenthood' but do not make them into a recognised instrument. For example: a guitar is made of wood and metal and, possibly, nylon. An infra-guitar would use those materials, but would not be a guitar. (Sounding materials might include: wood, metal, string, water, stone, skin, plastic, glass, etc.)

Notes

Bowers and Archer's own instructions include the following additional notes that may be helpful in realising this project:

- *Take an instrument and make it less.* Break an existing instrument (irreversible procedures) or restrict its operation and/or how one interacts with it (reversible procedures).
- *Build an instrument but include obvious mistakes.* Like selecting fresh vegetables as the material for construction.
- *Take something non-instrumental and find the instrument within.* A DTMF phone dialer can be regarded as an infra-synthesiser, a Geiger counter as infra-percussion, and so forth.
- *Find infra-instruments readymade.* In contrast to the above, here we have in mind instruments which already are infra in status, at least in the minds of aesthetic snobs. This would include many musical toys or musical boxes and other 'amusements'.[9]

● Project: *Sound byte for voice or percussion*

Introduction

This is a combination of sonic analysis and creative work. The object is to investigate the properties of the chosen sounds. The process will lead to a better understanding of how the voice or percussion instrumental sounds are formed and how digital processes might be successfully applied to them.

The project

Create a 20- to 30-second sound byte based on vocal or percussion sounds, demonstrating how elements of vocal sound can be 'taken apart'. Use any digital processing tools available to you, such as filtering, transposition and stretching.

Notes

The word 'demonstrating' is important here. This is not so much a compositional piece as a technical exercise. However, the 'demonstration' is likely to be better understood if it makes musical sense too.

● Project: *Restricted instruments*

Introduction

These instruments can be built on computer or using a sampler. There is no attempt here to prescribe the interactivity, so that is very much a matter of free invention. In some cases, a controller that reflects the sonic materials used may well be appropriate.

The project

Make a restricted instrument from a single sound source. Devise performances on the instrument to show as much variation and virtuosity as possible.

Notes

The instrument should reflect the acoustic properties of its sources in all its aspects. The challenge in this project is to make musical interest from very limited materials, so no additional processing or effects may be added. Working with a highly restricted palette like this can be a very effective way of developing the craft of digital sound manipulation.

● Project: *Improvisation ensemble*

Introduction

There are many ways to approach improvisation, but the main thing to bear in mind in the context of this book is that it is not helpful to allow improvisers simply to demonstrate their technical prowess on a given instrument or with the computer. In fact, there can be a positive advantage in having only limited technique on the given instrument. Virtuoso improvising is not about showing off, but rather about collective understanding and collaboration.

The project

Form an ensemble that does nothing but improvise. The ensemble must have more than three members.

Notes

The important thing is to develop aural awareness to the point of being able to make only meaningful sounds in the improvisation. It is acceptable to make no sound at all. A highly constrained improvisation might allow each musician only three sounds, which have to be carefully chosen and timed. Often, improvising in the dark can help to focus the ear. One exercise is to try to imitate a sound, passing it around the room 'Chinese whispers'-style. Another is to try to make the opposite sound each time (so a high, loud, long sound would be followed by a low, quiet, short one).

It is normally a good idea to time-limit an improvisation until the group has got to know one another to the point that they can 'feel' when to stop. Starting and finishing are often key moments in any ensemble improvisation, and various solutions will be found to what constitutes an appropriate ending. A 'riff' can sometimes be the death of a good improvisation, because it tends to encourage a 'jam-session' mentality, leading to an abandonment of careful listening. On the other hand, a well-constructed and careful use of repetition at the right time can be very successful. The key to a good improvisation is the right mix of repetition and variation. This is probably true of music in general.

● Project: *I hate . . .*

Introduction

'Music appreciation' has traditionally been taught by enthusiasts who are keen to awaken listeners to the marvellous features of the work they love. They have often done this very well. In extreme cases (such as Leonard Bernstein, whose passionate advocacy of Gustav Mahler rescued his music from relative obscurity), this has had far-reaching effects on the evolution of music itself. However, this project has a somewhat different purpose: to help understand individual taste.

The project

Find some music you hate. Listen to it over and over again. Try to understand exactly why you hate it. Write down your reasons. Do you get to like it better the more you listen, or does your hatred increase? Why? Is the problem in the music itself, or is there some other factor? When you can't take it any more, listen to something you love as a reward!

Notes

This may seem like torture, but it is a way of reaching self-knowledge and aural awareness. The ability to articulate what you are not is a good way to understand what you are. A deliberate attempt to reach this understanding can also produce surprising results. You may even find out you like things you thought you did not, and vice versa.

● Project: *Hydroponics 1 for Laptop Orchestra* (2007) by Ambrose Field

For: As many performers as there are available laptops and equipment, and conductor. Duration: twelve minutes minimum.

Equipment

Each performer will need: one laptop computer, microphone, any sound-processing or sound-generation program and an individual loudspeaker so that the computer system is a self-contained instrument without need for a unified, external PA system.

Each performer will need a small Perspex tank of water. Size may vary between performers, but the audience must be able to see your hand gestures.

Construction of a basic hydrophone

You will need a hydrophone microphone for this task. If you do not have one, you can construct your own. The following web reference (last checked March 2007) has good, detailed construction details: sonar-fs.lboro.ac.uk/uag/downloads/bender2.pdf.

The following basic version also works well. Use a small Piezo Ceramic microphone disk. These are extremely inexpensive. Solder two wires from a shielded connecting cable to a jack plug suitable for your equipment directly from the contacts on the surface of the disk. Cover the disk and exposed connections in an epoxy-resin-based solution and leave to harden.

Electrical safety in the work is your responsibility, so remember to consult your health and safety manual before undertaking electronics work, and keep all electrical equipment and power cables safely away from water!

Conductor

The role of the conductor in the work is to synchronise the performance and split the composition into sections: (1) smooth sounds, (2) waves, (3) drips and (4) turbulence. Write the section number on the back of a large card, and hold it up when three minutes has elapsed. You may freely repeat sections, and are free to experiment with the order of the sections.

Performance instructions

Place hydrophone in water tank. Keep laptop and mains electricity well away from water tank! In rehearsal, assign *one* processing algorithm of your choice to the sounds picked up live by your hydrophone. This processing can be as simple or as complex as you like: filtering, reverberation, resampling, sample triggering are all good examples. Decide as a group whether you wish to share information with each other on the choice of processing algorithms, or not. You may not change your processing algorithm during the piece: your task is to explore the sounds it can make by changing the nature of the water sounds arriving at your computer. Dry your hands if you need to operate the computer, do this carefully and visually each time.

Create sounds in your water tank as indicated by the conductor. Each section lasts roughly three minutes, and note that section timing and order is controlled by the conductor.

● Project: *Mood music*

Introduction

The idea of this project is to place the musical experience in the hands of the user. At its simplest, it can be realised by a 'point-and-click' method which enables the user to choose what to listen to and when. More elegant solutions involve a degree of animation and interactivity which will require some technical abilities in appropriate software and possibly hardware.

The project

Devise a multimedia interface which allows users to configure the musical experience according to their mood. The music they hear may be original or otherwise, but the results of user choice should either create or respond to a mood state.

Notes

It is notoriously hard to be precise about mood, so part of the challenge in this project is to find a way to satisfy the majority of users, but without expecting that everyone will be convinced. Colour and shape may be useful elements of the interface design in order to help establish the mood in the user's mind.

● **Project: *music-is-life* (2006) by Rob Godman**

Assign a letter, a number, to a pitch, a rhythm, a dynamic, a sample, a MIDI value, a . . .

● Project: *Random play*

Introduction

Download culture has significantly changed the way we experience music. Whereas previously to jump tracks on an LP, or worse still a cassette, required some tricky physical manipulation, the CD has automated the 'random play'. Music can be heard in any order, even if that was never the intention of the artists. The mp3 player takes this one stage further and allows all the tracks of an entire record collection to be randomly played. The results can be startling.

The project

First, simply listen to a succession of completely unrelated (the more unrelated the better) tracks in a random order. Do any surprising connections emerge? Try it again.

Next, assemble a collection of short excerpts or sounds. Make each one under five seconds. Now randomly play these back a few times. Make sure there is no time gap between each track, so as to create a seamless composition.

Finally, try to repeat the second step using ever-shorter clips of music or sound. How short can they be before the musical sense is lost?

Notes

The final step will probably involve some editing work. This is a crude exercise, and the editing can be done quite arbitrarily. The best effects are achieved when the 'jump-cuts' are violent or shocking.

● Project: *Digital minimalism*

Introduction

This is a project with a strong research element and a possible performative or compositional outcome. It could, however, equally well form the basis of an essay or seminar presentation.

The project

Investigate and research musical 'minimalism'. To what extent does it relate to minimalism in the other arts and architecture? And to what extent is it evident in digital music? Extend the research by making and/or performing a piece of digital minimalist music.

Notes

The following books and recordings may be useful:

■ Baker, K. (1988) *Minimalism: Art of Circumstance.* London: Abbeville Press.
■ Batchelor, D. (1997) *Minimalism.* London: Tate Gallery Publishing.
■ Battock, G. (ed.) (1969) *Minimal Art: A Critical Anthology.* London: Studio Vista.
■ Griffiths, P. (1979) *A Guide to Electronic Music.* London: Thames and Hudson.
■ Mertens, W. (1983) *American Minimal Music.* London: Kahn and Averill.
■ Nyman, M. (1999) *Experimental Music: Cage and Beyond.* 2nd edition. Cambridge: Cambridge University Press.
■ Potter, K. (2000) *Four Musical Minimalists.* Cambridge: Cambridge University Press.
■ Prendergast, M. (2000) *The Ambient Century: From Mahler to Trance – The Evolution of Sound in the Electronic Age.* London: Bloomsbury Publishing.
■ Salzman, E. (1974) *Twentieth-Century Music: An Introduction.* New York: Prentice-Hall. (Chapters 12–18 are particularly relevant.)
■ Toop, D. (1995, 2001) *Ocean of Sound: Aether Talk, Ambient Sound and Imaginary Worlds.* London: Serpent's Tail.
■ Meyer, J. (ed.) (2000) *Minimalism.* New York: Phaidon Press.

▲ Terry Riley (1964) *In C.* 20th Cantaloupe CA 21004.
▲ Philip Glass (1969) *Music in Similar Motion.* Nonesuch 79326-2.
▲ La Monte Young (1969) 'Excerpts from Map of 49's Dream The Two Systems of Eleven Sets of Galactic Intervals' on *OHM – The Early Gurus of Electronic Music: 1948– 1980.* Ellipsis Arts M1473 O46 2000.
▲ Steve Reich (1970) *Drumming.* Deutsches Grammophon 427-428-2.
▲ Mike Oldfield (1973) *Tubular Bells.* Virgin V2001.
▲ Gavin Bryars (1975) *Jesus' Blood Never Failed Me Yet.* Point Music 438-823-2.
▲ Kraftwerk (1976) *TransEurope Express.* EMI/Capitol 000 70095.
▲ CHIC (1979) 'Good Times' on *Risqué.* Atlantic 3584.
▲ Brian Eno, Harold Budd (1979) *Music for Airports #2: The Plateaux of Mirror.* EG Records EG 2335 205.
▲ Philip Glass (1983) *Koyaanisqatsi.* Antilles/Island 422-814 042-2.
▲ Alvin Lucier (1992) *Music on a Long Thin Wire.* Lovely LCD 1011.
▲ Orbital (1993) 'Halcyon + on + on' on *Orbital 2.* FFRR Records 162 351 026-2.
▲ Derrick May (1996) *Innovator.* Transmat TMT 2CD.
▲ Bernhard Günter (1999) *univers/temporel/espoirs.* Trente Oiseaux TOC991.
▲ Tetsu Inoue (1994, reissued 2000) *Ambiant Otaku*, Fax. Aw 017. (Although this album is a classic work of digital minimalism, its deliberately restricted release can make it hard to find. In the event of difficulty, try Inoue's collaboration with Carl Stone: *pict. soul.* Cycling '74 c74-005).
▲ Steve Roden (2003) *three roots carved to look like stones.* Sonoris sns-01 CD.

● Project: *Balloon debate*

Introduction

This project is a spin on an old favourite of debating societies: the balloon debate. In this format, each person is required to take on the defence of a chosen figure from history and defend their right to remain in an imaginary balloon which needs to jettison ballast. The person who remains after the rest have been voted out, one by one, is the winner.

The project

Scenario: all of culture is to be destroyed, except for the one thing that is worth keeping. What is that one thing? Make a presentation to defend the choice. Trick answers which try to avoid the spirit of the project automatically fail. The 'thing' should be an artefact or a body of work, but not a landmass or a people.

Notes

This is a good way of understanding and articulating the idea of cultural value. The presentation will need to give clear reasons for the choice, from which a value system and set of critical judgements may be deduced. If done in a group situation, the subsequent voting can also be revealing of the collective set of shared values.

● Project: *Evocative transcription*

Introduction

In traditional music, a transcription is a rewritten version of something previously heard in a different medium. One classic example is the piano transcription; very popular in the nineteenth century, when whole operas or symphonies would be reduced to a playable version for the home pianist. The composer Ferruccio Busoni, who was a master of the technique of piano transcription, took this idea one step further and, in his seminal text of 1911, *Sketch of a New Aesthetic of Music*, suggested that notated music is itself the transcription of a musical idea: 'from the moment the pen touches the paper, the idea loses its original form'.[10]

For Busoni, this was a loss, and his essay may in many ways be seen as a protest against the limitations of the musical language of his day and even an anticipation of technological developments that were to follow. It is not necessary to follow Busoni all the way down this path in order to recognise that a transcription is not, and can never be, the same as what it transcribes, and yet contains sufficiently recognisable features to *evoke* the music in the mind of the listener.

The notation of digital music, particularly where it is based upon spectral information, can often be problematic, because the emphasis is upon the aural element. However, in order to develop the ear, it can be beneficial to attempt to transcribe what is heard into some form of visual (or even verbal) representation. This is not in order to use the result as a basis for a reconstruction of its model, but rather as an evocation, or a reference for understanding the content of what is heard.

The project

Make an evocative transcription of a chosen piece of electronic or electro-acoustic music. The first step is to devise a system of symbols. This is rather subjective, but might include a time and frequency line (possibly a graph) and a system of colours or shapes to indicate sound types, intensities, behaviours and so on.

This can be done on paper, then extended into a digital format. Start by making a paper evocative transcription, using colours and shapes as described. Next, scan the image into the computer, and use animation software, such as Flash, to create a movie that corresponds to the music.

Notes

The evocative transcription reveals to what extent, and how accurately, the transcriber has heard. Although such visualisations are not notations of music in the traditional sense, and certainly are no substitute for actual listening, their value lies in the extent to which they represent an act of conscious listening and reflection. The Flash version of this project makes explicit the similarities between, and limitations of, the process of digitising sounds and images. The book website contains some excellent examples of evocative transcriptions made by students.

● Project: *Pecha kucha*

Introduction

Pecha kucha nights are now an established format for presentations in the creative industries. They began in 2003 in Tokyo, and were started by Astrid Klein and Mark Dytham of Klein Dytham Architecture as a way to attract customers to their nightclub. They now take place in many major cities around the world. The name derives from the Japanese for 'chit-chat'.

The project

Up to fourteen presenters each give a slideshow of twenty images. Each slide is shown for twenty seconds, giving a total time of 6 minutes 40 seconds per presentation. Sounds may be included freely within the allotted time span. The presentations should focus upon a particular project or may be used as a summary of the presenter's work as a whole.

Notes

The advantage of the very tight timings is that presenters are obliged to be extremely focused. The format also allows for an uninterrupted flow of presentations, and Pecha kucha nights normally develop a very convivial and energised atmosphere quite quickly. The range and diversity of the presentations can be both exciting and energising, as well as informative.

● Project: *Sonic branding*

Introduction

The ability to produce numerous versions of a single idea for a client is an indispensable skill in a commercial situation. Even if there are only slight variations between each version, the client must be offered a choice. This project is the aural equivalent of logo design and, despite its musical insignificance, may be the most lucrative activity ever undertaken by a digital musician.

The project

Find a short video clip that could be suitable for a 'sonic brand'. Produce at least ten different audio clips to accompany the video. Make a presentation to a 'client' to sell the audio brand.

Notes

The following book may be useful for this project:

■ Jackson, D. L. (2003) *Sonic Branding: An Essential Guide to the Art and Science of Sonic Branding.* London: Palgrave Macmillan.

Notes

I New technologies, new musicians

1 The word 'electro-acoustic' comes from engineering, where it is defined as 'an adjective describing any process involving the transfer of a signal from acoustic to electrical form, or vice versa'. B. Truax (ed.) (1999) *Handbook for Acoustic Ecology.*(www.sfu.ca/sonic-studio/handbook/Electro-Acoustic.html).

2 'Radiophonic' refers to the experimental use of sound in radio.

3 It will be noticed that this discussion is entirely concerned with human musicians using technology. The extent to which a computer may itself be a 'digital musician' is explored later in the book.

4 Tarkovsky, A. (1986, 1989) *Sculpting in Time*. Austin, TX: University of Texas Press.

5 The term 'nobrow' was coined by John Seabrook in his book of that title, published in 2000, and more recently used by Peter Swirski in his *From Lowbrow to Nobrow* (2005).

6 Benjamin, W. (1936) 'The Work of Art in the Age of Mechanical Reproduction' reprinted in W. Benjamin, trans. H. Zohn (1970) *Illuminations*. London: Jonathan Cape, pp. 219–253.

7 Casella, A. (1924) *Matter and Timbre*. 'Tone-Problems of Today' in *Musical* Quarterly, vol. 10, pp. 159–171.

8 Busoni, F. (1911) *Sketch of a New Aesthetic of Music* reprinted in *Three Classics in the Aesthetic of Music* (1962). New York: Dover Editions, pp. 89–95.

9 Russolo, L., trans B. Brown (1986) *The Art of Noises*. New York: Pendragon Press, pp. 27–28.

10 Varèse, E. (1936) *The Liberation of Sound* reprinted in E. Schwartz and B. Childs (1998) *Contemporary Composers on Contemporary Music*. New York: Da Capo Press, pp. 195–208.

11 'Musique concrète', or concrete music, is a somewhat misunderstood term. Traditional classical music is 'abstract', in the sense that it begins as notations on paper, which are then translated into sounds by performers. 'Concrete' music takes the opposite approach by beginning with actual sounds and abstracting a musical composition from them. By extension, the term *musique concrète* has become a commonly used shorthand for music made from 'real world' sounds rather than musical notes.

12 Cage, J. (1971) *Silence*. London: Marion Boyars, pp. 3–6.

13 Described as: '20-minute solos for one to 7 amplified harpsichords and tapes for one to 52 amplified monaural machines to be used in whole or in part in any combination with or without interruptions, etc., to make an indeterminate concert of any agreed-upon length having 2 to 59 channels with loud-speakers around the audience.' See J. Rivest (1999) 'In Advance of the Avant Garde: John Cage at the University of Illinois, 1952–69'. Electronic Music Foundation. (www.emfinstitute.emf.org/).

14 See A. Culver (2007) 'John Cage Computer Programs' (www.anarchicharmony.org).

15 Taylor, R., Menabrea, L. F. and Lovelace, A. A. (eds) 'Sketch of the Analytical Engine' in *Scientific Memoirs No.3*, London: Taylor, pp. 666–731.
16 United Nations Environment Program, Electricity Report. Available at www.unep.fr/en/ (visited 13 September 2007).
17 The picture was created by NASA from data gathered by the Defense Meteorological Satellite Program.
18 Source: Telecompaper. Available at www.telecompaper.com/ (visited 15 August 2005).
19 US Census Bureau, International Programs Center, www.census.gov/ipc/www/ (visited 9 September 2005).
20 *The Edge*. Available at www.edge.org/ (visited 12 February 2006).

2 Aural awareness

1 This is a logical consequence for Western music of the colouristic discoveries made in the late nineteenth century by Claude Debussy and others.
2 An anechoic chamber is, literally, a room without reflections, in other words: completely without reverberation. It is the ideal 'neutral' space for work in acoustics.
3 Cage, J. (1967) *A Year from Monday*. Middletown, CT: Wesleyan University Press.
4 Truax, B. (2001) *Acoustic Communication*. Westport, CT: Ablex, p. 15.
5 Ibid., p. 22.
6 Ibid.
7 Ibid., p. 24.
8 Oliveros, P. (1984) *Some Sound Observations* in *Software for People: Collected Writings 1963–80*. Baltimore, MD: Smith Publications.
9 Eno, B. (1996) *Ambient Music*, in *A Year with Swollen Appendices*. London: Faber & Faber.
10 Schaeffer, P. (1966) *Traité des objets musicaux*. Paris: Le Seuil. In 1983, Michel Chion published his *Guide des Objets Sonorés* (*Guide to Sound Objects*) as a general introduction to this volume. The English translation of Chion's text by John Dack and Christine North is soon to be published on EARS: The Electroacoustic Resource Site (www.ears.dmu.ac.uk).
11 Chion, M., trans. Dack, J. and North, C. (1982) *Guide des Objets Sonores: Pierre Schaeffer et la recherche musicale*. Paris: Buchet/Chastel, p. 25.
12 The examples given of the four modes are based on Emmerson, S. (2001) 'New Spaces/New Places: A Sound House for the Performance of Electro-Acoustic Music and Sonic Art' in *Organised Sound*, vol. 6, no. 2, pp. 103–105.
13 Chion, M., trans. Dack, J. and North, C. (1982) *Guide des Objets Sonores: Pierre Schaeffer et la recherche musicale*. Paris: Buchet/Chastel, p. 25.
14 Ibid.
15 Ibid.
16 Ibid.
17 Ibid.
18 The French word for this is 'époché', a term borrowed from the philosopher and phenomenologist Husserl, meaning: 'a deconditioning of habitual listening patterns, to return to the original experience of perception, enabling us to grasp the sound object at its own level which takes it as the vehicle of a meaning to be understood or a cause to be identified.' Source: *EARS: The Electroacoustic Resource Site* (www.ears.dmu.ac.uk).
19 Chion, M., trans. Dack, J. and North, C. (1982) *Guide des Objets Sonores: Pierre Schaeffer et la recherche musicale*. Paris: Buchet/Chastel, p. 26.
20 Smalley, D. (1997) 'Spectromorphology: Explaining Sound-shapes' in *Organised Sound*, vol. 2, no. 2, pp. 107–126.
21 Brün, H. (2004) *When Music Resists Meaning*. Middletown, CT: Wesleyan University Press, p. 58.

22   Masking is a perceptual phenomenon in which one sound apparently masks another. There are several ways in which it can occur. If a single tone pitched at 1,000 Hz is played simultaneously with one of 1,100 Hz, but with a slight difference in volume level between the two, the quieter wave will be inaudible. Also, humans cannot hear a quieter sound against a louder sound if there is up to a 5 millisecond delay between the two. Where two similar sounds are played at similar volume levels, the relationship becomes more dynamic between the masker and the masked.

23   Glennie, E. (2005) *Evelyn's Hearing*. (www.evelyn.co.uk/hearing.htm (quoted with permission).

24   Stelarc (1999) *The Extra Ear (or an ear on an arm)*. (www.stelarc.va.com.au/extra_ear/index.htm).

25   Frequency, or the number of cycles or periods of a sound wave per unit of time (normally seconds), is measured in hertz (Hz) and kilohertz (kHz) (1 kHz = 1,000 Hz). A fundamental frequency of 4 kHz is high – above the natural range of the female voice, for example.

26   In particular, those of Georg von Békésy (1899–1972), who won the Nobel Prize for his discovery that sound travels along the basilar membrane in waves. He showed how these waves peak at different places on the membrane, and he discovered that the location of the nerve receptors and the number of receptors involved are the most important factors in determining pitch and loudness. This has now become known as 'Place Theory'.

27   There are many complex overlaps in neuroscience between *cognitive psychology* (which studies cognition, the mental processes that are presumed to underlie behaviour), *cognition* (information processing, but also extending to knowledge in general), and *biological psychology* (the study of the organic basis of mental processes).

28   'Positron Emission Tomography, a type of scan that measures changes in blood flow associated with brain function by detecting positrons, positively charged particles emitted by radioactively labelled substances that have been injected into the body.' Source: Howard Hughes Medical Institute (www.hhmi.org).

29   'Functional Magnetic Resonance Imaging, a new method of scanning the brain's activity that needs no radioactive materials and produces images at a higher resolution than PET. It is based on differences in the magnetic resonance of certain atomic nuclei in areas of neuronal activity' Source: Howard Hughes Medical Institute (www.hhmi.org).

30   These images were produced by Morten Kringelbach to illustrate the sculpture *SENSE* by Annie Cattrell. The sculpture is owned by the Wellcome Trust and housed in its museum. The concept of using FMRI scans of the five senses of the human brain made into RP models and suspended in resin was Cattrell's. The sculpture itself was made with the help of Drs Mark Lythgoe, Steve Smith and Morten Kringelbach.

31   See www.opte.org.

32   The Connection Machine, built at the Massachusetts Institute of Technology in 1987–1988, was one such that has sometimes been used for music.

33   For a full account, see T. Myatt (2002) 'Strategies for Interaction in *Construction 3*' *Organised Sound*, vol. 7, no. 2, pp. 157–169.

34   Ibid., p. 168.

35   See www.spacedog.biz/infrasonic/infrasonicindex.htm.

36   The *Doppler* effect is created when the sound source itself is in motion. A sound source moving quickly towards you will seem to *rise* in pitch, whereas a sound source moving quickly away from you will seem to *fall* in pitch (hear a passing emergency vehicle siren to recognise this effect). The amount of frequency bending depends on the ratio of the speed of sound to the speed at which the object is travelling.

37   Difference tone is the result of subtracting the value of the lower of two frequencies from the higher. This result is normally a smaller number than the highest original frequency and is, consequently, a lower sound. The extent to which such difference

tones are audible will greatly depend on the purity of the original pitches, the nature of space in which they are being produced, and the aural awareness of the listener.

38 See in particular D. Deutsch (ed.) (1999) *The Psychology of Music*. 2nd edition. San Diego: Academic Press.

3 Understanding sound

1   The British Broadcasting Corporation's Radiophonic Workshop was set up in 1958 to provide soundtracks, sound effects and music for BBC broadcasts. Early projects included Samuel Beckett's play *All that Fall* and 'radiophonic poems', and many more radio and television programmes. The workshop was renowned for its experimentation with unlikely sound objects and new technologies.

2   *Doctor Who* is a popular UK television series featuring a time-travelling central character and numerous companions and enemies, including the famous Daleks. The series began in 1963, and was recently revived after a fifteen-year gap (at least on television) to great acclaim in the UK.

3   The pascal (symbol Pa) is the SI unit of pressure, and is equivalent to 1 newton per square metre. It is named after Blaise Pascal (1623–1662), the French mathematician, physicist and philosopher.

4   Phase is the fraction of the time required to complete a full cycle that a point completes after last passing through an arbitrary reference position.

5   Named after Heinrich Rudolf Hertz (1857–1894), a German physicist.

6   This experiment has since been redone many times, and various standard equal-loudness curves have resulted.

7   One Watt is 1 joule of energy per second, i.e., power.

8   For example 'lowercase' music, which generally comprises extremely quiet recordings of small or overlooked sounds and is related to 'microsound', made from sounds of extremely short – up to 100 milliseconds' – duration.

9   A semitone is the distance in pitch between one note and the next in the standard Western twelve-note equal temperament. There are twelve semitone steps in an octave (i.e., from 1:1 to 2:1), represented by the black and white keys on a keyboard.

10 Clarke, J. J. (2006) *Advanced Programming Techniques for Modular Synthesizers* (www.cim.mcgill.ca/~clark).

11 The name 'noise music' is an apparent contradiction in terms, since 'noise' usually refers to unwanted sound. However, the Japanese noise musician Merzbow has remarked: 'If by noise you mean uncomfortable sound, then pop music is noise to me' (interview with Oskari Mertalo, 1991).

12 This power supply may come from a battery, or from a phantom power line from a mixer. Phantom power supplies vary from between 9 and 48 volts.

13 After Alan Blumlein (1903–1942), the inventor of stereophonic sound.

14 Attractive though this idea may be, it should be noted that it is unethical to record *people* without their consent.

15 *Phase* is an acoustic phenomenon. When two or more waves (for example, from independent microphones) of the same frequency meet, their amplitudes combine, adding to each other. If the peaks and troughs of the wave forms line up, they are said to be 'in phase'. In this situation, each peak adds to the peak on the other wave form, and each trough adds to the other troughs, resulting in a wave form which is twice the amplitude of the original wave form. If the peaks of one wave form match the troughs of another wave form, the peaks and the troughs will cancel each other out, resulting in no wave form at all. Such wave forms are said to be 180 degrees 'out of phase'. This is rare, however, and in most cases, the waves are out of phase by a different amount. This results in a more complicated wave form than either of the original waves, as the amplitudes at each point along the wave form are added together.

16 There are a number of examples of colour spectrograms at the book website (www. digitalmusician.org).

17 Named after Harry Nyquist (1889–1976), an engineer who worked on information theory.

18 There is no single definition of the word 'bandwidth'. It is used fairly loosely to describe the measure of a function's width in the frequency domain.

19 One kilobit (Kbps) = 1,000 bits per second. One kilobyte per second is worth eight times that amount (1 byte = 8 bits).

20 In this case, 140 dB.

4 Organising sound

1 For an exploration of the difficulties of translation and making definitions, see Leigh Landy's review of H. de la Motte-Haber (1999) *Klangkunst: Tönende Objekte und kligende Räume. Volume 12. Handbuch der Musik im 20. Jahrhundert.* Laaber: Laaber-Verlag and the CD-ROM *Klangkunst in Deutschland, Organised Sound* (2000) vol. 5, no. 3, pp. 191–194.

2 Sound-art here owes a great deal to Marcel Duchamp, whose invention of the 'ready-made', a found or bought object that was then exhibited in an art gallery, first defined the artistic potential of such recontextualisation.

3 Jem Finer, interviewed by Steven Poole in *The Guardian*, September 2001.

4 Murch, W. (2005) 'Dense Clarity – Clear Density'. The Transom Review, 5/1. www. transom.org.

5 Campbell, D. and Greated, C. (1987) *The Musicians Guide to Acoustics.* London: Dent, pp. 542–545.

6 A good example of lateral restriction is making a sound down a cardboard tube. When the sound waves emerge from the tube, they spread out in all directions.

7 Sabine's formula: $T_r = 0.16$ x (V / A), where T_r = reverberation time, V = volume of the room in cubic metres and A = total absorption (absorbency × area).

8 Tanaka, A. and Toeplitz, K. (1998) *Global String.* (www.sensorband.com/atau/global-string/globalstring.pdf).

9 In 1931, Alan Blumlein patented a method of recreating the phase difference between human ears using amplitude, which he called 'binaural audio'. This was the beginning of stereophonic sound.

10 This is a typical set-up of the Birmingham ElectroAcoustic Sound Theatre (BEAST), adapted, with permission, from J. Harrison (1998) 'Sound, Space, Sculpture: Some Thoughts on the "What", "How" and (Most Importantly) "Why" of Diffusion . . . and related topics', *Journal of Electroacoustic Music* 11, p. 19.

11 Christian Huygens (1629–1695) was a Dutch physicist.

12 Normandeau, R. (2001) *Clair de Terre.* Empreintes digitales IMED 0157 (liner notes).

13 The traditional musical terms for these are *monophony* and *polyphony* or *counterpoint*.

14 Negroponte, N. (1996) *Being Digital.* New York: First Vintage Books.

15 Peter Traub (1999) *bits and pieces* (www.fictive.org/bits).

16 Roads, C. (2001) *Microsound.* Cambridge, MA: MIT Press, pp. 3–4.

17 Ibid., p. 55.

18 See www.notam02.no/9/.

19 XLR was originally a registered trademark of ITT-Cannon but has now become a standard format for microphone cables.

20 Named after the mathematician Jean-Baptiste Joseph Fourier (1768–1830) who first elaborated the theoretical principles.

21 An algorithm is a set of instructions for accomplishing a task which, given an initial state, will produce a corresponding and recognisable end state. A recipe is a typical algorithm. Algorithms are used widely in computer processes.

22 These envelopes will not correct all of the errors that typically arise in such complex calculations, so overlap is sometimes used to increase the overall accuracy.

23 Werner Heisenberg (1901–1976) laid the foundations of quantum mechanics in the 1920s.

24 For example, the acoustic phenomenon that a rhythmically repeated impulse becomes continuous pitch when the rate increases beyond the point at which a human ear can differentiate the individual impulses. Herbert Eimert was the first to synthesise this, and it became an important aspect of Karlheinz Stockhausen's music in the 1950s.

25 'The *envelope* of a sound is the profile of the evolution of its intensity and/or spectrum during its duration'. EARS: The Electroacoustic Resource Site (www.ears.dmu.ac.uk).

26 *Phase cancellation* occurs when two sound waves that are out of phase with each other are added together, resulting in a wave that has less overall amplitude than either of the original waves.

27 There are many other types of digital filter: the Butterworth filter is a band-pass filter designed to have as flat a frequency response as possible; the Bessel, the Cauer, and the Chebyshev filters all take slightly different approaches to the minimising of error in the passband and stopband of a band-pass filter.

28 Wishart specifically mentions the transformations of 'lis' (from the word 'listen') into bird song, 'rea' (from the word 'reason') to animal sounds, and 'reasonabl' into water. He also describes ways of manipulating sound using *wavesets*, which are sound packets grouped together by zero-crossings of the wave form (i.e., where the amplitude is zero). This way of dividing up sound enables a number of DSP processes such as waveset inversion, omission, reversal, shaking, shuffling, substitution, averaging, harmonic distortion and 'power-distortion', in which the amplitude of each sample of the sound is raised mathematically by a 'power', such as squared, cubed and so on. See his 1994 book *Audible Design* and the essay 'Computer Sound Transformation', available from his website (www.trevorwishart.co.uk).

29 Schoenberg, A. (1967) *Fundamentals of Musical Composition*. London, Faber & Faber. First published in 1948, this book, although it discusses exclusively classical music, nevertheless contains some extremely useful ideas for anyone embarking on composition.

30 'Montage' is a term derived from cinema, in which rapid editing, special effects, sound and music combine to present compressed narrative information.

31 Johann Wolfgang von Goethe (1749–1832) was a German writer, scientist and painter, and the author of *Faust* and *A Theory of Colours*.

32 Smalley, D. (1986) 'Spectro-morphology and Structuring Processes' in S. Emmerson (ed.) *The Language of Electroacoustic Music*. London: Macmillan, p. 71.

33 Xenakis formed the CEMAMu (Centre d'Études de Mathématiques et Automatiques Musicales/Centre for Studies in Mathematics and Automated Music) in Paris in 1972. He then developed UPIC (Unité Polyagogique Informatique du CEMAMu) in 1977.

34 Source: The Electroacoustic Resource Site (www.ears.dmu.ac.uk).

35 Smalley, D. (1986) 'Spectro-Morphology and Structuring Processes' in Emmerson, S. (ed.) *The Language of Electroacoustic Music*. London: Macmillan.

36 Smalley, D. (1992) *Valley Flow*. Concert programme, University of East Anglia.

5 Creating music

1 This literal interpretation of the word is even more explicit in post-production of visual effects and cinema, where 'compositing' (rather than composition) refers to the combination of images from various sources. 'Composition' is not quite the same as 'compositing' but is a conceptual neighbour, sharing some similar characteristics.

2 Based in part on an e-mail exchange with Bret Battey (bbattey@dmu.ac.uk) 21 May

2005. *RE: what is music for?* E-mail to A. Hugill (ahu@dmu.ac.uk).

3 Stravinsky, I. (1939) *Poetics of Music*. Cambridge, MA: Harvard University Press.

4 See Weale, R. (2005) 'Intention/Reception in Electroacoustic Music'. Unpublished PhD thesis, De Montfort University, Leicester.

5 Rhodes, M. (1961) 'An Analysis of Creativity', *Phi Delta Kappan* 42, pp. 305–310.

6 For a more detailed examination of this idea, see N. Barrett (2002) 'Spatio-Musical Composition Strategies', in *Organised Sound*, vol. 7, no. 3, pp. 313–323.

7 Brown, E. quoted in R. Kostelanetz and J. Darby (1996) *Classic Essays on Twentieth-Century Music*. New York: Schirmer, p. 202.

8 An interval is the pitch relationship between two notes in music.

9 John Richards calls this 'Sonic Magnification'. See J. Richards (2001) *New Modality: Sonic Magnification*. Paper given at the 'Music without Walls? Music without Instruments?' conference, De Montfort University, Leicester.

10 Yavelow, C. (1997) *The Music is the Message*. Installation at The New Metropolis Centre for Science and Technology in Amsterdam, The Netherlands.

11 Zorn, J. (2000) *Arcana: Musicians on Music*. New York: Granary Books, Preface.

6 Performing

1 Chanan, M. (1994) *Musica Practica: The Social Practice of Western Music from Gregorian Chant to Postmodernism*. London: Verso, p. 23.

2 Wyatt, S. *et al.* (2005) *Investigative Studies on Sound Diffuson/Projection at the University of Illinois: A Report on an Explorative Collaboration*. University of Illinois.

3 Barbosa, Á. (2003) 'Displaced Soundscapes: A Survey of Network Systems for Music and Sonic Art Creation' in *Leonardo Music Journal*, vol. 13, pp. 53–59.

4 Developed by Phil Burk and others, it is distributed through Burk's company, Soft-Synth.

5 www.electrotap.com/jade.

6 Most notably *Second Life* (www.secondlife.com).

7 Barry Truax, conversation with the author, 2005.

8 'Gradus ad Parnassum' was the title of a treatise by J. J. Fux, written in 1725, which described 'species counterpoint', a compositional method that subsequently became the basis of most academic tuition and that still underpins the teaching of music in many conservatoires and universities. The title refers to the Greek myth of Mount Parnassus, home to the Muses, who were the embodiment of music, poetry and other arts. Step by step, from the base to the peak, 'Gradus ad Parnassum' climbs that mythical mountain.

9 See Wishart, T. (1996) *On Sonic Art*. Amsterdam: Harwood Academic Publishers.

10 Small, C. (1998) *Musicking*. Middletown, CT: Wesleyan University Press, p. 5.

11 Thomas, S. (2005) 'Transliteracy – reading in the digital age' in *Higher Education Academy, English Subject Centre Newsletter*, November 2005. 'Transliteracies' were first discussed by Professor Alan Liu in the Department of English at the University of California Santa Barbara and applied exclusively to the written word. 'Transliteracy', as defined by Professor Sue Thomas of De Montfort University, Leicester, extends that concept to new media.

12 A highly developed example of this kind of environment is the CAVE (Cave Automatic Virtual Environment), an immersive, cuboid space in which the user may wear stereoscopic glasses, data gloves and other devices to assist in moving through a virtual world presented using multiple projectors and mirrors. Various versions of this concept exist at many institutions around the world. Their musical use has so far been rather limited, and their scale and difficulty of use mean that it is unlikely that the digital musician will get much opportunity to work in such an environment. Instead, a stereo (often binaural) reduced version of the same idea, presented on a flat

panel display, is a more familiar tool.

13 Paine, G. (1998) *MAP1* (notes) (www.activatedspace.com).

14 [R]egardless of the style of music performed, creativity is a fundamental part of musical skill development, as musicians constantly work towards an ideal sound which itself is constantly being refined.' S. Amitani, E. Edmonds and A. Johnston (2005) 'Amplifying Reflective Thinking in Musical Performance', paper given at the Creativity and Cognition Conference, 2005, University of London: Goldsmiths College.

15 Schön, D. (1983) *The Reflective Practitioner*. London: Temple Smith, p. 68.

16 Ibid.

17 Magnusson, T. and Hurtado, M. E. (2007) 'The Acoustic, the Digital and the Body: A Survey of Musical Instruments', *Proceedings of the NIME Conference, New York University*, NY, USA. pp. 94–99.

18 Ibid.

19 Ibid.

20 Ibid.

21 For detailed accounts of the physiological effects and health benefits of music, see D. J. Schneck and D. S. Berger (2006) *The Music Effect: Music Physiology and Clinical Applications*. Philadelphia, PA: Jessica Kingsley Publishers; and D. Aldridge (1996) *Music Therapy Research and Practice in Medicine: From Out of the Silence*. Philadelphia, PA: Jessica Kingsley Publishers.

22 For more information about Kaffe Matthews, see www.annetteworks.com.

23 www.steim.org/steim/info.html.

24 NIME is also the name of a leading annual conference on the subject. See hct.ece.ubc.ca/nime.

25 Image source (www.mis.atr.jp/~mlyons/nime02.html).

26 Bailey, D. (1993) *Improvisation: Its Nature and Practice in Music*. New York: Da Capo Press.

27 For example, Cornelius Cardew's *The Tiger's Mind*.

28 Collins, N. (2007) 'Live Coding Practice' in *Proceedings of the NIME Conference*, New York University, New York, USA. pp. 112–117.

29 Collins, N. (2007) 'Live Coding Practice', unpublished paper.

30 Cook, P. R. and Wang, G. (2004) 'On-the-Fly Programming: Using Code as an Expressive Musical Instrument' in *Proceedings of the 2004 International Conference on New Interfaces for Musical Expression (NIME-04)*. Hamamatsu, Japan, p. 138–143.

31 See deprogramming.us/perfs.

32 See www.pawfal.org/index.php?page=BetaBlocker.

33 TOPLAP, the (Temporary/Transnational/Terrestrial/Transdimensional) Organisation for the (Promotion/Proliferation/Permanence/Purity) of Live (Algorithm/Audio/Art/Artistic) Programming, may be found at www.toplap.org.

34 Collins, N. *op. cit.*

7 Cultural context

1 Leigh Landy, conversation with A. Hugill, 2005.

2 Chanan, M. (1994) *Musica Practica: The Social Practice of Western Music from Gregorian Chant to Postmodernism*. London: Verso, Prologue.

3 Available at, respectively: www.ubu.com/ethno/soundings/tuva.html, musicmavericks.publicradio.org/features/highband/boo.html, www.bmic.co.uk/collection, www.ebay.com secondlife.com.

4 Manovich, L. (2001) *The Language of New Media*. Cambridge, MA: MIT Press, pp. 27–45.

5 Some writers, notably Kim Cascone, have labelled this tendency 'post-digital'. See

K. Cascone (2002) 'The Aesthetics of Failure: "Post-Digital" Tendencies in Contemporary Computer Music', *Computer Music Journal*, vol. 24, no. 4, pp. 12–18.

6 An ethnomusicologist studies the music of a given culture with a view to understanding its ethnicity first and foremost.

7 Timar, A. (2006) 'What is *gamelan*?', Deep Down Productions. (www.deepdownproductions.com/what-gamelan-a-3.html?osCsid=3fce7aa59863b36087adc8b5a2b51559).

8 See www.gatesstreet.com/Heavy_Metal_512.mov.

9 Kapur, A. *et al.* (2003) 'GigaPop Ritual', *Proceedings of the 2003 Conference on New Instruments for Musical Expression (NIME)*, Montreal Canada, pp. 23–26.

10 Battey, B. (2003) 'Bézier Spline Modeling of Pitch-continuous Melodic Expression and Ornamentation', *Computer Music Journal*, vol. 28, no. 4, pp. 25–39.

11 See www.mti.dmu.ac.uk/~bbattey/Gallery/autark.html.

12 Bret Battey, interviewed by the author, 2006.

13 Steve Reich, quoted in W. Duckworth (1995) *Talking Music*. New York: Schirmer, p. 293.

14 Ligeti, L. (2000) 'Beta Foley: Experiments with Tradition and Technology in West Africa', *Leonardo Music Journal*, vol. 10, pp. 41–47.

15 Small, C. (1977) *Music, Society, Education*. London: John Calder, p. 47.

16 The word 'blog' is an abbreviation for 'weblog', which is an online diary created using easily writable web pages.

17 A 'wiki' is an online collaborative tool, a website that can easily be edited by many users. The most extensive example is a collaborative encyclopedia called Wikipedia (en.wikipedia.org).

18 These developments are often grouped together under the name 'Web 2.0'.

19 Fractals are geometrically self-similar objects at all levels of magnification, such as the famous Mandelbrot set, or a fern.

20 An L-system or Lindenmayer system is a formal grammar (a set of rules and symbols) often used to model the growth processes of plant development, although able to model the morphology of a variety of organisms.

21 In fact, it is not necessary to use a computer to make an algorithm, and 'algorithmic music' may be found in the medieval period and earlier. In this context, however, the meaning is restricted to the digital domain.

22 See www.plunderphonics.com.

23 This is one of many such charts that circulate around the Internet. This one came from the wikipedia site (www.en.wikipedia.org) but a general search on 'electronic dance music' will produce more extensive examples listing hundreds of genres and sub-genres.

8 Critical engagement

1 McClary, S. (1994) 'Constructions of Subjectivity in Schubert's Music' in P. Brett, E. Wood and G. C. Thomas (eds), *Queering the Pitch: The New Gay and Lesbian Musicology*. New York: Routledge, pp. 205–233.

2 Probably the most authoritative account is given in P. Manning (2004) *Electronic and Computer Music*, revised edition. Oxford: Oxford University Press.

3 Also known as a Tannerin, after its inventor Paul Tanner, the slide theremin is an electronic instrument that produces a somewhat similar sound to the original theremin, with the difference that it is controlled by a keyboard rather than the motion of the hands in the air.

4 For a full discussion of these and many other similar examples, see P. Greene and T. Porcello (eds) (2005) *Wired for Sound: Engineering and Technologies in Sonic Cultures*. Middletown, CT: Wesleyan University Press.

5 An interesting way to tackle this list in a classroom situation is to play one or two of

these without revealing the artists or the background to the music, then to question the students about their perception of the work. One anecdote, frequently told by Leigh Landy, about just such an exercise was that, when asked their politics, students almost uniformly expressed radical, even left-wing, views. When asked their taste in music, on the other hand, it tended to be conservative.

6 Stravinsky composed only one film score, for *The Commandos Strike at Dawn*, which was rejected by the studio. He did have several other offers, but none of them came to anything. Schoenberg was asked by Irving Thalberg to write the music for *The Good Earth*, but this project also fell through when the composer demanded final editing rights. In the end, Schoenberg only composed the soundtrack to an imaginary film: *Music to Accompany a Film Scene*.

7 Genette, G. (1966) 'Structuralism and Literary Criticism', reproduced in D. Lodge and N. Wood (eds) (1999) *Modern Criticism and Theory: A Reader*. London: Longman, p. 67 fn.

8 Statement attributed to Marshall McLuhan, 1969.

9 Attali, J. (trans B. Massumi) (1977) *Noise: The Political Economy of Music*. Minneapolis, MN: University of Minnesota Press, p. 4 *et seq*.

10 Ibid., p. 8.

11 Ibid., p. 9.

12 Hume, D. (1777) 'On the Standard of Taste' Essay XXIII in *Essays, Moral, Political and Literary*. Reproduced in E. F. Miller (ed.) (1985) *David Hume: Essays, Moral, Political and Literary*. Indianapolis: Liberty Fund, p. 241.

13 Kant, I. (trans. J. H. Bernard) (1790) *Critique of Judgment*. New York: Hafner Press, Macmillan, e.g. §§V–VIII and §17.

14 See Lerdahl, F. and Jackendoff, R. (1983, 1999) *A Generative Theory of Tonal Music*. Cambridge, MA and London: MIT Press.

15 See Blacking, J. (1973) *How Musical is Man?* Seattle, WA: University of Washington Press.

16 Tagg, P. (1999) *Introductory Notes to the Semiotics of Music* (www.tagg.org/xpdfs/semio tug.pdf).

17 Tagg, P. (2000) *Kojak: 50 Seconds of Television Music*. New York State: Mass Media Music Scholars' Press.

18 Nattiez, J.-J. (1990) *Music and Discourses: Towards a Semiology of Music*. Princeton, NJ: Princeton University Press, p. 101.

19 Bohm, D. (1951) *The Quantum Theory*. New York: Dover.

20 From the liner notes.

21 Mabbett, A. (1995) *The Complete Guide to the Music of Pink Floyd*. London: Omnibus Press.

22 Jaffé, D. (1999) "The Compleat Jonathan Harvey' (www.musicwrite.demon.co.uk/harvey.html.

23 McClary, S. (1991) *Feminine Endings: Music, Gender and Sexuality*. Minnesota: University of Minnesota Press. p. 110.

24 Coldcut (1998) *Timber*. Hexstatic ZencdS65A. Press release. Available at www.ninja-tune.net/ninja/release.php?id=90.

25 *Squarepusher* (Jenkinson, T.) (2004) 'Philosophy'. Available at www.squarepusher.net.

9 The digital musician

1 Dimitris Moraitis, conversation with A. Hugill, 2005.

2 Herrema, R., conversation with A. Hugill, 2005.

3 Cage, J. (1968) 'Lecture on Nothing', *Silence*. London: Marion Boyars, p. 109.

4 See www.collectionscanada.ca/glenngould/index-e.html.

5 See Paddison, M. (2000) 'Frank Zappa' in S. Sadie and J. Tyrrell (eds) *The New Grove Dictionary of Music and Musicians*. London: Macmillan; and Watson, B. (1995) *Frank Zappa: The Negative Dialectics of Poodle Play*. London: Quartet.

6 *Son et lumière* is a form of night-time entertainment usually presented outdoors at a site of historical interest, which combines lighting, image and sound in a spectacular show. *Cirque de soleil* is a modern circus franchise that does not use animals and features colourful costumes, extraordinary design and specially created music and light, along with the acrobatics.

7 The term 'audio-vision' was coined by Michel Chion. See M. Chion (1990) *Audio-Vision – Sound on Screen*. New York: Columbia University Press.

8 The Foley artist on a film crew is the person who creates and records many of the sound effects. This is a highly specialised job. The name comes from Jack Foley (1891–1967), one of the first, who helped to introduce sound effects into the movies.

9 Adkins, M. (2005) 'The Changing Skillset of the Contemporary Musician', paper given at the *National Association of Music in Higher Education* Conference, University of Southampton.

10 Freiberger, M. (2006) 'Nick Collins. Career Interview: Computer Music Researcher' in *+plus10 magazine*, no. 38. Available at http://plus.maths.org/issue38/interview.html.

10 Projects and performance repertoire

1 Truax, B. (ed.) (1999) *Handbook for Acoustic Ecology*. Vancouver: Cambridge St Publishing (www.sfu.ca/sonic-studio/handbook).

2 Truax, B. (2007) Soundscape Composition (www.sfu.ca/~truax/scomp.html).

3 Truax, B. (2002) 'Genres and Techniques of Soundscape Composition as developed at Simon Fraser University', *Organised Sound*, vol. 7, no. 1, pp. 5–14 (www.sfu.ca/~truax/OS5.html).

4 Cage, J., 'Statements Re Duchamp' in J. Masheck (ed.) (1975) *Marcel Duchamp in Perspective*. New York: Da Capo Press, pp. 67–68.

5 Duchamp, M. (1934) *Green Box*. Reproduced in R. Hamilton (1960) *The Bride Stripped Bare by Her Bachelors Even*, a typographical version by Richard Hamilton of Marcel Duchamp's Green Box. London: Lund, Humphries.

6 Denis Smalley (1991) 'L'Espace du Son II' in a special edition of *Lien: revue d'esthetique musicale*. Ohain, Belgium: Éditions Musiques et Recherchés, pp. 121–124.

7 Appleton, J. (1992) 'Machine Songs III: Music in the Service of Science – Science in the Service of Music', *Computer Music Journal*, vol. 16, no. 3, p. 18.

8 Bowers, J. and Archer, P. (2005) 'Not Hyper, Not Meta, Not Cyber but Infra-Instruments', *Proceedings of the NIME (New Interfaces for Musical Expression) Conference*, Vancouver, Canada, pp. 63–69.

9 Ibid.

10 Busoni, F. (1911) *Sketch of a New Aesthetic of Music* reprinted in *Three Classics in the Aesthetic of Music* (1962). New York: Dover Editions, p. 85.

Index

Pages in **bold** type refer to major discussions